DATA STRUCTURES DEMYSTIFIED

JAMES KEOGH
& KEN DAVIDSON

McGraw-Hill/Osborne

New York   Chicago   San Francisco   Lisbon   London
Madrid   Mexico City   Milan   New Delhi   San Juan
Seoul   Singapore   Sydney   Toronto

The McGraw·Hill Companies

McGraw-Hill/Osborne
2100 Powell Street, 10th Floor
Emeryville, California 94608
U.S.A.

To arrange bulk purchase discounts for sales promotions, premiums, or fund-raisers, please contact **McGraw-Hill**/Osborne at the above address. For information on translations or book distributors outside the U.S.A., please see the International Contact Information page immediately following the index of this book.

Data Structures Demystified

1234567890 FGR FGR 01987654

ISBN 0-07-225359-2

Publisher	**Proofreader**
Brandon A. Nordin	Linda Medoff
Vice President & Associate Publisher	**Indexer**
Scott Rogers	Claire Splan
Editorial Director	**Composition**
Wendy Rinaldi	Jean Butterfield, Tara A. Davis
Project Editor	**Illustrators**
Jennifer Malnick	Kathleen Edwards, Melinda Lytle
Acquisitions Coordinator	**Cover Series Design**
Athena Honore	Margaret Webster-Shapiro
Technical Editor	**Cover Illustration**
Jeff Kent	Lance Lekander
Copy Editor	
Sally Engelfried	

This book was composed with Corel VENTURA™ Publisher.

*This book is dedicated to Anne, Sandy, Joanne,
Amber-Leigh Christine, and Graaf, without whose
help and support this book couldn't be written.
—Jim*

*To Janice, Jack, Alex, and Liz.
—Ken*

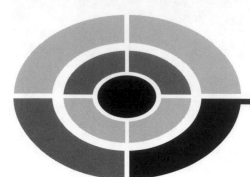

ABOUT THE AUTHORS

Jim Keogh is a member of the faculty of Columbia University, where he teaches courses on Java Application Development, and is a member of the Java Community Process Program. He developed the first e-commerce track at Columbia and became its first chairperson. Jim spent more than a decade developing advanced systems for major Wall Street firms and is also the author of several best-selling computer books.

Ken Davidson is a member of the faculty of Columbia University, where he teaches courses on Java Application Development. Ken has spent more than a decade developing advanced systems for major international firms.

CONTENTS AT A GLANCE

CONTENTS

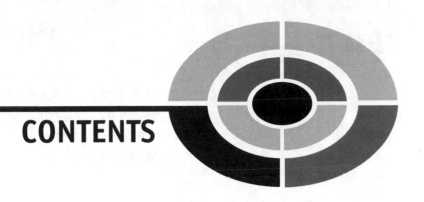

CONTENTS

INTRODUCTION

This book is for everyone who wants to learn basic data structures using C++ and Java without taking a formal course. It also serves as a supplemental classroom text. For the best results, start at the beginning and go straight through.

If you are confident about your basic knowledge of how computer memory is allocated and addressed, then skip the first two chapters, but take the quiz at the end of those chapters to see if you are actually ready to jump into data structures.

If you get 90 percent of the answers correct, you're ready. If you get 75 to 89 percent correct, skim through the text of Chapters 1 and 2. If you get less than 75 percent of the answers correct, then find a quiet place and begin reading Chapters 1 and 2. Doing so will get you in shape to tackle the rest of the chapters on data structures. In order to learn data structures, you must have some computer programming skills—computer programming is the language used to create data structures. But don't be intimidated; none of the programming knowledge you need goes beyond basic programming in C++ and Java.

This book contains a lot of practice quizzes and exam questions, which are similar to the kind of questions used in a data structures course. You may and should refer to the chapter texts when taking them. When you think you're ready, take the quiz, write down your answers, and then give your list of answers to a friend. Have your friend tell you your score, but not which questions were wrong. Stay with one chapter until you pass the quiz. You'll find the answers in Appendix B.

There is a final exam in Appendix A, at the end of the book, with practical questions drawn from all chapters of this book. Take the exam when you have finished all the chapters and have completed all the quizzes. A satisfactory score is at least 75 percent correct answers. Have a friend tell you your score without letting you know which questions you missed on the exam.

We recommend that you spend an hour or two each day; expect to complete one chapter each week. Don't rush. Take it at a steady pace. Take time to absorb the material. You'll complete the course in a few months; then you can use this book as a comprehensive permanent reference.

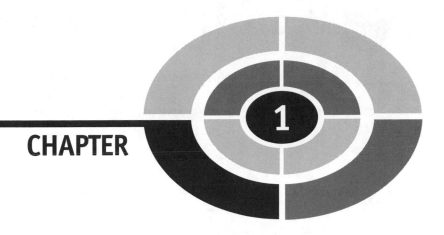

CHAPTER

Memory, Abstract Data Types, and Addresses

What is the maximum number of tries you'd need to find your name in a list of a million names? A million? No, not even close. The answer is 20—if you structure the list to make it easy to search and if you search the structure with an efficient searching technique. Searching lists is one of the many ways data structures help you manipulate data that is stored in your computer's memory. However, before you can understand how to use data structures, you need to have a firm grip on how computer memory works. In this chapter, you'll explore what computer memory is and why only zeros and ones are stored in memory. You'll also learn what a Java data type is and how to select the best Java data type to reserve memory for data used by your program.

A Tour of Memory

Computer memory is divided into three sections: main memory, cache memory in the central processing unit (CPU), and persistent storage. *Main memory*, also called *random access memory* (RAM), is where instructions (programs) and data are stored. Main memory is volatile; that is, instructions and data contained in main memory are lost once the computer is powered down.

Cache memory in the CPU is used to store frequently used instructions and data that either is, will be, or has been used by the CPU. A segment of the CPU's cache memory is called a register. A *register* is a small amount of memory within the CPU that is used to temporarily store instructions and data.

A bus connects the CPU and main memory. A *bus* is a set of etched wires on the motherboard that is similar to a highway and transports instructions and data between the CPU, main memory, and other devices connected to a computer (see Figure 1-1).

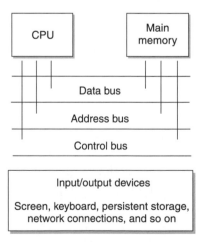

Figure 1-1 A bus connects the CPU, main memory, persistent storage, and other devices.

Persistent storage is an external storage device such as a hard disk that stores instructions and data. Persistent storage is nonvolatile; that is, instructions and data remain stored even when the computer is powered down.

Persistent storage is commonly used by the operating system as virtual memory. *Virtual memory* is a technique an operating system uses to increase the main memory capacity beyond the random access memory (RAM) inside the computer. When main memory capacity is exceeded, the operating system temporarily copies the contents of a block of memory to persistent storage. If a program needs access to instructions or data contained in the block, the operating system switches the block stored in persistent storage with a block of main memory that isn't being used.

CPU cache memory is the type of memory that has the fastest access speed. A close second is main memory. Persistent storage is a distant third because persistent storage devices usually involve a mechanical process that inhibits the quick transfer of instructions and data.

Throughout this book, we'll focus on main memory because this is the type of memory used by data structures (although the data structures and techniques presented can also be applied to file systems on persistent storage).

Data and Memory

Data used by your program is stored in memory and manipulated by various data structure techniques, depending on the nature of your program. Let's take a close look at main memory and how data is stored in memory before exploring how to manipulate data using data structures.

Memory is a bunch of electronic switches called *transistors* that can be placed in one of two states: on or off. The state of a switch is meaningless unless you assign a value to each state, which you do using the binary numbering system.

The *binary numbering system* consists of two digits called *binary digits* (bits): zero and one. A switch in the off state represents zero, and a switch in the on state represents one. This means that one transistor can represent one of two digits.

However, two digits don't provide you with sufficient data to do anything but store the number zero or one in memory. You can store more data in memory by logically grouping together switches. For example, two switches enable you to store two binary digits, which gives you four combinations, as shown Table 1-1, and these combinations can store numbers 0 through 3. Digits are zero-based, meaning that the first digit in the binary numbering system is zero, not 1. Memory is organized into groups of eight bits called a *byte*, enabling 256 combinations of zeros and ones that can store numbers from 0 through 255.

Switch 1	Switch 2	Decimal Value
0	0	0
0	1	1
1	0	2
1	1	3

Table 1-1   Combinations of Two Bits and Their Decimal Value Equivalents

The Binary Numbering System

A *numbering system* is a way to count things and perform arithmetic. For example, humans use the decimal numbering system, and computers use the binary numbering system. Both these numbering systems do exactly the same thing: they enable us to count things and perform arithmetic. You can add, subtract, multiply, and divide using the binary numbering system and you'll arrive at the same answer as if you used the decimal numbering system.

However, there is a noticeable difference between the decimal and binary numbering systems: the decimal numbering system consists of 10 digits (0 through 9) and the binary numbering system consists of 2 digits (0 and 1).

To jog your memory a bit, remember back in elementary school when the teacher showed you how to "carry over" a value from the right column to the left column when adding two numbers? If you had 9 in the right column and added 1, you changed the 9 to a 0 and placed a 1 to the left of the 0 to give you 10:

$$\begin{array}{r} 9 \\ +1 \\ \hline 10 \end{array}$$

The same "carry over" technique is used when adding numbers in the binary numbering system except you carry over when the value in the right column is 1 instead of 9. If you have 1 in the right column and add 1, you change the 1 to a 0 and place a 1 to the left of the 0 to give you 10:

$$\begin{array}{r} 1 \\ +1 \\ \hline 10 \end{array}$$

Now the confusion begins. Both the decimal number and the binary number seem to have the same value, which is ten. Don't believe everything you see. The decimal number does represent the number 10. However, the binary number 10 isn't the value 10 but the value 2.

The digits in the binary numbering system represent the state of a switch. A computer performs arithmetic by using the binary numbering system to change the state of sets of switches.

Reserving Memory

Although a unit of memory holds a byte, data used in a program can be larger than a byte and require 2, 4, or 8 bytes to be stored in memory. Before any data can be stored in memory, you must tell the computer how much space to reserve for data by using an abstract data type.

An *abstract data type* is a keyword of a programming language that specifies the amount of memory needed to store data and the kind of data that will be stored in that memory location. However, an abstract data type does not tell the computer how many bytes to reserve for the data. The number of bytes reserved for an abstract data type varies, depending on the programming language used to write the program and the type of computer used to compile the program.

Abstract data types in Java have a fixed size in order for programs to run in all Java runtime environments. In C and C++, the size of an abstract data type is based on the register size of the computer used to compile the program. The `int` and `float` data types are the size of the register. A `short` data type is half the size of an `int`, and a `long` data type is double the size of an `int`.

Think of an abstract data type as the term "case of tomatoes." You call the warehouse manager and say that you need to reserve enough shelf space to hold five cases of tomatoes. The warehouse manager knows how many shelves to reserve because she knows the size of a case of tomatoes.

The same is true about an abstract data type. You tell the computer to reserve space for an integer by using the abstract data type `int`. The computer already knows how much memory to reserve to store an integer.

The abstract data type also tells the computer the kind of data that will be stored at the memory location. This is important because computers manipulate data of some abstract data types differently than data of other abstract data types. This is similar to how the warehouse manager treats a case of paper plates differently than a case of tomatoes.

Table 1-2 contains a list of abstract data types. The first column contains keywords for each abstract data type. The second column lists the corresponding number of bits that are reserved in memory for a Java program. The third column shows the range of values that can be stored in the abstract data type. And the last column is the group within which the abstract data type belongs.

You choose the abstract data type that best suits the data that you want stored in memory, then use the abstract data type in a declaration statement to declare a variable. A *variable* is a reference to the memory location that you reserved using the declaration statement (see Chapter 2).

You should always reserve the proper amount of memory needed to store data because you might lose data if you reserve too small a space. This is like sending ten cases of tomatoes to the warehouse when you only reserved space for five cases. If you do this, the other five cases will get tossed aside.

Data Type	Data Type Size in Bits	Range of Values	Group
byte	8	–128 to 127	Integers
short	16	–32,768 to 32,767	Integers
int	32	–2,147,483,648 to 2,147,483,647	Integers
long	64	–9,223,372,036,854,775,808 to 9,223,372,036,854,775,807	Integers
char	16 (Unicode)	65,536 (Unicode)	Characters
float	32	3.4e-038 to 3.4e+038	Floating-point
double	64	1.7e-308 to 1.7e+308	Floating-point
boolean	1	0 or 1	Boolean

Table 1-2　Simple Java Data Types

Abstract Data Type Groups

You determine the amount of memory to reserve by determining the appropriate abstract data type group to use and then deciding which abstract data type within the group is right for the data.

There are four data type groups:

- **Integer**　Stores whole numbers and signed numbers. Great for storing the number of dollars in your wallet when you don't need a decimal value.
- **Floating-point**　Stores real numbers (fractional values). Perfect for storing bank deposits where pennies (fractions of a dollar) can quickly add up to a few dollars.
- **Character**　Stores a character. Ideal for storing names of things.
- **Boolean**　Stores a true or false value. The correct choice for storing a yes or no or true or false response to a question.

Integers

The *integer* abstract data type group consists of four abstract data types used to reserve memory to store whole numbers: byte, short, int, and long, as described in Table 1-2.

Depending on the nature of the data, sometimes an integer must be stored using a positive or negative sign, such as a +10 or –5. Other times an integer is assumed to be positive so there isn't any need to use a positive sign. An integer that is stored with a sign is called a *signed number*; an integer that isn't stored with a sign is called an *unsigned number*.

What's all this hoopla about signed numbers? The sign takes up 1 bit of memory that could otherwise be used to represent a value. For example, a byte has 8 bits, all of which can be used to store an unsigned number from 0 to 255. You can store a signed number in the range of –128 to +127.

C and C++ support unsigned integers. Java does not. An *unsigned integer* is a value that is implied to be positive. The positive sign is not stored in memory. All integers in Java are represented with a sign. Zero is stored as a positive number.

byte Abstract Data Type

The byte abstract data type is the smallest abstract data type in the integer group and is declared by using the keyword byte (see Figure 1-2). Programmers typically use a byte abstract data type when sending data to and receiving data from a file or across a network. The byte abstract data type is also commonly used when working with binary data that may not be compatible with other abstract data types. Choose a byte whenever you need to move data to and from a file or across a network.

Main memory

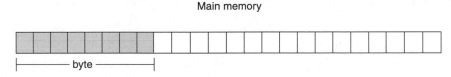

byte

Figure 1-2   A byte abstract data type in Java reserves 8 bits of main memory.

short Abstract Data Type

The short abstract data type is ideal for use in programs that run on 16-bit computers. However, most of those computers are on the trash heap and have been replaced by 32-bit and 64-bit computers! (See Figure 1-3.) Therefore, the short is the least used integer abstract data type. Choose a short if you ever need to store an integer in a program that runs on a very old computer.

Main memory

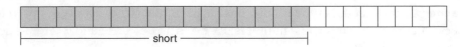

Figure 1-3   A `short` abstract data type in Java reserves 16 bits of main memory.

int Abstract Data Type

The `int` abstract data type is the most frequently used abstract data type of the integer group for a number of reasons (see Figure 1-4). Choose an `int`:

- For control variables in control loops
- In array indexes
- When performing integer math

Main memory

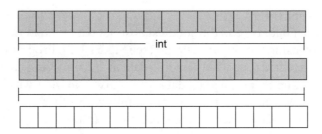

Figure 1-4   An `int` abstract data type in Java reserves 32 bits of main memory.

long Abstract Data Type

A `long` abstract data type (see Figure 1-5) is used whenever using whole numbers that are beyond the range of an `int` data type (refer to Table 1-2). Choose a `long` when storing the net worths of Bill Gates, Warren Buffet, and you in a program.

Floating-Point

Abstract data types in the *floating-point* group are used to store real numbers in memory. A *real number* contains a decimal value. There are two kinds of floating-point data types: `float` and `double` (as described in Table 1-2). The `float`

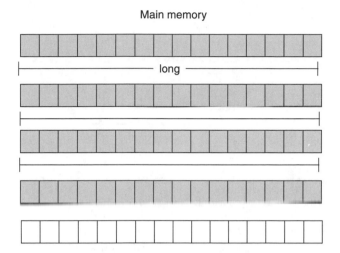

Figure 1-5   A `long` abstract data type in Java reserves 64 bits of main memory.

abstract data type is a single precision number, and a `double` is a double precision number. *Precision* of a number is the number of places after the decimal point that contains an accurate value.

The term *floating-point* refers to the way decimals are referenced in memory. There are two parts of a floating-point number: the real number, which is stored as a whole number, and the position of the decimal point within the whole number. This is why it is said that the decimal point "floats" within the number.

For example, the floating-point value 43.23 is stored as 4323 (no decimal point). Reference is made in the number indicating that the decimal point is placed after the second digit.

float Abstract Data Type

The `float` abstract data type (see Figure 1-6) is used for real numbers that require single precision, such as United States currency. *Single precision* means the value is precise up to 7 digits to the right of the decimal. For example, suppose you divide $53.50 evenly among 17 people. Each person would get $3.147058823529. Digits to the right of $3.1470588 are not guaranteed to be precise because of the way a `float` is stored in memory. Choose a `float` whenever you need to store a decimal value where only 7 digits to the right of the decimal must be accurate.

Main memory

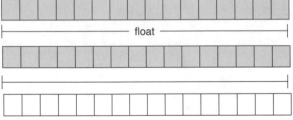

Figure 1-6   A float abstract data type in Java reserves 32 bits of main memory.

double Abstract Data Type

The double abstract data type (see Figure 1-7) is used to store real numbers that are very large or very small and require double the amount of memory that is reserved with a float abstract data type. Choose a double whenever you need to store a decimal value where more than 7 digits to the right of the decimal must be accurate.

Main memory

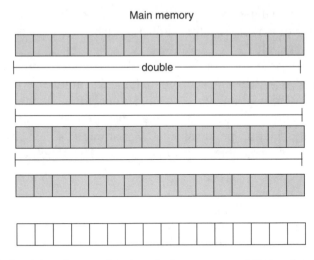

Figure 1-7   A double abstract data type in Java reserves 64 bits of main memory.

Characters

A *character* abstract data type (see Figure 1-8) is represented as an integer value that corresponds to a character set. A *character set* assigns an integer value to each character, punctuation, and symbol used in a language.

For example, the letter *A* is stored in memory as the value 65, which corresponds to the letter *A* in a character set. The computer knows to treat the value 65 as the letter *A* rather than the number 65 because memory was reserved using the `char` abstract data type. The keyword `char` tells the computer that the integer stored in that memory location is treated as a character and not a number.

There are two character sets used in programming, the American Standard Code for Information Interchange (ASCII) and Unicode. ASCII is the granddaddy of character sets and uses a byte to represent a maximum of 256 characters. However, a serious problem was evident after years of using ASCII. Many languages such as Russian, Arabic, Japanese, and Chinese have more than 256 characters in their language. A new character set called Unicode was developed to resolve this problem. Unicode uses 2 bytes to represent each character. Choose a `char` whenever you need to store a single character in memory.

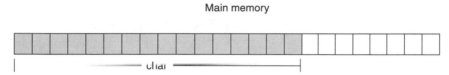

Main memory

Figure 1-8   A `char` abstract data type in Java reserves 16 bits of main memory.

Boolean Abstract Data Type

A `boolean` abstract data type (see Figure 1-9) reserves memory to store a `boolean` value, which is a `true` or `false` represented as a zero or one. Choose a `boolean` whenever you need to store one of two possibilities in memory.

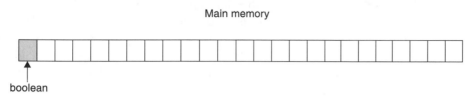

Main memory

boolean

Figure 1-9   A `boolean` abstract data type in Java reserves 1 bit of main memory.

Memory Addresses

Imagine main memory as a series of seemingly endless boxes organized into groups of eight. Each box holds a zero or one. Each group of eight boxes (1 byte) is assigned a unique number called a *memory address*, as shown in Figure 1-10. It is very important

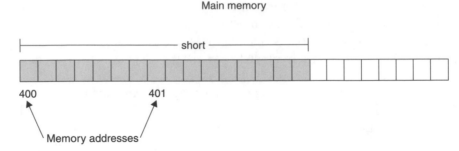

Figure 1-10   The memory address of the first byte is used to reference all bytes
reserved for an abstract data type.

to keep this in mind as you learn about data structures; otherwise, you can easily
become confused.

A memory address is indirectly or directly used within a program to access all eight
boxes. For example, say your program tells the computer that you want to copy data
stored in memory location 423—that is, the box whose address is 423. The computer
goes to that memory location and copies the data (zero or one) from box 423 and copies
data from the next seven boxes. Those next seven boxes don't have a memory address.
You could say that those seven boxes share the memory address of box 423.

Real Memory Addresses

Memory addresses are represented so far throughout this chapter as a decimal value,
such as "box 423." In reality, memory addresses are a 32-bit or 64-bit number, depending on the computer's operating system, and are represented as a hexadecimal value.

Hexadecimal is a numbering system similar to the decimal and binary numbering
systems. That is, hexadecimal values are used to count and they are used in arithmetic.
The hexadecimal numbering system has 16 digits from 0 through 9 and A through F,
which represents 10 through 15. Here is how memory address 258,425,506 is represented in hexadecimal notation 0x0F6742A2.

Abstract Data Types and Memory Addresses

Previously in this chapter you learned that you reserve memory for data by using an
abstract data type. Some abstract data types reserve memory in a size that is greater
than 1 byte. For example, the `short` abstract data type in Java reserves 2 bytes of
memory.

Since each byte of memory has its own memory address, you might assume a `short` has two memory addresses because it uses 2 bytes of memory. That's not the case. The computer uses the memory address of the first byte to reference any abstract data type that reserves multiple bytes of memory.

Let's say that space was reserved in memory for a `short` abstract data type (see Figure 1-10). Two memory locations are reserved, memory addresses 400 and 401. However, only memory address 400 is used to reference the `short`. The computer automatically knows that the value stored in memory address 401 is part of the value stored in memory address 400 because the space was reserved using an `short` abstract data type. Therefore, the computer copies all the bits from memory address 400 *and* all the bits from memory address 401 whenever a request is made by the program to copy the integer stored at memory address 400.

Quiz

1. What is an abstract data type?

2. What abstract data type would be used to store a whole number?

3. Explain how a memory address is used to access an abstract data type that is larger than 1 byte.

4. What is the difference between a `float` abstract data type and a `double` abstract data type?

5. What is precision?

6. Explain how memory is organized within a computer.

7. What is a numbering system?

8. Why is the binary numbering system used in computing?

9. Why don't you directly specify the number of bytes to reserve in memory to store data?

10. Explain the impact signed and unsigned numbers have on memory.

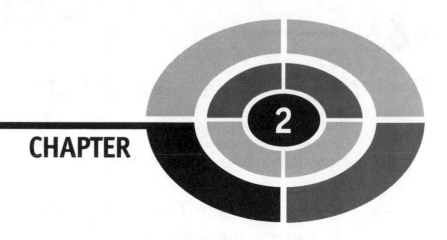

The Point About Variables and Pointers

Some programmers cringe at the mere mention of the word "pointer" because it brings to mind complex, low-level programming techniques that are confounding. Hogwash. Pointers are child play, literally. Watch a 15-month-old carefully and you'll notice that she points to things she wants, and that's a pointer in a nutshell. A pointer is a variable that is used to point to a memory address whose content you want to use in your program. You'll learn all about pointer variables in this chapter.

Declaring Variables and Objects

Memory is reserved by using a data type in a declaration statement. The form of a declaration statement varies depending on the programming language you use. Here is a declaration statement for C, C++, and Java:

```
int myVariable;
```

There are three parts to this declaration statement:

- **Data type**   Tells how much memory to reserve and the kind of data that will be stored in that memory location
- **Variable name**   A name used within the program to refer to the contents of that memory location
- **Semicolon**   Tells the computer this is an instruction (statement)

Primitive Data Types and User-Defined Data Types

In Chapter 1, you were introduced to the concept of abstract data types, which are used to reserve computer memory. Abstract data types are divided into two categories, primitive data types and user-defined data types. A primitive data type is defined by the programming language, such as the data types you learned about in the previous chapter. Some programmers call these built-in data types.

The other category of abstract data type, a user-defined data type, is a group of primitive data types defined by the programmer. For example, let's say you want to store students' grades in memory. You'll need to store 4 data elements: the student's ID, first name, last name, and grade. You could use primitive data types for each data element, but primitive data types are not grouped together; each exists as separate data elements.

A better approach is to group primitive data types into a user-defined data type to form a record. You probably heard the term "record" used when you learned about databases. Remember that a database consists of one or more tables. A table is similar to a spreadsheet consisting of columns and rows. A row is also known as a record. A user-defined data type defines columns (primitive data types) that comprise a row (a user-defined data type).

The form used to define a user-defined data type varies depending on the programming language used to write the program. Some programming languages, such as Java, do not support user-defined data types. Instead, attributes of a class are used to group together primitive data types; this is discussed later in this chapter.

In the C and C++ programming languages, you define a user-defined data type by defining a structure. Think of a structure as a stencil of the letter *A*. The stencil isn't the letter *A*, but it defines what the letter *A* looks like. If you want a letter *A*, you place the stencil on a piece of paper and trace the letter *A*. If you want to make another letter *A*, you use the same stencil and repeat the process. You can make as many letter *A*'s as you wish by using the stencil.

The same is true about a structure. When you want the group of primitive data types represented by the structure, you create an *instance* of the structure. An instance is the same as the letter *A* appearing on the paper after you remove the stencil.

Each instance contains the same primitive data types that are defined in the structure, although each instance has its own copy of those primitive data types.

Defining a User-Defined Data Type

A structure definition consists of four elements:

- **struct**   Tells the computer that you are defining a structure
- **Structure name**   The name used to uniquely identify the structure and used to declare instances of a structure
- **Structure body**   Open and close braces within which are primitive data types that are declared when an instance of the structure is declared
- **Semicolon**   Tells the computer this is an instruction (statement)

The body of a structure can contain any combination of primitive data types and previously defined user-defined data types depending on the nature of the data required by your program. Here is a structure that defines a student record consisting of a student number and grade. The name of this user-defined data type is StudentRecord:

```
struct StudentRecord
{
   int studentNumber;
   char grade;
};
```

Declaring a User-Defined Data Type

You declare an instance of a user-defined data type using basically the same technique that you used to declare a variable. However, you use the name of the structure in place of the name of the primitive data type in the declaration station.

Let's say that you want to create an instance of the `StudentRecord` structure defined in the previous section. Here's the declaration statement that you need to declare in your program:

```cpp
#include <iostream>
using namespace std;
struct StudentRecord
{
    int studentNumber;
    char grade;
} ;
void main()
{
    StudentRecord myStudent;
    myStudent.studentNumber = 10;
    myStudent.grade = 'A';
    cout << "grades: " << myStudent.studentNumber << " "
        << myStudent.grade << endl;
}
```

The declaration statement tells the computer to reserve memory the size required to store the `StudentRecord` user-defined data type and to associate `myStudent` with that memory location. The size of a user-defined data type is equal to the sum of the sizes of the primitive data types declared in the body of the structure.

The size of the `StudentRecord` user-defined data type is the sum of the sizes of an `integer` and a `char`. As you recall from Chapter 1, the size of a primitive data type is measured in bits. The number of bits for the same primitive data type varies depending on the programming language. Therefore, programmers refer to the name of the primitive data type rather than the number of bits when reserving memory. The computer knows how many bits to reserve for each primitive data type.

User-Defined Data Types and Memory

Data elements within the body of a structure are placed sequentially in memory when an instance of the structure is declared within a program. Figure 2-1 illustrates memory reserved when the `myStudent` instance of `StudentRecord` is declared.

The instance name `myStructure` is an alias for the memory address that is reserved for the first primitive data type defined in the `StudentRecord` structure, which is memory address 1 in Figure 2-1. For the sake of simplicity, let's say each block shown in Figure 2-1 represents 1 byte of memory and the size of an `int` is 2 bytes.

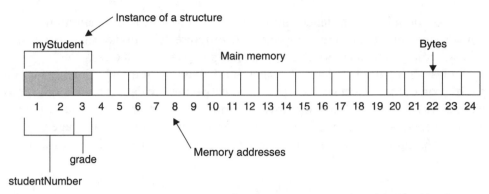

Figure 2-1   Memory for elements of a structure are placed in sequential memory locations when an instance of the structure is declared.

Each primitive data type of a structure has its own memory address. The first primitive data type in this example is studentNumber, and its name references memory location 1. The second primitive data type is grade, and its name references memory location 2.

What happened to memory location 1? This can be confusing. Remember that each byte of memory is assigned a unique memory address. Some primitive data types are larger than a byte and therefore must occupy more than one memory address, which is the case in this example with an int. The first primitive data type takes up the first 2 bytes of memory. Therefore, the second primitive data type defined in the structure is placed in the next available byte of memory, which is memory location 2.

Accessing Elements of a User-Defined Data Type

Elements of a data structure are accessed by using the name of the instance of the structure and the name of the element separated by a dot operator. Let's say that you want to assign the grade A to the grade element of the myStudent instance of the StudentRecord structure. Here's how you would write the assignment statement:

```
myStudent.grade = 'A';
```

You use elements of a structure the same way you use a variable within your program except you must reference both the name of the instance and the name of the element in order to access the element. The combination of instance name and element name is the alias for the memory location of the element.

User-Defined Data Type and Classes

Structures are used in procedure languages such as C. Object-oriented languages such as C++ and Java use both structures and classes to group together unlike primitive data types into a cohesive unit.

A class definition is a stencil similar in concept to a structure definition in that both use the definition to create instances. A structure definition creates an instance of a structure, while a class definition creates an instance of a class.

A class definition translates attributes and behaviors of a real life object into a simulation of that object within a program. Attributes are data elements similar to elements of a structure. Behaviors are instructions that perform specific tasks known as either methods or functions, depending on the programming language used to write the program. Java references these as methods and C++ references them as functions.

Defining a Class

A class definition resembles a definition of a structure, as you can see in the following example. A class definition consists of four elements:

- **class** Tells the computer that you are defining a class
- **Class name** The name used to uniquely identify the class and used to declare instances of a class
- **Class body** Open and close braces within which are primitive data types that are declared when an instance of the class is declared and definitions of methods and functions that are members of the class
- **Semicolon** Tells the computer this is an instruction (statement)

The following class definition written in C++ defines the same student record that is defined in the structure defined in the previous section of this chapter. However, the class definition also defines a function that displays the student number and grade on the screen.

```
class StudentRecord {
    int studentNumber;
    char grade;
    void displayGrade() {
        cout<<"Student: " << studentNumber << " Grade: "
        << grade << endl;
    }
};
```

Declaring an Instance of a Class and a Look at Memory

You declare an instance of a class much the same way you declare a structure. That is, you use the name of the class followed by the name of the instance of the class in a declaration statement. Here is how an instance of the StudentRecord class is declared:

```
StudentRecord myStudent;
```

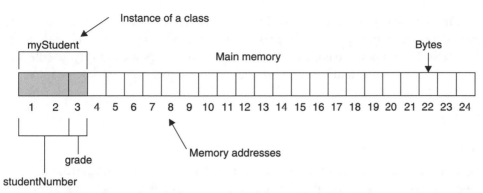

Figure 2-2   Memory for attributes of a class are placed in sequential memory locations when an instance of the class is declared.

Memory is reserved for attributes of a class definition sequentially when an instance is declared, much the same way as memory is reserved for elements of a structure. Figure 2-2 shows memory allocation for the `myStudent` instances of the `StudentRecord` class. Notice that this is basically the same way memory for a structure is allocated.

Methods and functions are stored separately in memory from attributes when an instance is declared because methods and functions are shared among all instances of the same class.

Accessing Members of a Class

Attributes, methods, and functions are referred to as members of a class. You access members of an instance of a class using the name of the instance, the dot operator and the name of the member, much the same ways as you access an element of a structure.

Here is how to access the grade attribute of the `myStudent` instance of the `StudentRecord` class and call the `displayGrade()` method:

```
myStudent.grade = 'A';
myStudent.displayGrade();
```

Pointers

Whenever you reference the name of a variable, the name of an element of a structure, or the name of an attribute of a class, you are telling the computer that you want to do something with the contents stored at the corresponding memory location.

In the first statement in the following example, the computer is told to store the letter *A* into the memory location represented by the variable `grade`. The last statement tells the computer to copy the contents of the memory location represented by the `grade` variable and store it in the memory location represented by the `oldGrade` variable.

```
char grade = 'A';
char oldGrade;
oldGrade = grade;
```

A pointer is a variable and can be used as an element of a structure and as an attribute of a class in some programming languages such as C++, but not Java. However, the contents of a pointer is a memory address of another location of memory, which is usually the memory address of another variable, element of a structure, or attribute of a class.

Declaring a Pointer

A pointer is declared similar to how you declare a variable but with a slight twist. The following example declares a pointer called `ptGrade`. There are four parts of this declaration:

- **Data type**   The data type of the memory address stored in the pointer
- **Asterisk (*)**   Tells the computer that you are declaring a pointer
- **Variable name**   The name that uniquely identifies the pointer and is used to reference the pointer within your program
- **Semicolon**   Tells the computer this is an instruction (statement)

```
char *ptGrade;
```

Data Type and Pointers

As you will recall, a data type tells the computer the amount of memory to reserve and the kind of data that will be stored at that memory location. However, the data type of a pointer tells the computer something different. It tells the computer the data type of the value at the memory location whose address is contained in the pointer.

Confused? Many programmers are confused about the meaning of the data type used to declare a pointer, so you're in good company. The best way to clear any confusion is to get back to basics.

The asterisk (*) used when declaring a pointer tells the computer the amount of memory to reserve and the kind of data that will be stored at that location. That is, the memory size is sufficient to hold a memory address, and the kind of data stored there is a memory address.

You're probably wondering why you use a data type when declaring a pointer. Before answering that question, let's make sure you have a firm understanding of pointers. The following example declares four variables. The first statement declares an integer variable called studentNumber. The second statement declares a char variable called grade. The last two statements each declare a pointer. Figure 2-3 depicts memory reserved by these statements. Assume that a memory address is 4 bytes for this example.

```
int studentNumber;
char grade;
char *ptGrade;
int *ptStudentNumber;
```

The char data type in the ptGrade pointer declaration tells the computer that the address that will be stored in ptGrade is the address of a character. As you'll see in the next section, the contents of the memory location associated with ptGrade will contain the address of the grade variable.

Likewise, the int data type of the ptStudentNumber pointer states that the contents of the memory location associated with ptStudentNumber will contain the address of an integer variable, which will be the address of the studentNumber variable.

Why does the computer need to know this? For now, let's simply say that programmers instruct the computer to manipulate memory addresses using pointer arithmetic. In order for the computer to carry out those instructions, the computer must know the data type of the address contained in a pointer. You'll learn pointer arithmetic later in this chapter.

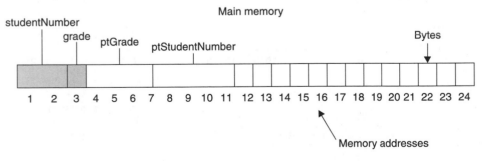

Figure 2-3   Memory allocated when two pointers and two variables are declared

Assigning an Address to a Pointer

An address of a variable is assigned to a pointer variable by using the address operator (&). Before you learn about dereferencing a variable, let's review an assignment statement. The following assignment statement tells the computer to copy the value stored at the memory location that is associated with the `grade` variable and store the value into the memory location associated with the `oldGrade` variable:

```
oldGrade = grade;
```

An assignment statement implies that you want the contents of a variable and not the address of the variable. The address operator tells the computer to ignore the implied assignment and assign the memory address of the variable and not the content of the variable.

The next example tells the computer by using the address operator to copy the address of the variable to the pointer variable. That is, the memory address of the grade variable is copied to the `ptGrade` pointer variable, and the memory address of the `studentNumber` variable is assigned to the `ptStudentNumber` pointer:

```
ptGrade = &grade;
ptStudentNumber = &studentNumber;
```

Figure 2-4 depicts memory after the previous two statements execute. Notice that the `grade` variable is an alias for memory address 3 and the `studentNumber` variable is the alias for memory address 1. The content of `ptGrade` pointer is 3, which is the memory address of the grade variable. Likewise, the content of pointer `ptStudentNumber` is 1, which is the memory address of `studentNumber`.

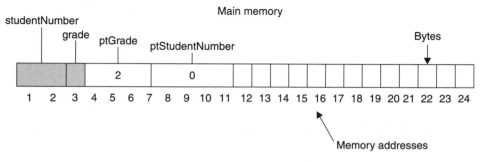

Figure 2-4   Memory allocated after pointers are assigned memory addresses

Accessing Data Pointed to by a Pointer

A pointer variable references a memory location that contains a memory address. Sometimes a programmer wants to copy that memory address to another pointer variable. This is accomplished by using an assignment statement as shown here:

```
ptOldGrade = ptNewGrade;
```

You'll notice that this assignment statement is identical to assignment statements used with any variable. Remember that the assignment statement tells the computer to copy the contents of a variable regardless if the content is a memory address or any other value.

Other times, programmers want to the use the content of the memory address stored in the pointer variable. This may be tricky to understand, so let's look at an example to clear up any confusion. The following statements will be familiar to you because we've used them in examples throughout this chapter.

The first two statements declare variables, one of which is initialized with a value. The next two statements declare pointer variables. And the last statement assigns the address of the first variable to pointer variables. Figure 2-5 shows how memory looks after these statements execute.

```
char oldGrade;
char grade = 'A';
char *ptGrade;
char *ptOldGrade;
ptGrade = &grade;
```

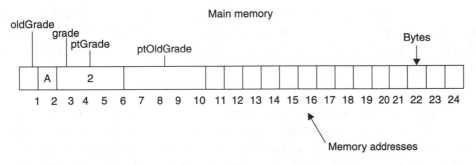

Figure 2-5   Memory allocated after values are assigned to variables

Let's say a programmer wants to use the value stored in the `grade` variable to display the grade on the screen. However, the programmer wants to use only the `ptGrade` pointer to do this. Here's how it is done.

The programmer uses the pointer dereferencing operator (sometimes called the dereferencing operator), which is the asterisk (*), to dereference the point variable. Think of dereferencing as telling the computer you are referring to to go to the memory address contained in the pointer and then perform the operation. Without dereferencing, the computer is told to use the contents of the pointer when performing the operation.

Let's say that you want to copy the content of `ptGrade` to `ptOldGrade`. Here's how you would do it:

```
ptOldGrade = ptGrade;
```

Figure 2-6 shows you the effect this statement has on memory.

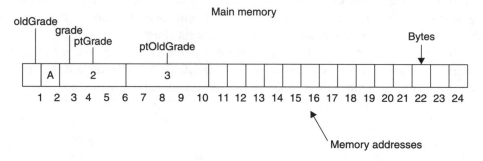

Figure 2-6   Memory allocated after the value of the `ptGrade` is copied to `ptOldGrade`.

Now let's suppose you want to copy the contents of `grade` to the `oldGrade` variable, but you only want to use the `ptGrade` pointer. You do this by dereferencing the `ptGrade` pointer variable using the asterisk (*) as the dereferencing pointer operator as shown here:

```
char oldGrade = *ptGrade;
```

The previous statement tells the computer to go to the memory address contained in the `ptGrade` pointer variable and then perform the assignment operation, which copies the value of memory address 2 to the memory address represented by the `oldGrade` variable, which is memory address 1. The result is shown in Figure 2-7.

You can dereference a pointer variable any time you want to use the contents of the memory address pointed to by the variable and use the dereference pointer variable in any statement that you would use a variable.

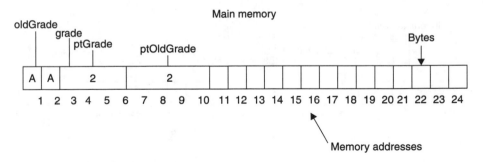

Figure 2-7   Memory allocated after the contents of the memory address pointed to by
ptGrade is copied to the oldGrade variable.

Pointer Arithmetic

Pointers are used to step through memory sequentially by using pointer arithmetic
and the incremental (++) or decremental (– –) operator. The incremental operator
increases the value of a variable by 1, and the decremental operator decreases the
value of a variable by 1.

In the following example, the value of the studentNumber variable is incremented by 1, making the final value 1235.

```
int studentNumber = 1234;
studentNumber++;
```

Likewise, the next example decreases the value of the studentNumber variable by 1, resulting in the final value of 1233.

```
int studentNumber = 1234;
studentNumber--;
```

Pointer arithmetic uses the incremental and decremental operator in a similar but
slightly different way. The following statements declare two variables used to store
student numbers and two pointers each pointing to one of those variables. Figure 2-8
depicts memory allocation after these statements execute.

```
int studentNumber1 = 1234;
int studentNumber2 = 5678;
int *ptStudentNumber1;
int *ptStudentNumber2;
ptStudentNumber1 = &studentNumber1;
ptStudentNumber2 = &studentNumber2;
```

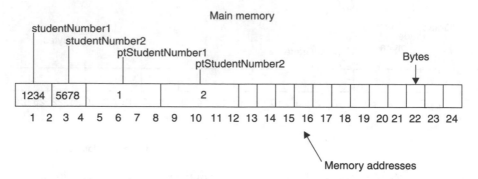

Figure 2-8 Memory allocation before incrementing `ptStudentNumber1`

What would be the value stored in the pointer variable `studentNumber1` if the `studentNumber1` is incremented by 1 using the following statement?

```
ptStudentNumber1++;
```

This is tricky because the value of `ptStudentNumber1` is 0. If you increment it by one, the new value is 1. However, memory address 2 is the second half of the memory location reserved for `studentNumber1`. This means that `ptStudentNumber1` would point to the middle of the values of `studentNumber1`, which doesn't make sense.

That's not what happens. The computer uses pointer arithmetic. Values are incremented and decremented in pointer arithmetic using the size of a data type. That is, if the memory address contains an integer and the memory address is incremented, the computer adds the size of an integer to the current memory address.

Let's return to Figure 2-8 and see how this works. `ptStudentNumber1` contains the memory address 1. If you go to memory address 1, you'll notice that the memory address stores an integer. In the example, the size of an integer is 2 bytes. When `ptStudentNumber1` is incremented using pointer arithmetic, the computer adds 2 bytes to the address stored in `ptStudentNumber1` making the new value 2, which is stored in `ptStudentNumber1`. Figure 2-9 shows the results of incrementing using pointer arithmetic.

Decrementing a value using pointer arithmetic is very similar to incrementing a value, except the size of a data type is subtracted from the value. Let's return to Figure 2-8 for a moment. If the following statement executed, the value of `ptStudentNumber2` would be 1 because the computer subtracts the size of an integer (2 bytes) from the current value of the `ptStudentNumber2` (2).

```
ptStudentNumber2--;
```

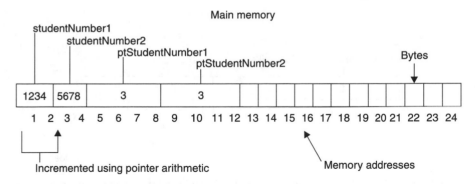

Figure 2-9　Memory allocation after incrementing `ptStudentNumber1`

Pointers to Pointers

Imagine having a list of a million students along with their final grades and student numbers and being asked to sort the list by last name, first name, and student number. Intuitively, you might think about making two copies of this list, each placed in one of the sort orders. However, this wastes memory. There is a better approach to sort the list: use pointers to pointers.

You learned that a pointer is a variable that contains the memory address of another variable. A *pointer to a pointer* is also a variable that contains the memory address, except a pointer to a pointer contains the memory address of another pointer variable.

Confused? You're not alone. The concept of a pointer to a pointer isn't intuitive to understand. However, we can clear up any confusion by declaring variables and storing values into memory.

Let's begin by declaring four `char` variables and initializing them with letters of the alphabet. This is shown in the first statement of the following example. The second statement declares a pointer called `ptInitial` and a pointer to a pointer called `ptPtInitial`. A pointer is declared using a signal asterisk (*). A pointer to a pointer is declared using a double asterisk (**).

```
char inital1 = 'D', inital2 = 'A', inital3 = 'C', inital4 = 'B';
char *ptInitial, **ptPtInitial;
ptInitial = &inital1;
ptPtInitial = &ptInitial;
```

With variables declared, the next two statements assign values to the pointer and to the pointer to a pointer. In both cases, the ampersand (&) is used as the dereferencing operator.

The `ptInitial` pointer variable is assigned the address of variable `inital1`, which is memory address 1. The `ptPtInitial` pointer to a pointer variable is

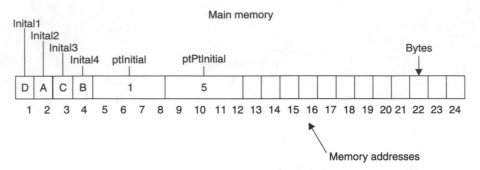

Figure 2-10 The pointer to a pointer variable is assigned the memory address of the `ptInitial` pointer.

assigned the memory address of `ptInitial`. The address of `ptInitial` is memory address 5. Figure 2-10 shows the allocated memory after these statements execute.

Programmers use a pointer to a pointer to tell a computer to use the contents of the memory address contained in the pointer variable that the pointer to a pointer is pointing to. This is a mouthful, so we'll restate this using an example:

You can use the content of the `initall` variable by referencing the `ptPtInitial` variable. Here's how this is done:

```
cout << **ptPtInitial;
```

The `cout` statement is used in C++ to display something on the screen. In this example, you're displaying the content of the `initall` variable, although it doesn't seem to be doing so. This statement is telling the computer to go to the memory address stored in the `ptPtInitial` pointer to a pointer variable, which is memory address 5 (see Figure 2-11). The content of that memory address is another memory address, which is memory address 1. The computer is told to go to memory address 1 and display the content of that memory address, which is the letter *D*.

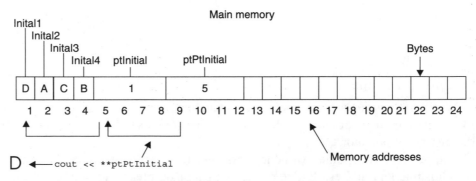

Figure 2-11 Two memory addresses are referenced when using a pointer to a pointer to display a value on the screen.

Quiz

1. What is a user-defined data type?
2. How do you determine the size of a structure?
3. Why would you use a structure?
4. Why happens when you declare an instance of a structure?
5. How do you access parts of a structure?
6. What is a pointer?
7. Why would you use a pointer in a program?
8. What is a pointer to a pointer?
9. Why would you use a pointer to a pointer in a program?
10. What is shown on the screen if you display the content of a pointer variable?

CHAPTER 3

What Is an Array?

Computer memory is like a small town—or a large town, depending on the amount of memory available in the computer. Each byte of memory is a building that has its own address called a *memory address*, and the town's people are bits of data living in those buildings. The small town inside your computer is a neighborly place. A program refers to buildings by name rather than by address, and puts Mary's grade in the maryGrade building. However, being personable is troublesome when you need to come up with hundreds of names for these buildings. That is, unless you use an array. You'll explore arrays, multidimensional arrays, pointer arrays, and an array of pointers to pointers in this chapter.

An Array

An *array* is a way to reference a series of memory locations using the same name. Each memory location is represented by an array element. An *array element* is similar to one variable except it is identified by an index value instead of a name. An *index* value is a number used to identify an array element.

Now we'll show you what an array looks like, with the three array elements shown next. The array is called `grades`. The first array element is called `grades[0]`. The zero is the index value. The square bracket tells the computer that the value inside the square bracket is an index.

```
grades[0]
grades[1]
grades[2]
```

Each array element is like a variable name. For example, the following variables are equivalent to array elements. There is no difference between array elements and variables—well, *almost* no difference, but we'll get to the differences in a moment. For now, let's explore how they are the same. Here are three integer variables:

```
int maryGrade;
int bobGrade;
int amberGrade;
```

You probably recall from your programming class that you store a value into a memory location by using an assignment statement. Here are two assignment statements. The first assigns a value to a variable, and the other assigns a value to an array element. Notice that these statements are practically the same except reference is made to the index of the array element in the second statement:

```
int grades[1];
maryGrade = 90;
 grades[0] = 90;
```

Suppose you want to use the value stored in a memory location. There are a number of ways to do this in a program, but a common way is to use another assignment statement like the ones shown in the next example. The first assignment statement uses two variables, the next assignment statement uses two array elements, and the last assignment statement assigns the value referenced by a variable name and assigns that value to an array element:

```
bobGrade = maryGrade;
grades[0] = grades[1];
grades[0] = bobGrade;
```

You've probably noticed a pattern developing. You use an array element the same way you use a variable.

Why an Array?

There are two important differences between an array element and a variable, and those differences make working with large amounts of data a breeze. Suppose you had to work with 100 grades to calculate the average grade. How would you do this?

The challenge isn't applying the formula for calculating an average. You know how that's done. The challenge is to come up with 100 variable names and then reference all those variable names in a program. Ouch!

First, you'd need to sum all the grades by writing a statement similar to the following. (We'll stop at three variables because it's difficult to identify 100 variables—and we'd run out of space on this page.)

```
sum = maryGrade + bobGrade + amberGrade;
```

Now, here's how a smart programmer meets this challenge using an array:

```
sum = 0;
for (int i = 0; i < 100; i++)
   sum = sum + grades[i];
```

Big difference. The control variable of the for loop is the index for the array element, enabling the program to quickly walk through all array elements in two lines of code. (The first statement has nothing to do with walking through all the array elements. It only initializes the sum variable with the total grades.)

The other difference between an array and a variable is that all the array elements are next to each other in memory. Variables can be anywhere in memory. For example, grades[0] is next to grades[1] in memory, grades[1] is next to grades[2] in memory, and so on. In contrast, maryGrade and bobGrade variables can be anywhere in memory, even if they are declared in the same declaration statement.

You might be scratching your head right now thinking, that's an interesting bit of computer trivia. So what? But the location of array elements is important when pointers (see Chapter 2) are used to manipulate data stored in memory. It is more efficient to point to array elements than variables because the computer moves to the next memory location when you point to the next array element.

Arrays and Data Structures

Some programmers might say that arrays are the backbone of data structures because an array enables a programmer to easily reorganize hundreds of values stored in memory by using an array of pointers to pointers.

This is a mouthful to say. So we drew a picture to show you the importance of arrays in data structures. Figure 3-1 shows memory; you'll remember this from the previous chapters in this book. Each block is a byte. We'll say that two bytes are needed to store a memory address in memory. You need to store a memory address in memory because you'll use it to refer to other memory addresses in the "An Array of Pointers" section of this chapter.

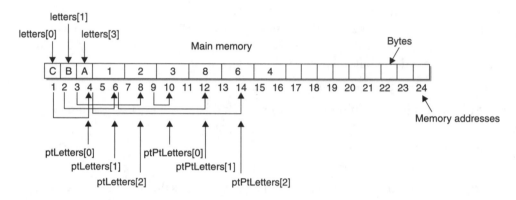

Figure 3-1   Elements of an array are stored sequentially in memory.

First, create an array called letters and assign characters to it, as shown here:

```
char letters[3];
letters[0] = 'C';
letters[1] = 'B';
letters[2] = 'A';
```

You'll notice in Figure 3-1 that each letter appears one after the other in memory. This is because these values are assigned to elements of an array, and each array element is placed sequentially in memory.

Next, create an array of pointers. As you'll recall from Chapter 2, a *pointer* is a variable that contains a memory address of another variable. In this example, you'll use an array of pointers instead of a pointer variable.

An *array of pointers* is nearly identical to a pointer variable except each array element contains a memory address. Assign the memory address of each element of the letters array to elements of the ptLetters array, which is an array of pointers. Here's how this is done in C and C++:

```
char * ptLetters[3];
for (int i = 0; i < 3; i++)
   ptLetters[i] = &letters[i];
```

Remember from Chapter 2 that the ampersand (&), which is called the address operator, tells the computer to assign the memory address of the element of the letters array and not the contents of the element.

The final step is to create an array of pointers to pointers and then use it to change the order of the letters array when printing the letters array on the screen. A *pointer to a pointer* is a variable that contains the address of another pointer. In the example, you use an array of pointers to a pointer where each element of the array is like a pointer to a pointer variable. That is, each element is assigned an address of a pointer.

Use the following code to assign the memory address of each element of the ptLetters pointer array to the ptPtLetters pointer to pointer array. Notice that you don't use a for loop. This is because you need to change the order of the letters array without changing the letters array itself. Figure 3-1 shows how memory looks after the following code executes. If you printed elements of the ptPtLetters array, what would be displayed on the screen?

```
char ** ptPTLetters[3];
ptPtLetters[0] = &ptLetters[2];
ptPtLetters[1] = &ptLetters[1];
ptPtLetters[2] = &ptLetters[0];
```

Here is the code that prints the ptPtLetters array:

```
for ( i = 0; i <3; i++)
   cout << **ptPtLetters[i] << endl;
```

The answer to the question is A B C. Follow Figure 3-1 as we explain how this works. The first element of the ptPtLetters array is located at memory address 10. The content of memory address 10 is 8, which is memory address 8 because memory address 10 is the last element of the array ptLetters—a pointer. The value of memory address 8 is 3, which is the memory address of the third element of the array letters.

When the computer sees the ptPtLetters[i] statement for the first time, it goes to the array element ptPtLetters[0] and reads its value, which is 8. The computer then goes to memory address 8 and reads its content because memory address 8 is a pointer. The content of memory address 8 is 3, which is the memory address of the third element of the letters array. The computer reads the content of memory address 3 and displays the content on the screen.

This can be a bit tricky to follow unless you use Figure 3-1 as a guide; you can also use Figure 3-1 to explain how the computer displays the other letters.

The importance of using arrays for data structures is that you can easily change the order of data by using pointers and pointers to pointers without having to touch the original data. Some smart programmer might tell you that you're not saving any time or memory by using pointers and pointers to pointers to rearrange an array of characters. The programmer is correct. However, we're juggling characters to illustrate how arrays and pointers to pointers work. In the real world, pointers typically point to a whole group of information such as a client's name, address, phone number, and other pertinent data. Instead of juggling all that information, you need only to juggle memory addresses.

Declaring an Array

The way to declare an array depends on the programming language used to write your program. In Java, there are two techniques for declaring an array. You can declare and initialize an array either where memory is allocated at compile time or where memory is dynamically allocated at runtime. *Allocation* is another way of saying reserving memory.

Let's begin by declaring an array where memory is reserved when you compile your program. This technique is similar in Java, C, and C++, except in Java you must initialize the array when the array is declared. There are four components of a statement that declares an array. These components are a data type, an array name, the total number of array element to create, and a semicolon (;). The semicolon tells the computer that the preceding is a statement. Here's the declaration statement in C and C++:

```
int grades[10];
```

In Java, you must initialize the array when the array is declared as shown here. The size of the array is automatically determined by counting the number of values within the braces. Therefore, there isn't any need to place the size of the array within the square brackets:

```
int[] grades = {0,0,0,0,0,0,0,0,0,0};
```

The *data type* is a keyword that tells the computer the amount of memory to reserve for each element of the array. In this example, the computer is told to reserve enough memory to store an integer for each array element.

The *array name* is the name you use within a program to reference an array element. The array name in this example is `grades`. The number within the square brackets is the total number of elements that will be in the array. The previous statements tell the computer to create an array of 10 elements.

Avoid making a common rookie mistake. Previously in this chapter you learned that the index for the first array element is zero, not one. Therefore, the tenth array element has the index value 9, not 10.

Some programs confuse an index with the total number of array elements. That is, they use the value 9 within the square brackets when declaring an array because they assume they are declaring 10 elements. In reality, they are declaring an array of 9 elements. The confusion stems from the fact that 9 is the index to reference the tenth array element.

With a little practice you can avoid making this mistake. Remember that the value within the square brackets in the statement that creates an array is not an index, although it resembles an index. This value is the number of array elements you need. That is, you insert the number 10 within the square brackets if you need 10 array elements. You use the index value of 9 if you want to access the tenth element.

In order to allocate memory at compile time, you must know the number of array elements that you need. Sometimes you don't know this, especially if your program loads the array with data stored in a database. The amount of data stored in a database typically fluctuates.

The solution in Java is to allocate memory at runtime. Programmers call this *dynamically allocating memory*. You dynamically allocate memory by using the new operator when declaring the array, as shown here:

```
int grades[] = new int[10];
```

This example looks a little strange, but it creates the same array as is created in the previous example. There are three things happening in this statement.

First, the new operator tells the computer to reserve 10 array elements, each the size of an int data type. The new operator returns a reference to the allocated memory.

Next, a reference to an int data type called grades is declared (int grades[]).

Last, the reference to the memory allocation returned by the new operator is assigned to the reference declared in the program.

This can be confusing even for experienced programmers to understand. If you're confused, remember this visitor's locker room example: a stadium has a locker room with "Visitors" on the door. This is similar to the reference grades[]. The visitor's locker room refers to the visiting team similar to the way grades[] refers to allocated memory: each game brings in a different visiting team who is assigned to the visitor's locker room. This is similar to assigning allocated memory to the reference grades[].

Multidimensional Arrays

The array described in this chapter is referred to as a *one-dimensional array* because the array consists of one series of elements. However, an array can have more than one series of elements. This is called a *multidimensional array*.

A multidimensional array consists of two or more arrays defined by sets of array elements, as shown in Figure 3-2. Each set of array elements is an array. The first set of array elements is considered the primary array, and the second and subsequent sets of array elements are considered subarrays.

There are two arrays in the multidimensional array shown in Figure 3-2. Each element of the first array points to a corresponding array. For example, `letters[1]` in Figure 3-2 points to the array beginning with array element `letters[1][0]` where the zero is the first element of the second array.

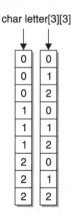

Figure 3-2   A two-dimensional array is a multidimensional array consisting of two arrays.

Although you can create an array with any size multidimension, many programmers limit an array to two dimensions. Any size greater than two dimensions becomes unwieldy to manage.

An analogy we find helpful is visualizing a table (rows and columns) for a two-dimensional array and a cube (or similar figure) for a three-dimensional array.

Why Use a Multidimensional Array?

A multidimensional array can be useful to organize subgroups of data within an array. Let's say that a student has three grades, a mid-term grade, a final exam grade, and a final grade. You can store all three grades for an endless number of students in a two-dimensional array, as shown in Figure 3-3.

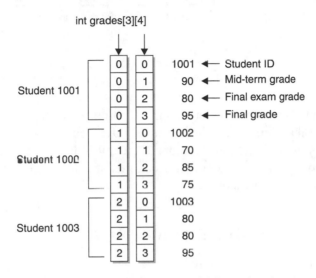

Figure 3-3   All three grades can be stored in a multidimensional array.

Figure 3-3 declares a multidimensional array of integers. The first set of array elements contains three array elements, one for each student. The second set of array elements has four array elements. The first of the four elements contains the `student ID` and the other three contain the three grades for that student ID.

In addition to organizing data stored in elements of an array, a multidimensional array can store memory addresses of data in a pointer array and an array of pointers to pointers, which are discussed later in "An Array of Pointers to Pointers."

Multidimensional Array in Memory

Data stored in a multidimensional array is stored sequentially by sets of elements, as shown in Figure 3-4. The first set of four array elements is placed in memory, followed by the second set of four array elements, and so on.

The name of a multidimensional array references the memory address of the first element of the first set of four elements. That is, `grades` is the equivalent of using memory address 1 in Figure 3-4. You can use the name of a multidimensional array as a pointer to the entire array.

The index of the first element of the first set of array elements points to the memory address where values assigned to array elements are stored.

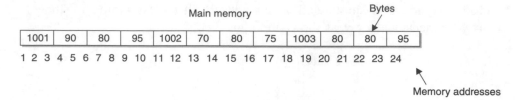

Figure 3-4 Elements of a multidimensional array are stored sequentially in memory.

Referencing the index of the first dimension points to the memory address of the first element of that dimension. For example, referencing `grades[1]` points to memory address 9 in Figure 3-4. Memory address 9 is the first memory address of contiguous memory where values of the second set of array elements that are associated with `grades[1]` are stored.

Declaring a Multidimensional Array

A multidimensional array is declared similar to the way you declare a one-dimensional array except you specify the number of elements in both dimensions. For example, the multidimensional array shown in Figure 3-3 is declared as follows in C or C++:

```
int grades[3][4];
```

The first bracket ([3]) tells the compiler that you're declaring 3 pointers, each pointing to an array. This concept might be confusing because the term "pointer" may make some programmers think of pointer variable or pointer array, which you'll learn about later in this chapter. However, we are not talking about a pointer variable or pointer array. Instead, we are saying that each element of the first dimension of a multidimensional array reference a corresponding second dimension, which is an array.

In this example, all the arrays pointed to by the first index are of the same size. The second index can be of variable size. For example, the previous statement declares a two-dimensional array where there are 3 elements in the first dimension and 4 elements in the second dimension.

The element `grades[0]` is said to "point" (just as you use your finger to point) to the second dimension of the array, which is referenced as `grades[0][0]`. The second dimension is considered an array. Therefore, programmers say that the first element of a multidimensional array points to another array (that is, the second dimension).

The data type tells the computer that each element of the array will contain an `integer` data type. The data type is followed by the array name and two values that

indicate the size of each dimension used for the array. In this case, there are three sets of four array elements.

You declare a multidimensional array and initialize its elements by using French braces, as shown in Figure 3-5. There are three sets of inner French braces. Each of these sets represents the first dimension of the array. There are four values within each set of inner French braces. These values are assigned to each element of the second dimension of the array.

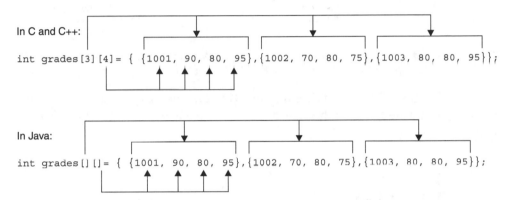

Figure 3-5   Braces define sets of values to be assigned to array elements (the top example is C and C++ and the bottom example is Java).

Assigning Values to a Multidimensional Array

You assign a value to an element of a multidimensional array with an assignment statement similar to the assignment statement that assigns a value to a single-dimensional array, as shown here:

```
grades[0][0] = 1001;
```

You must specify the index for both dimensions. In this example, the integer 1001, which is a student ID, is assigned to the first element of the first set of elements in the grades array.

Referencing the Contents of a Multidimensional Array

The contents of elements of a multidimensional array can be used in a program by referencing the index of both dimensions of the array element. Figure 3-6 shows you how to display the final exam grade for the second student.

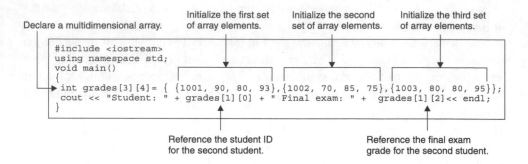

Figure 3-6 Display the contents of array elements by referencing the index of both sets of array elements.

In this example, the student ID is displayed by referencing the first element of the second set, and the grade for the final exam is displayed by referencing the third element of the second set.

Pointers and Arrays

There is a close-knit relationship between a pointer and an array. The array name is like a pointer variable in that the array name by itself references the address of the first element of the array. Confused? We'll give you an example (see Figure 3-7) to show how this works.

Java doesn't permit a programmer to use pointers, so we use C++ code in Figure 3-7. The example begins by declaring an array of characters called letters that consists of

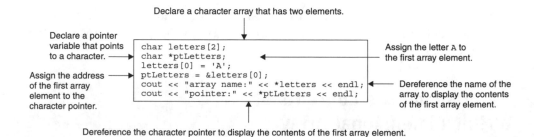

Figure 3-7 Use the array name as a pointer to the first array element.

2 elements. Also declared is a character pointer called ptLetters. (You learned about pointers in Chapter 2.)

Next, the character A is assigned to the first element of the array. The address of the first array element is then assigned to the pointer variable. Figure 3-8 gives you a glimpse of memory once the address of the first array element is assigned to the pointer.

Figure 3-7 displays the letter A twice. The first time is by using the name of the array as a pointer. Only the name of the array is used—the square brackets and index are not. The A is displayed the second time by using the pointer. Using the asterisk dereferences both the array name and the pointer. (You learned about dereferencing in Chapter 2.)

You might be wondering why you'd use the array name as a pointer to the first element of the array. Programmers do this to use pointer arithmetic (see the "Pointer Arithmetic" section of Chapter 2) to access each array element without having to reference an array index.

An Array of Pointers

Previously, you learned that pointers are the backbone of data structures. Some programmers feel that an array of pointers, also known as a pointer array, is the backbone of pointers. An array of pointers is an array whose elements are pointers. That is, the value of each array element is a memory address similar to a pointer variable, which you learned about in Chapter 2.

The benefit of using an array of pointers instead of several pointer variables is that you can use a for loop to step through each element of the array to access memory addresses that are assigned to the array. You'll need to do this to efficiently access and reorder values stored in memory.

An array of pointers is not available in all programming languages. For example, Java doesn't let programmers use pointers, so you won't be able to create an array of pointers in Java. However, you can create an array of pointers in C and C++.

NOTE: It is technically incorrect to say that Java doesn't use pointers. Java does use pointers, but a programmer doesn't explicitly declare them. You can declare an array whose data type is a Java object, and this is in fact an array of pointers. The value of each array element is an object. When you switch those values to other array elements, you are moving memory addresses and not the object itself.

An array of pointers is declared using nearly the same format as declaring an array of data types, with one exception. The name of the array must be preceded with an asterisk, as shown here:

```
char *grades[10];
```

The asterisk tells the computer that the array is a pointer array where each element can contain a memory address. The data type in this declaration statement tells the computer that memory addresses stored in array elements are memory addresses that contain a char value. This is the same pointer variable concept you learned in Chapter 2.

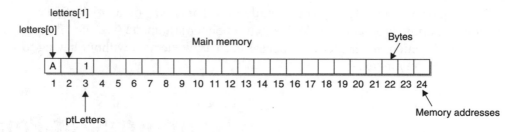

Figure 3-8   Memory allocation after the pointer is assigned the address of the first array element

As you probably recall from your programming course, a computer copies the value of a variable in an assignment statement, as shown in the next example. The first two statements in this example reserve a memory location large enough to store a char and associate those memory addresses with the names finalGrade and recordedGrade. The first statement also stores the value A in memory. The last statement copies the value stored in the memory location represented by finalGrade to the memory address represented by the recordedGrade.

```
char finalGrade = 'A';
char recordedGrade;
recordedGrade = finalGrade;
```

You assign a memory address of a variable to an element of an array of pointers by placing the address operator (&) in front of a variable name in an assignment statement to reference the variable. The ampersand (&) returns a pointer, and an asterisk (*) dereferences the pointer and tells the computer that you want the value pointed to by the pointer.

Referencing tells the computer to copy the memory address of the variable instead of copying the value stored in the memory address. This is illustrated in the next example where the address of the `finalGrade` variable is referenced, resulting in the memory address of the `finalGrade` variable being assigned to the first element of the `ptRecordedGrades` array. The `ptRecordedGrades` is an array of pointers.

```
char finalGrade = 'A';
char *ptRecordedGrades[10];
ptRecordedGrades[0] = &finalGrade;
```

Programmers use an array of pointers in two ways: they use the address assigned to array elements, and they use the content of the memory address assigned to an array element. Let's take a look at how to use addresses stored in an array of pointers.

The following example initializes three variables with grades and declares two pointer arrays called `ptGradeBook` and `ptRecordedGrade`. The addresses of the three variables are then assigned to each element of the `ptGradeBook` pointer array. A `for` loop then copies memory addresses stored in the `ptGradeBook` array to the `ptRecordedGrade` array. Notice that the ampersand is not used in this assignment expression because we want the content of each array element to be copied to the `ptRecordedGrade` array.

```
char bobGrade = 'A';
char maryGrade = 'B';
char amberGrade = 'A';
char *ptGradeBook[3];
char *ptRecordedGrade[3];
ptGradeBook [0] = &bobGrade;
ptGradeBook [1] = &maryGrade;
ptGradeBook [2] = &amberGrade;
for (int i = 0; i < 3; i++)
    ptRecordedGrade[i] = ptGradeBook[i];
```

Now we'll modify this program slightly in the next example by changing the `ptRecordedGrade` array from an array of pointers to an array of integers. We'll then use the `for` loop to copy the contents of the variables to the `recordedGrade` by using the pointer array, as shown here:

```
char bobGrade = 'A';
char maryGrade = 'B';
char amberGrade = 'A';
char *ptGradeBook[3];
char recordedGrade[3];
ptGradeBook [0] = &bobGrade;
ptGradeBook [1] = &maryGrade;
ptGradeBook [2] = &amberGrade;
```

```
for (int i = 0; i < 3; i++)
    recordedGrade[i] = *ptGradeBook[i];
```

The last statement in this example dereferences each element of the ptGradeBook array by preceding the name of the array with an asterisk. This tells the computer to first go to the memory address stored in the array element and then copy the value stored at the memory address to the element of the recordedGrade array element (see Figure 3-9).

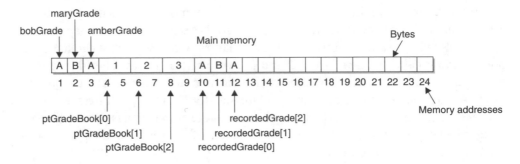

Figure 3-9   Using the content pointed to by an array of pointers

An Array of Pointers to Pointers

The supercharger of pointers is an array of pointers to pointers because an array of pointers to pointers enables you to reorganize tons of data in memory by simply referring to memory addresses. You were introduced to arrays of pointers to pointers at the beginning of this chapter. You'll now learn the ins and outs of using them.

Be forewarned: an array of pointers to pointers is one of the most abstract concepts to grasp in programming. Therefore, it is critical that you draw a picture of computer memory as you analyze a program that uses an array of pointers to pointers; otherwise, you are bound to become unnecessarily frustrated.

Let's begin by recalling the basics. It probably seems that you read these terms countless times in the last chapter and this chapter, but these terms are so important to understanding an array of pointers to pointers that we'll talk about them one more time.

A *variable* is a reference to a memory location used to store data that is described in a data type. A *pointer variable* is the same as a variable except its contents are the memory address of another variable. A *pointer to a pointer*, which you learned about in Chapter 2, is a pointer variable. The contents of the pointer variable is a memory address of another pointer variable.

More on an Array of Pointers to Pointers

Before we show you how to use an array of pointers to pointers, let's be sure that you understand how arrays, arrays of pointers, and arrays of pointers to pointers join forces to rearrange tons of data efficiently.

Think of an array as the storage place of the tons of data. The last thing you want to do is to physically reorganize a lot of data in computer memory because it is inefficient.

Think of an array of pointers as the storage place for memory addresses of data stored in an array. This is like a notepad where you jot down memory addresses of data.

Think of an array of pointers to pointers as the place where you reorganize the data contained in the array by indirectly rearranging memory addresses contained in the array of pointers. You can have any number of arrays of pointers to pointers, each indirectly ordering the content of the array of pointers in a different order.

Let's say that you have a list of three names, as shown in Figure 3-10. Each name is assigned to elements of an array in reverse alphabetical order. You can reorder those names without changing their order in the array by using an array of pointers and an array of pointers to pointers.

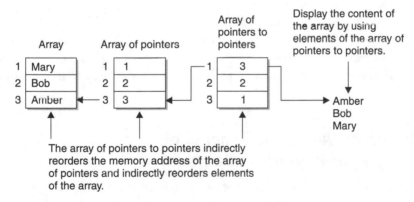

Figure 3-10   An array of pointers to pointers reorganizes names without changing the order of the array that contains the names.

In Figure 3-10, elements of the array of pointers are assigned the memory addresses of each element of the array. Elements of the array of pointers to pointers are assigned the memory addresses of elements of the array of pointers. Notice that these memory addresses are assigned in the reverse order that they appear in the array of pointers, which indirectly references the array of names in reverse order—that is, in alphabetical order.

Declaring and Using an Array of Pointers to Pointers

An array of pointers to pointers is declared nearly the same way as you declare an array of pointers, except two asterisks (**) are used before the name of the array, as shown here:

```
string **ptPTStudents[3];
```

The data type of an array of pointers to pointers is used a little differently than the data type of an array of pointers. Previously in this chapter, you learned that the data type of an array of pointers refers to the data type stored at memory addresses that are assigned to elements of the pointer array.

Suppose you declared an array of strings and an array of pointers to strings and then assigned memory addresses of the string array to the pointer array. The data type of the pointer array is a string data type, which tells the computer that elements of the pointer array contain memory addresses of strings.

The data type of the array of pointers to pointers corresponds to the data type of the pointers that are assigned to elements of the array of pointers to pointers. Let's say you assign elements of the pointer array to elements of the array of pointers to pointers. Because the pointer array points to strings, the array of pointers to pointers must also use the `string` data type.

The data type of an array of pointers to pointers tells the computer that the memory address contains a memory address that is a pointer. This pointer contains a memory address of a string or whatever the data type specified when the pointer is declared.

Assigning Values to Elements of an Array of Pointers to Pointers

You assign a value to an element of an array of pointers to pointers the same way you assign a value to an element of an array of pointers. That is, use the address operator (&) to reference either a pointer variable or an element of an array of pointers, as shown here:

```
ptPTStudents[0] = &ptStudents[0];
```

You'll recall that the address operator tells the computer to assign the memory address of a pointer variable or array element to the element of the array of pointers to pointers, not the value stored at that address. The previous example assigns the memory address of a pointer array to the element of the array of pointers to pointers. It does not assign the contents of the `ptStudents[0]`, which is also a memory address.

Using the Contents of an Array of Pointers to Pointers

Accessing the contents of an element of an array of pointers to pointers is nearly identical to the way the content of an element of a pointer array is accessed. Previously, you learned that you dereference an element of a pointer array when you want to tell the computer to use the content of the element, as shown here:

```
cout << *ptStudents[0] << endl;
```

An element of an array of pointers to pointers is accessed by using two asterisks (**), as shown in this statement:

```
cout << **ptPTStudents[0] << endl;
```

Pointers to Pointers in Action

Now that you have a firm grasp on arrays and an array of pointers to pointers, we'll show you how you can harness the power of the array. Figure 3-10 is a diagram of how an array containing three names is reordered using a pointer array and an array of pointers to pointers. Figure 3-11 shows how to do this in C and C++. Remember that Java does not permit programmers to use pointers directly, but understanding how pointers work in C and C++ will help you understand how pointers are used in Java.

The program begins by declaring an array of strings called students that is initialized with the names of three students. Notice the order of these names. The program will use an array of pointers to pointers to reverse this order.

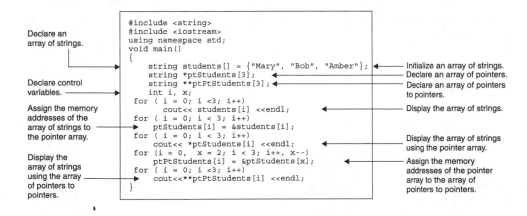

Figure 3-11   Using a pointer array and an array of pointers to pointers to display the contents of an array of strings

Once the array of strings is declared, the program declares a pointer array and an array of pointers to pointers, both of which have three elements. Two integers are then declared and used as control variables for the `for` loop.

The first `for` loop displays elements of the `students` array to show the original order in which names are stored in the array, as shown in the left stack in Figure 3-10.

The second `for` loop assigns memory addresses of each element of the `students` array to elements of the pointer array, as shown in the center stack in Figure 3-10.

The third `for` loop uses the `ptStudents` array of pointers to display students contained in the `students` array. Names appear in the same order shown in the left stack in Figure 3-10.

The fourth `for` loop assigns the memory address of each element in the pointer array to elements of the array of pointers to pointers, which is called `ptPtStudents`. This is where the program reorders names of the `students` array. It may look confusing at first glance, but here's what is happening.

The `i` control variable is initialized to 0, and the `x` control variable is initialized to 2. These determine the starting points in the array of pointers to pointers and the pointer array. The `ptPtStudents` pointer to pointer array begins with the first element, while the `ptStudents` array pointer begins with the last element. This is because the program reverses the order in which names appear in the `students` array. The last name will appear first in the reordered list.

Each time the `for` loop is looped, the value of the `i` variable is incremented, causing the program to move to the second and third elements of the `ptPtStudents` array of pointers to pointers. At the same time, the value of the `x` variable is decremented, causing the `ptStudents` pointer array to move to the second and first elements, as shown in the right stack in Figure 3-10.

The fifth `for` loop steps through elements of the `ptPtStudents` array of pointers to pointers displaying the corresponding name in the `students` array on the screen.

Quiz

1. What is the difference between an array element and a variable?

2. What is an array of pointers?

3. How do you assign an address to an element of a pointer array?

4. What is an array of pointers to pointers?

5. How do you assign a value to an element of an array of pointers to pointers?

6. How do you display the contents of the memory addresses stored in an element of a pointer array?

7. Why would you use an array of pointers to pointers?

8. How do you declare an array?

9. How do you display the contents of the memory addresses stored in an element of an array of pointers to pointers?

10. How are elements of an array stored in memory?

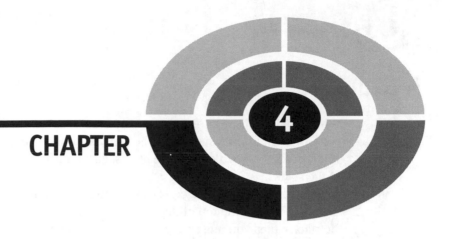

Stacks Using an Array

The term "stack" is one of the magical and sometimes imposing terms used in computer programming that seems to imply an abstract concept that only a Ph.D. from MIT—whoops, we should say Columbia University—can understand. Yet you actually know all about stacks because you use a stack when playing cards, making pancakes, and storing laundry. A *stack* is the way you groups things together by placing one thing on top of another and then removing things one at a time from the top of the stack. It is amazing that something this simple is a critical component of nearly every program that is written. In this chapter, you'll learn how to create and use a stack in your programs.

A Stack

When you hear the term "stack" used outside the context of computer programming, you might envision a stack of dishes on your kitchen counter. This organization is structured in a particular way: the newest dish is on top and the oldest is on the bottom of the stack.

Each dish in a stack is accessed using fifo: first in, first out. The only way to access each dish is from the top of the stack. If you want the third dish (the third oldest on the stack), then you must remove the first two dishes from the top of the stack. This places the third dish at the top of the stack making it available to be removed.

There's no way to access a dish unless the dish is at the top of the stack. You might be thinking stacks are inefficient, and you'd be correct if the objective was to randomly access things on the stack. There are other data structures that are ideal for random access, which you'll learn about throughout this book.

However, if the object is to access things in the order in which they were placed on the stack, such as computer instructions, stacks *are* efficient. In these situations, using a stack makes a lot of sense.

NOTE: Stacks and arrays are often bantered about in the same discussion, which can easily lead to confusion, but they are really two separate things (see Figure 4-1). An array *stores values in memory; a* stack *tracks which array element is at the top of the stack. When a value is popped off the stack, the value remains in memory because the value is still assigned to an array element. Popping it only changes the array element that is at the top of the stack.*

Inside a Stack

Programmers use arrays to store values that are referenced by a stack. As you'll recall from Chapter 3, an array consists of a series of array elements, each of which is similar in concept to a variable. The stack contains the index of the array element that is at the top of the stack.

Figure 4-1 is the way some programmers envision an array used with a stack. This example shows an array called `stack` with 8 array elements. The entire array contains values that are referenced by the stack. Three array elements are assigned values, while the other array elements are empty and can be used when new items are placed on the stack (see the upcoming section "Push").

Mike is the first value placed on the stack. You know this because Mike is at the bottom of the stack. Bob is the last item placed on the stack because Bob is the top item on the stack.

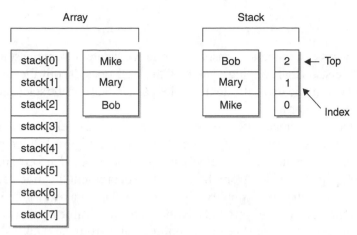

Figure 4-1   A stack and an array are two different things: an array stores values in memory; a stack tracks which of the array elements is at the top of the stack.

Push

Programmers use the term "push" to mean placing an item on a stack. *Push* is the direction that data is being added to the stack. Think of this as pushing items down on the stack to move the items already on the stack down to make room for the next item.

Here's what actually happens. The new value is assigned to the next available array element and the index of that array element becomes the top of the stack, as shown in Figure 4-2. The program increments the current index of the stack by 1. In this example, the index is incremented by 1, resulting in index 3 being at the top of the stack, which is the index of the new values assigned to the array.

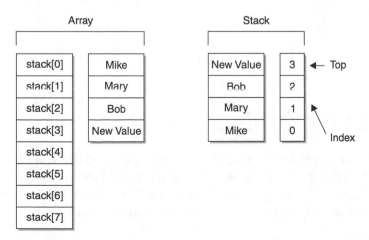

Figure 4-2   The new value is assigned to the next array element and its index becomes the top of the stack.

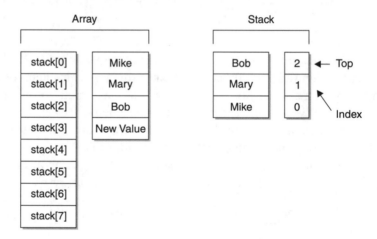
Pop

Popping is the reverse process of pushing: it removes an item from the stack. It is important to understand that popping an item off the stack doesn't copy the item. Once an item is popped from the stack, the item is no longer available on the stack, although the value remains in the array.

Here's what really happens. Remember that the top of the stack contains an index of the array element whose value is at the top of the stack. In Figure 4-2, index 3 is at the top of the stack, which means New Value in array element 3 is at the top of the stack.

When you pop New Value from the stack, you decrement the index at the top of the stack. That is, you make its index 2 instead of 3. This makes Bob the new value at the top of the stack (see Figure 4-3). Notice that New Value and array element 3 remain untouched in the array because popping a value from the stack only alters the stack, not the underlying array.

Figure 4-3   All values move toward the top of the stack when the top item is popped off the stack.

Creating a Stack in C++

You can create a stack in C++ by defining a stack class and declaring an instance of the class. The Stack class requires three attributes and several member functions, which are defined as you learn about them. You'll begin by defining a basic stack class that has only the components needed to create the stack.

The class is called `Stack`, but you can call it any name you wish. This class definition is divided into a private access specifier section and a public access specifier section. The *private access specifier* section has attributes and member functions (although not in this example) that are accessible only by a member function defined in this class. The *public access specifier* section has attributes (although not in this example) and member functions that are accessible by using an instance of the class.

The private access specifier section of the `Stack` class defines three attributes: `size`, `top`, and `values`, all of which are integers. The `size` attribute stores the number of elements in the stack, the `top` attribute stores the index of the top element of the stack, and the `values` attribute is a pointer to the stack, which is an array. The stack in this example is a stack of integer values, but you can use an array of any data type, depending on the nature of your program.

Only one member function is defined in the `Stack` class, although we'll define other member functions for the class in upcoming sections of this chapter. For now, let's keep the example simple and easy to understand.

This member function is called `Stack`, which is the constructor of the class. A *constructor* is a member function that has the same name as the class and is called when an instance of the class is created. The code for this is on the next page.

Several things are happening in the constructor. First, the constructor receives an integer as an argument that is passed when the instance of the `Stack` class is declared. The integer determines the number of elements in the stack and is assigned to the `size` variable.

The first statement might look a bit confusing. It appears that the value of the `size` variable from the argument list is being assigned to itself, but that's not the case. Actually, the size variable from the argument list is local to the `Stack` member function. The `this->size` combination refers to the size attribute of the `Stack` class, as shown here:

```
this->size = size;
```

Programmers use the `this` pointer within a member function to refer to the current instance of the class. In this example, the `this` pointer uses the pointer reference (`->`) to tell the computer to use the `size` attribute of the class. As you'll remember from your C++ programming class, the pointer reference is used when indirectly working with a class member, and the dot operator is used when you are directly working with a class member.

This allows the compiler to distinguish between a class variable and local variable that have the same name. This means that the value of the `size` variable that is passed as an argument to the `Stack` member function is assigned to the `size` attribute, making the value available to other members of the `Stack` class.

You can see how the `size` attribute is used in the next statement. This statement does two things. First, it allocates memory for the stack by using the `new` operator (`new int[size]`). The `new` operator returns a pointer to the reserved memory location. The size is the `size` attribute of the class and determines the size of the array. The array is an array of integers.

Next, the pointer to the array of integers is assigned to the values attribute of the class. The `values` attribute is a pointer variable that is defined in the private attribute section of the `Stack` class.

The last statement in the `Stack` member function assigns a −1 to the `top` attribute. The value of the top attribute is the index of the top element of the stack. A −1 means that that stack doesn't have any elements. Remember from your programming class that index values are memory offsets from the start of the array. Index 0 means "move 0 bytes from the start of the array." So index −1 is just a convenient way to say that the stack is empty.

We'll expand on the definition of the `Stack` class in the next section, but for now let's create an instance of the `Stack` class. The instance is declared within the `main()` function of this example. Three things are happening here. First, the `new` operator is creating an instance of the stack in memory. The `new` operator returns a pointer to that memory location.

Next, the statement declares a reference to the stack, which is called `myStack`. The reference is a pointer. The final step is to assign the pointer returned by the new operator to the reference. You then use the reference (`myStack`) as the name of the instance of the `Stack` class throughout the program.

```
public class Stack
{
    private:
        int size;
        int top;
        int* values;
    public:
        Stack(int size)
        {
            this->size = size;
            values = new int[size];
            top = -1;
        }
};
void main(){
    Stack *myStack = new Stack(10);
}
```

Creating a Push Member Function in C++

Now that you've seen how to define a class that creates a stack, we'll show you how to define additional member functions that enable the class to push values onto the stack. Pushing a value onto the stack is a two-step process. First, you must determine if there is room on the stack for another value. If there is, you push the value onto the stack; otherwise, you don't.

We'll create different member functions for each step, beginning by defining a member function that determines if there is room on the stack. We'll call it `isFull()` and define it in the following code. The `isFull()` member function is simple. It compares the value of the `top` attribute with the one less than the value of the `size` attribute.

The value of the `top` attribute is −1 when the instance of the stack is declared. Suppose the value of `size` is 10. The condition expression in the `if` statement of the `isFull()` member function determines if the value of `top`, which is −1, is 1 less than the value of `size`. Since the value of `size` is 10, the condition expression compares −1 < 9. If `top` is greater than or equal to 9, then a `true` is returned; otherwise, a `false` is returned.

Why do you subtract 1 from the size of the stack? The value of the `top` attribute is an index of an array element. Remember that the index begins with zero. In contrast, the size is actually the number of array elements in the stack. Therefore, the tenth array element on the stack has an index of 9.

```
bool isFull()
{
    if(top < size-1)
    {
        return false;
    }
    else
    {
        return true;
    }
}
```

With the `isFull()` member function defined, we'll move on to defining the `push()` member function, as shown in the next example. The `push()` member function pushes a value onto the stack. The value being pushed onto the stack is passed as an argument to the `push()` member function and is assigned to the variable `x` in this example.

Before doing anything else, the `push()` member function determines if there is room on the stack by calling the `isFull()` member function in the condition expression of the `if` statement. The condition expression might look a little strange because the call is preceded by an exclamation point (!) so we'll take apart the condition expression to explain what is really happening here.

Remember from your programming classes that statements within an `if` statement execute only if the condition expression is `true`. This means the condition expression must be `true` for the value passed to the `push()` member function to be placed on the stack.

Here's a slight problem. We're calling the `isFull()` member function to determine if there is room on the stack for another value. However, the `isFull()` member function returns `false` if there is room and `true` if there isn't room. A `false` causes the `push()` member function to skip statements that place the value on the stack. We really need the `isFull()` member function to return a `true` if there is room available, not a `false`. Rather than rewrite the `isFull()` member function, we use the exclamation point to reverse the logic. As you remember from your programming class, the exclamation point is the not operator—that is, a `false` is treated as a `true`, which causes the value to be placed on the stack.

There are two statements within the `if` statement. The first statement increments the value of the `top` attribute, which is the index of the last value placed on the stack. If the stack is empty, then the current value of the top attribute is –1. Incrementing –1 changes the value of the `top` attribute to 0, which is the index of the first array element of the stack. The last statement in the `if` statement assigns the value passed to the `push()` member function to the next available array element.

```
void push(int x)
{
    if(!isFull())
    {
        top++;
        values[top] = x;
    }
}
```

Creating a Pop Member Function in C++

We still need a way to remove values from the stack. To do this, we need to define two additional member functions, `isEmpty()` and `pop()`. The `isEmpty()` member function determines if there are any values on the stack. The `pop()` member function removes the value from the top of the stack.

Let's define the `isEmpty()` member function in this next example. The `isEmpty()` member function contains an `if` statement. The condition expression of the `if` statement compares the value of the `top` attribute to –1. Remember that –1 is the initial value of the top attribute when the instance of a stack is declared. If the top attribute is equal to –1, then a `true` is returned because the stack is empty; other-wise, a `false` is returned.

```
bool isEmpty()
{
   if(top == -1)
   {
      return true;
   }
   else
   {
      return false;
   }
}
```

The `pop()` member function of the `Stack` class has the job of changing the index that is at the top of the stack and returning the value of the corresponding array to the statement that calls the `pop()` member function. The next example defines the `pop()` member function.

The first statement in the definition declares an integer variable called `retVal` that stores the value returned by the `pop()` member function. The `retVal` is ini-tialized to zero.

Next, the `isEmpty()` member function is called in the condition expression of the `if` statement to determine if there is a value at the top of the stack. Notice the exclamation point reverses the logic as it did in the `pop()` member function.

Statements within the `if` statement should only execute if the `isEmpty()` member function returns a `false`, meaning the stack is not empty. Therefore, we need to use the exclamation point to reverse the logic of the condition expression to make the condition expression `true` if the `isEmpty()` member function returns a `false`.

Two steps occur within the `if` statement. First, the value at the top of the stack is assigned to the `retVal` variable by referencing the values array using the index contained in the `top` attribute. Next, the value of the `top` attribute is decremented. The return `retVal` is then returned by the `pop()` member function.

```
int pop()
{
   int retVal = 0;
   if(!isEmpty())
   {
      retVal = values[top];
      top--;
   }
   return retVal;
}
```

Creating a Stack in Java

Many of the basic concepts that create a stack in C++ also create a stack in Java, as you'll see in the following example. The `Stack` class definition contains all the members that are found in the definition of the `Stack` class in the C++ example, although the format of these class definitions is slightly different.

Java doesn't permit the class definition to be grouped into private and public access specifier sections. Instead, the keywords `private` and `public` precede the name of the member. In this example, the attributes `size` and `top` and the reference to the values array are private and accessible only by a member method of the class.

`Stack` is a member method that is a constructor of the `Stack` class. Previously, you learned that a constructor is a member method that is called when an instance of the class is created. The `Stack` constructor requires that an integer representing the size of the stack be passed to its argument list.

Statements within the `Stack` constructor are similar to the statements within the `Stack` constructor in the C++ version of the `Stack` class. The first statement assigns the integer passed to the `Stack` constructor to the `size` attribute of the Stack class by using the `this` pointer.

The next statement declares an array of integers using the `new` operator, which returns a reference to the memory location of the array. This reference is assigned to the values attribute, which is a reference to an array of integers.

The last statement assigns –1 to the `top` attribute. As you'll recall, the `top` attribute contains the index of the array element that is at the top of the stack. The value –1 means that the stack is empty.

Beneath the `Stack` definition in this example is the definition of the `StackExample` application class, which is the Java application that creates an instance of the `Stack` class. You'll remember this statement from your Java programming class. Three things are happening here. On the right side of the assignment operator, the `new` operator declares an instance of the `Stack` class and passes 10 to the constructor as the size of the stack. On the left side of the assignment operator, the statement declares a reference to an instance of the `Stack` class called `myStack`. The last step is that the assignment operator assigns a reference to the instance of the `Stack` class returned by the `new` operator to the `myStack` reference. You'll then use the `myStack` reference to access public members of the `Stack` class.

```
public class Stack
{
    private int size;
    private int top;
```

```
    private int[] values;
    public Stack(int size)
    {
        this.size = size;
        values = new int[size];
        top = -1;
    }
}
public class StackExample {
    void main( String args[]){
        Stack myStack = new Stack(10);
    }
}
```

Creating a Push Member Method in Java

The Java versions of the push() member method also require that you define an isFull() member method to determine if room is available to place another value on the stack. The next example shows the definition of the isFull() member method.

Notice that this is nearly identical to the C++ version, with two exceptions. The method name begins with the keyword public making it callable from within the program using the instance of the Stack class. In the C++ version, the isFull() member method was placed beneath the public access specifier section of the class definition. The other difference is the keyword that designates the data type of the return value. In C++, bool is the keyword for a Boolean data type; the equivalent in Java is boolean.

Inside the isFull() member method, the condition expression in the if statement determines if the value of the top attribute (index) is less than one less the value of the size attribute (total number of array elements).

```
public boolean isFull()
{
    if(top < size-1)
    {
        return false;
    }
    else
    {
        return true;
    }
}
```

The Java version of the push() member method is defined in the next example. This too is nearly identical to the C++ push() member function except the keyword public precedes the signature of the member method.

The statement calling the push() member method passes it the value that is to be placed on the top of the stack. This value is assigned to the variable *x*. Inside the method, the isFull() member method is called in the condition expression of the if statement to determine if there is room for the new value on the stack. As with C++, you must reverse the logic of the value returned by the isFull() member method by using the exclamation point. That is, when a false is returned (room is available on the stack), the condition expression treats it as true, enabling statements within the if statement to be executed.

The first statement in the if statement increments the value of the top attribute, which you'll remember is an index. The other statement assigns the value of the variable *x* to the array element.

```
public void push(int x)
{
    if(!isFull())
    {
        top++;
        values[top] = x;
    }
}
```

Creating a Pop Member Method in Java

Two methods must be defined to pop a value off the top of the stack in Java. These are isEmpty() and pop(), both of which are similar to the C++ versions. The isEmpty() member method, shown in the next example, determines if there is a value at the top of the stack by comparing the value of the top attribute to −1. The value −1 is the initial value of the top attribute when the instance of the Stack class is declared. The comparison is made in the condition expression of the if statement. Depending on the result of the comparison, either a true or a false is returned.

```
public boolean isEmpty()
{
    if(top == -1)
    {
        return true;
    }
    else
    {
```

```
      return false;
   }
}
```

The `pop()` member method that is defined in the next example works the same way as the C++ version. First, an integer variable called `retVal` is declared and initialized to 0. This stores the value that is popped off the top of the stack and returned to the statement that calls the `pop()` member method.

The `isEmpty()` member method is called in the condition expression of the `if` statement to determine if there is a value at the top of the stack. Again, the exclamation point must be used to reverse the logic of the value returned by the `isEmpty()` member method. A `false` is returned if there is a value at the top of the stack. The exclamation point makes this a true enabling statement within the `if` statement to execute.

The first statement within the `if` statement assigns the value of the top element of the stack to the `retVal` variable. The other statement decrements the value of the `top` attribute, which brings the next index of the array to the top of the stack.

The last statement in the `pop()` member method returns the value of the variable `retVal`.

```
public int pop()
{
   int retVal = 0;
   if(!isEmpty())
   {
      retVal = values[top];
      top--;
   }
   return retVal;
}
```

Stack in Action Using C++

Now that you understand how to create and use a stack, we'll pick up the pace and explore an industrial-strength stack. You've may have heard the term *industrial strength* used in relation to programming and may be curious what this really means.

Industrial strength is a term used in industry that implies a product is designed to withstand stress. Industrial strength can be used to describe any kind of product, but in this case the product is the program that creates and uses a stack.

Programs used to illustrate the concepts of a stack in this chapter are bare bones and lack the robust features that are found in industrial-strength programs. A bare-bones program is what you need when you're learning the concepts of stacks and other data structures because the program contains only statements that pertain to what you are learning.

However, once you learn the concept, you need to see how it's applied in a real-world program. That's what we'll be exploring in the "Stack in Action" sections of this chapter. In this section, you'll take a look at how a stack is created and used in an industrial-strength C++ program. Later, you'll see the Java version of this program.

TIP: From your programming classes, you learned to always build error-trapping routines into your program to properly handle errors should they occur. Always include such routines in your stack program. Three common errors to trap are problems allocating memory for the stack, reacting to a full stack, and reacting to an empty stack.

We'll use as an example an industrial-strength C++ program that creates and uses a stack. The program is contained within three files, `stack.h`, `stack.cpp`, and `stackDemo.cpp`. The `stack.h` file is a header file that contains the definition of the `Stack` class, which is the "blueprint" of the `Stack` class. The `stack.cpp` file is a source code file that contains the implementation of the member functions of the `Stack` class. The `stackDemo.cpp` file contains the source code for the C++ program that declares the instance of the `Stack` class and calls its member functions. Let's begin by taking a look at the `stack.h` header file, which is shown in the next code example. As you'll recall from your C++ classes, a header file typically contains definitions and preprocessor instructions. A preprocessor is a program that applies preprocessor instructions to source code before the code is compiled.

The `stack.h` header file contains one preprocessor instruction, `#define`, which defines a symbol. Here we've defined the symbol `DEFAULT_SIZE` and given it a value of 10. The preprocessor then replaces all occurrences of `DEFAULT_SIZE` with 10 before the code is compiled. The `DEFAULT_SIZE` is the default size of the stack if the `no` argument is passed to the constructor. Function parameters in C and C++ can be assigned default values in the function prototype as long as those arguments are at the end of the argument list. If the size value is not passed in, it gets defaulted to the value of `DEFAULT_SIZE`, which is 10 in our example.

The `stack.h` file also contains the definition of the `Stack` class. The `Stack` class definition has the same `size`, `top`, and `values` attributes you saw in the previous C++ example. However, the definition of member functions is different from what you saw because member functions are implemented outside the class definition in the `stack.cpp` source code file. The header file contains only the prototype of the functions, which make up the blueprint for the class.

From your C++ class, you'll remember that only the prototype or signature of a member function needs to be included in a class definition. The implementation of the member function can be outside the class definition. There are two important reasons for keeping the definition (header file) and implementation (source) in separate files:

- It keeps your development environment cleaner and easier to understand.
- It allows you to provide a commercial software application programmer interface to a programmer without handing over your source code. You provide the programmer with your header files, which they will use to compile their code (they only need header files to compile the code). You provide your source code in the form of precompiled libraries that are referenced by the programmer's program during linking.

The class definition contains signatures of six member functions. The first member function is called `Stack`, which is the constructor that you learned about previously in this chapter. Previously, you learned that the constructor is passed an integer representing the size of the stack. In the real-world version, the program sets a default size that can be overridden when an instance of the class is created in the program. The default size is specified by using the `DEFAULT_SIZE`, which is 10 (see `#define`).

The next member function is `~Stack()` and is the destructor of the class. A destructor is the last member function that is called when the instance of the class goes out of scope and dies. A constructor must always be the same name as the class and begin with a tilde (~). By definition, destructors cannot accept any arguments. The purpose of the destructor is to free memory that is used by the stack or do any other sort of cleanup that's required.

The remaining member functions are the same functions that you learned about previously in this chapter.

```
//stack.h
#define DEFAULT_SIZE 10
class Stack
{
  private:
     int size;
     int top;
     int* values;
  public:
     Stack(int size = DEFAULT_SIZE);
     virtual ~Stack();
     bool isFull();
     bool isEmpty();
     void push(int);
     int pop();
};
```

The stack.cpp file is a source code file that contains the implementation of the Stack class's member functions. We placed these in a different file from the class definition because it is easier to read and maintain as well as for other reasons explained previously.

The file begins with the preprocessor instruction #include that tells the computer to evaluate the contents of the stack.h file before compiling the stack.cpp file so it "knows" about the Stack class definition before compiling the program.

Member functions in the stack.cpp file will be familiar to you because all except one are the same member functions that you learned about previously in the chapter. However, the names of the member functions might be confusing at first glance because each name begins with the name of the class followed by two colons (::). The two colons are called the *scope resolution operator*.

You must precede the name of a member function with the class name and scope resolution operator if the member function is defined outside the class definition. Think of this as telling the computer that the member function belongs to the Stack class.

The ~Stack() member function frees memory used by the stack. It does this by using the delete operator and referencing the name of the array used for the stack. In this example, values is the name of the array.

To avoid memory leaks, freeing memory is important whenever memory is dynamically allocated. The square brackets ([]) are used with delete because the object being removed from memory was dynamically created.

The stack.cpp is compiled as you would compile any source code. The result is an object file that is joined together with the compiled stackDemo.cpp source code file by the linker to create an executable program called a *load module*.

```
//stack.cpp
#include "stack.h"
Stack::Stack(int size)
{
   this->size = size;
   values = new int[size];
   top = -1;
}
Stack::~Stack()
{
   delete[] values;
}
bool Stack::isFull()
{
    if(top < size-1)
    {
```

```
            return false;
        }
        else
        {
            return true;
        }
}
bool Stack::isEmpty()
{
    if(top == -1)
    {
        return true;
    }
    else
    {
        return false;
    }
}
void Stack::push(int x)
{
    if(!isFull())
    {
        top++;
        values[top] = x;
    }
}
int Stack::pop()
{
        int retVal = 0;
        if(!isEmpty())
        {
        retVal = values[top];
        top--;
    }
    return retVal;
}
```

Finally, we come to the stackDemo.cpp program, which is the C++ program that creates the instance of the Stack class. The first statement creates the stack in a three-step process. The first step is to use the new operator to allocate space in memory for the Stack class by calling the constructor of the class. The new operator returns the memory location of the stack. The second step is to declare a pointer called stack. The last step is to assign the memory location returned by the new operator to the stack pointer.

In this example, we used the default size for the stack, which is 10 elements. We can pass the `Stack()` constructor an integer to change the size of the stack.

The `push()` member function is called three times. Each time a different value is placed on the stack. Notice that the `->` pointer is used instead of the dot operator. You must do this because `stack` is a pointer to an instance of the class and not the instance itself.

The last portion of the `stackDemo.cpp` program calls the `pop()` member three times. Each time a value is removed from the top of the stack and displayed on the screen.

```cpp
//stackDemo.cpp
void main() {
    Stack *stack = new Stack();
    stack->push(10);
    stack->push(20);
    stack->push(30);
    for(int i=0; i<3; i++)
    {
        cout << stack->pop() << endl;
    }
}
```

Stack in Action Using Java

The Java version of the `stackDemo` program combines the definition of the `Stack` class and the `stackDemo` application class definition in the same file, which is shown in the next example. Java doesn't provide any facility for separating the definition from the implementation as C and C++ do.

Usually, programmers will place the `Stack` class definition in a Java package rather than in the Java application class. As you'll recall from your Java programming class, a Java package is a collection of Java class definitions that can be incorporated into the Java source code. Packages are used partly to organize the classes into logical groups, but more importantly packages are used for name resolution. The JDK has three classes called `Element`, but they reside in three different packages. You can tell the JDK which one you're referring to by using the package name. C++ uses namespaces for the same purpose.

You'll notice as you read through the next example that the `Stack` class definition contains the same attributes and member methods as described in previous Java examples. However, there is a new attribute defined in the first statement of the class definition: the `DEFAULT_SIZE` attribute, whose value determines the default size of the stack, which is set to 10 elements.

The DEFAULT_SIZE attribute is available only to member methods of the class as is signified by the keyword private. The DEFAULT_SIZE is also designed as static and final. The keyword static means that one copy of this attribute is placed into memory, regardless of how many instances of the class are created. That is, any member method of any instance can change the value of DEFAULT_SIZE, and the change affects all instances. This is different than other nonstatic attributes because each instance has its own set of nonstatic attributes. A change in the value of one of the attributes doesn't affect the same attribute of another instance. The keyword final states that the value of DEFAULT_SIZE cannot be changed once this statement initializes it. Attempts to change its value will cause an error.

Notice that there are two constructors defined for the Stack class. The no argument constructor calls the second constructor, passing it a value of DEFAULT_SIZE to initialize the stack. Java does not permit default parameter values like C and C++, so this is a way to accomplish the same thing in Java.

The Java application class definition performs basically the same functionality as the statements in the main() function of the C++ program. The program creates a stack and then uses the reference name to the stack and the dot operator to call the push() method three times. The value passed to the push() member method is placed on the stack each time.

The last portion of the Java application class definition calls the pop() member method three times. The value returned by the pop() method is displayed on the screen each time.

```java
public class Stack
{
    private static final int DEFAULT_SIZE = 10;
    private int size;
    private int top;
    private int[] values;
    public Stack()
    {
        this(DEFAULT_SIZE);
    }
    public Stack(int size)
    {
        this.size = size;
        values = new int[size];
        top = -1;
    }
    public boolean isFull()
    {
        if(top < size-1)
        {
```

```
            return false;
        }
        else
        {
            return true;
        }
    }
    public boolean isEmpty()
    {
        if(top == -1)
        {
            return true;
        }
        else
        {
            return false;
        }
    }
    public void push(int x)
    {
        if(!isFull())
        {
            top++;
            values[top] = x;
        }
    }
    public int pop()
    {
        int retVal = 0;
        if(!isEmpty())
        {
            retVal = values[top];
            top--;
        }
        return retVal;
    }
}
public stackDemo{
    void main( String args[]){
        Stack stack = new Stack();
        stack.push(10);
        stack.push(20);
        stack.push(30);
        for(int i=0; i<3; i++)
```

```
        {
            System.out.println(stack.pop());
        }
    }
}
```

Quiz

1. What is a stack?
2. What is the purpose of the push() member method?
3. What is the purpose of the pop() member method?
4. What is the purpose of the isFull() member method?
5. What is the purpose of the isEmpty() member method?
6. What kind of value is assigned to the top attribute?
7. Why is the top attribute initialized to −1?
8. What is the purpose of the keyword private?
9. What is the purpose of the keyword public?
10. What is the difference between a constructor and a destructor?

CHAPTER

5

Queues Using an Array

You probably never thought that waiting in line in the supermarket would help you become a whiz at data structures, but it's a big help: the checkout line at a supermarket is similar to the way data structures are organized. We're the "things" organized by the supermarket line, and the same kind of organization is used for data within your program. The checkout line in your program is called a queue. In this chapter, you'll learn the ins and outs of implementing a queue within your program.

A Queue

A queue is like the checkout line at the supermarket where the first customer is at the front of the line, the second customer is next in line, and so on until you reach the last customer who is at the back of the line. Customers check out of the supermarket in the order they arrive in the line. That is, the first customer is the first one to check out. This is referred to as first in, first out (fifo).

The same concept applies to a queue in your program. A *queue* is a sequential organization of data. Data is accessible using fifo. That is, the first data in the queue is the first data that is accessible by your program. In this chapter, you will explore the simplest type of queue, a fixed size, first in, first out queue using an array. In Chapter 8, you will learn how to build a priority queue using a linked list. With a priority queue, the elements are removed based on two factors, the order they were placed in the queue and the priority of the element.

A Simple Queue vs. Priority Queue

Programmers use one of two kinds of queues depending in the objective of the program, a simple queue or a priority queue. A simple queue organizes items in a line where the first item is at the beginning of the line and the last item is at the back of the line. Each item is processed in the order in which it appears in the queue. The first item in line is processed first, followed by the second item and then the third until the last item on the line is processed. There isn't any way for an item to cut the line and be processed out of order.

A priority queue is similar to a simple queue in that items are organized in a line and processed sequentially. However, items on a priority queue can jump to the front of the line if they have priority. Priority is a value that is associated with each item placed in the queue. The program processes the queue by scanning the queue for items with high priority. These are processed first regardless of their position in the line. All the other items are then processed sequentially after high priority items are processed.

You'll learn how to create and use a priority queue in Chapter 8. For now, we'll keep things simple by creating and using a simple queue.

The Business of Queues

Queues are very important in business applications that require items to be processed in the order they are received. The supermarket checkout line is a queue that most of us have experienced, but you won't be creating a supermarket checkout line in a program unless the program is designed to simulate a checkout line.

In the real world, queues are used in programs that process transactions. A transaction is a set of information such as an order form. Transaction information is received by a program and then placed in a simple queue waiting to be processed by another part of the program.

Let's return to a supermarket to see how this works. The cash register is a computer that runs a transaction program that, among other things, processes the bar code on each product scanned at the checkout counter.

One of the first steps to processing the bar code is to look up the price. There could be 20 or more cash registers in a busy supermarket all trying to look up prices at the same time. However, the computer can process only one bar code at a time. The program that look ups prices manages the demand by using a simple queue in which each new request is placed at the back of the queue, and the program looks up the bar code that is at the front of the queue.

Many other applications use a simple queue to maintain the order in which to process items. These include programs that process stock and bond trades and those that process students registering for a course. Queues are also used within a computer to manage printing.

The Array and the Queue

Data organized by a queue may be stored in an array. The queue determines the array element that is at the front and back of the queue. The array is not the queue. Likewise, the queue is not the array. Both are two separate things. This is an important concept to grasp and one that may be difficult to understand at first.

Take a look at Figure 5-1 and you'll see how an array and a queue are different and yet are linked together to organize data. The array is pictured as a block of elements.

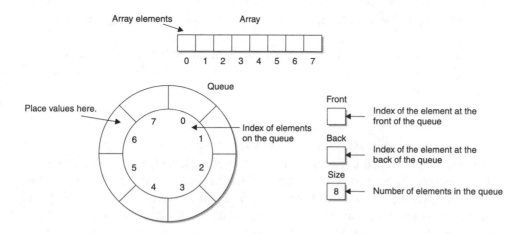

Figure 5-1   The queue is different from the array used to store data that appears in the queue.

The queue is pictured as a circle. The empty boxes are where values are stored in the queue, and the numbers correspond to the index of the array that is associated with the queue. To the right of the circle are three values. The `front` and `back` values store the index of the front and back of the queue. The `size` value is the number of elements in the queue, which is 8 in this example.

Enqueue

A value is placed in the queue by performing the enqueue process, which consists of two steps. The first step is to identify the array element that is at the back of the queue. However, this is not necessarily the last element of the array. Remember that the queue is not the array. The back of the queue is calculated by using the following formula:

$$back = (back+1) \% size$$

Figure 5-2 shows how to use the formula and gives the values for the front, back, and size of the queue. The `front` and `back` variables are set to zero because the queue is empty, and size is set to 8 because the array has 8 elements.

The next box shows the formula that identifies the back of the queue and assigns it the value 90. To the right of this box is the same formula with variable names replaced by actual values. Let's take a closer look at this and see how the back of the queue is calculated.

The first operation occurs within the parentheses, where 1 is added to the value of the `back` variable. The modulus operator determines where the next element should be placed in the queue by performing an integer division and returning the remainder of the division.

Although we've described a queue as a checkout line in the supermarket, a queue is actually circular. This is illustrated in the calculation used to determine the back of the queue, as shown here:

$$(7 + 1) \% 8$$

When you get to the last element in the array at index 7, the calculation returns 0 (8 divided by 8 is 1 and the remainder is 0). So after the last element in the array, you come around to the beginning of the array as the back of the queue. As you'll see in the "Queues Using an Array in C++" section of this chapter, you check to see if you're at the front of the queue before placing an item at the back of the queue so you don't overwrite the item at the front and corrupt the queue.

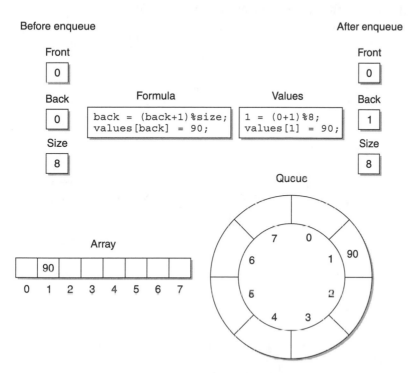

Figure 5-2   The enqueue process places a new value at the back of the queue.

The second step is to assign the value 90 to array element 1. That is, place the value 90 at the back of the queue. Remember that values are added to the queue from the back just as you go to the back of the checkout line to wait your turn at the supermarket. Notice that the value 90 is assigned to the array in Figure 5-2.

Dequeue

Dequeue is the process that removes a value from the front of the queue. It is important to understand that the value is removed from the queue, not the array. The value always remains assigned to the array until the value is either overwritten or the queue is abandoned. You'll see how to do overwrite later in this chapter.

There are two steps in the dequeue process, as illustrated in Figure 5-3. The initial step is to calculate the index of the array element at the front of the queue using the following expression:

$$front = (front+1) \% 8$$

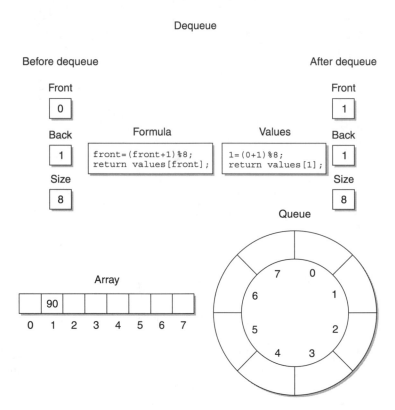

Figure 5-3   The dequeue process removes an item from the front of a queue.

Notice that this expression is very similar to the expression used in the enqueue process to calculate the index of the array element at the back of the queue. The first operation in this expression increments the value of the `front` variable. As you can see in Figure 5-3, the `front` variable is assigned the initial value zero. Therefore, the result of the first operation is 1. The next operation is to apply the modulus operator, which is identical to the modulus operation performed in the enqueue process. The result of this operation is 1, meaning that the front of the queue is the array element whose index is 1. This value is then assigned to the `front` variable. Previously in this chapter, you learned that if you were at index 7 in the array, the result of this calculation would be 0 ((7+1)%8 = 0), so you would chase the queue around in a circle.

The final step in the dequeue process is to use the value located at the front of the queue. Typically, the dequeue process is a method, and the front of the queue is returned to the statement that called the method.

In Figure 5-3, the array element values[1] is at the front of the queue. The value assigned to this element is 90, which was placed at the back of the queue by the previous enqueue process.

Notice that the value 90 remains assigned to the values[1] array element in Figure 5-3 because values assigned to the array associated with a queue are not affected when a value is removed from the front of the queue. The queue keeps track of array elements that are at the front and back of the queue, not the front or back of the array. In this case, we're using a simple integer array to illustrate the principles behind implementing the queue data structure. You may come across more complex implementations, where each element in the array is a pointer to a class object or structure. In these cases, you should be concerned about memory management when you perform enqueue and dequeue operations.

Queues Using an Array in C++

Now that you understand how queues work with an array, it is time to create a real queue. In this section, you'll create a queue using C++. You'll see the Java version of this program later in this chapter.

The C++ queue program is organized into three files: the queue.h file, the queue.cpp file, and the queueProgram.cpp file. The queue.h file, shown next, sets the default size of the array and defines the Queue class. The Queue class declares size, front, and back attributes that store the array size and the index of the front and back of the queue. The Queue class also declares a pointer that will point to the array. In addition to these, the Queue class defines a set of member functions that manipulate the queues. These are explained later in this section.

```
//queue.h
#define DEFAULT_SIZE 8
class Queue{
   private:
      const int size;
      int front;
      int back;
      int* values;
   public:
      Queue(int size = DEFAULT_SIZE);
      virtual ~Queue();
```

```
        bool isFull();
        bool isEmpty();
        void enqueue(int);
        int dequeue();
};
```

The `queue.cpp` file contains the implementation of the member functions for the `Queue` class. There are six member functions defined in this file: `Queue()`, `~Queue()`, `isFull()`, `isEmpty()`, `enqueue()`, and `dequeue()`.

The `Queue()` member function is a constructor, which is passed the size of the array when an instance of the `Queue` class is declared. If the constructor is called with no parameters, then the default size is used; otherwise, the value passed to the constructor is used. The value of the array size is assigned to the attribute size by the first statement within the constructor.

The second statement uses the `new` operator to declare an array of integers whose size is determined by the size passed to the constructor. The `new` operator returns a pointer to the array, which is assigned to the `values` pointer. The last two statements in the constructor initialize the `front` and `back` attributes to zero.

The `~Queue()` member function is the destructor and uses the delete operator to remove the array from memory when the instance of the `Queue` class goes out of scope.

The `isFull()` member function (see Figure 5-4) determines if there is room available in the queue by comparing the calculated value of the back of the queue with the value of the front of the queue, as in shown Figure 5-4. Notice that the expression that calculates the back of the queue is very similar to the expression in the enqueue process (see the "Enqueue" section of this chapter), and both produce the same result. The queue is full when the back index is 1 behind the front. Placing another element in the queue would overwrite the front element and corrupt the queue. The modulus operator is used again to make this a circular queue, so when you're at element 7 on the back, the next element to look at is element 0.

The `isFull()` member function is called by the `enqueue()` member function before an attempt is made to place a value on the back of the queue. The `isFull()` member function returns a `true` if no more room is available in the queue or a `false` if there is room available.

The `isEmpty()` member function determines (see Figure 5-5) if the queue is empty by comparing the `back` and `front` variables. If they have the same values, a `true` is returned; otherwise, a `false` is returned. The `isEmpty()` member function is called within the `dequeue()` member function before it attempts to remove the front item from the queue.

The `enqueue()` member function places an item at the back of the queue, as described in the "Enqueue" section of this chapter. The `enqueue()` member function is passed the value that is to be placed in the queue. However, before doing so, the

Before dequeue

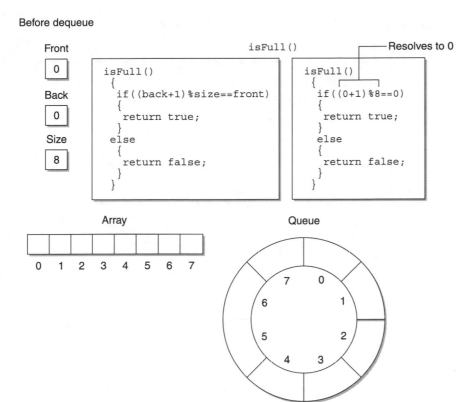

Figure 5-4   The isFull() member function determines if there is room to place
another item on the back of the queue.

isFull() member function is called to determine if there is room available in the
queue. Notice in the following example that the isFull() member function is
called as the condition expression of the if statement. Also notice that the not operator reverses the bool value returned by the isFull() method. That is, a false is returned by the isFull() member function if room is available in the queue. The
condition expression in the if statement reverses this logic to true so that statements within the if statement execute to place the new item on the back of the queue.

The dequeue() member function removes an item from the queue and returns
that item to the statement within the program that calls the dequeue() member
function. However, the isEmpty() member function is called in the condition expression of the if statement within the dequeue() member function, as shown in
the next code listing.

The not operator in this expression reverses the logic returned by the isEmpty()
member function. The isEmpty() member function returns a false if the queue is

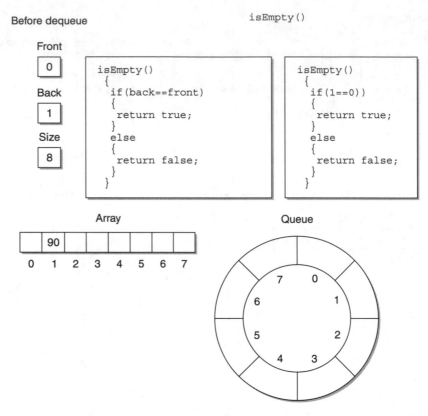

Figure 5-5   The isEmpty() member function determines if the queue contains any values.

not empty. The not operator changes this to true, enabling statements within the if statement to remove the front item from the queue and return it to the statement that calls the dequeue() member function.

```
//queue.cpp
#include "queue.h"
Queue::Queue(int size)
{
   this->size = size;
   values = new int[size];
   front = 0;
   back = 0;
}
Queue::~Queue()
{
   delete[] values;
}
```

```cpp
bool Queue::isFull()
{
   if( (back+1) % size == front)
   {
      return true;
   }
   else
   {
      return false;
   }
}
bool Queue::isEmpty()
{
   if(back == front)
   {
      return true;
   }
   else
   {
      return false;
   }
}
void Queue::enqueue(int x)
{
   if(!isFull())
   {
      back = (back+1) % size;
      values[back] = x;
   }
}
int Queue::dequeue()
{
   if(!isEmpty())
   {
      front = (front+1) % size;
      return queue[front];
   }
   return 0;
}
```

The queueProgram.cpp is where all the action takes place. It is here that an instance of the Queue class is declared and manipulated. As you can see in the next example, the first statement in the program uses the new operator to declare an instance of the Queue class and set the size to 8 elements. The new operator returns a pointer that is assigned to a pointer to an instance of the Queue class.

The next three statements call the enqueue() member function three times to place the values 10, 20, and 30 in the queue, respectively. The program concludes by calling the dequeue() member function three times to display the contents of the queue. Figure 5-6 shows the queue and the array after the last call to the enqueue() member function is made.

```cpp
//queueProgram.cpp
#include <iostream>
using namespace std;
void main(){
   Queue *queue = new Queue(8);
   queue->enqueue(10);
   queue->enqueue(20);
   queue->enqueue(30);
   for(int i=0; i<3; i++)
   {
      cout << queue->dequeue() << endl;
   }
}
```

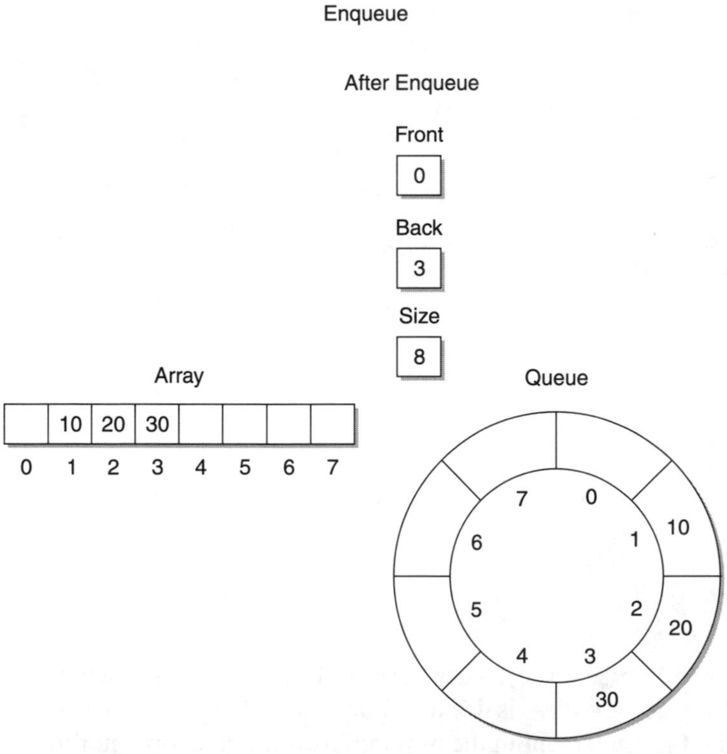

Figure 5-6   Here's the queue and the array after the last call to the enqueue() member function is made.

Queues Using An Array in Java

A queue is implemented in Java similar to the way you implement it in C++ except for a few tweaks, which we'll talk about in this section. The code example in this section is a queue using an array in a Java application. Two classes are defined in the example: the Queue class and the Java application class queueArrayDemo().

The Queue class defines the same set of attributes as is defined in the C++ version of this program. However, instead of declaring an integer pointer, the Java version of this program declares a reference to an array of integers, which is called values.

The Queue class defines seven member methods including two constructors. Most of the member methods are the same as the member functions in the C++ program. However, there are a few differences in the Java Queue class: it defines two constructors, which are the first couple of member methods in the class definition.

The first version of the constructor is Queue(). The Queue() constructor is called if the instance of the Queue() class is declared without the size of the queue passed as a parameter to the constructor. The Queue() constructor uses the default size for the queue. As you'll remember from your Java programming class, the this(DEFAULT_SIZE) statement calls the Queue(int size) constructor and passes it the default size of the queue. Java does not support default parameter values like C++, so this is one way to achieve the same result.

The second version of the constructor is Queue(int size). The Queue(int size) constructor is called whenever the size of the queue is passed as a parameter to the constructor. The size is then assigned to the size attribute of the Queue class and sets the size of the array. The array is created using the new operator, and reference to the location of the array in memory is assigned to the values attribute of the Queue class. The Queue(int size) constructor also initializes the front and back attributes.

The remaining member methods defined in the Queue class definition are the same as those defined in the Queue class definition in the C++ version of this program.

Beneath the Queue class definition is the Java application class definition called queueArrayDemo. This class defines the main() method of the application that contains nearly identical statements as those found in the main() function of the C++ program.

The first statement creates an instance of the Queue class that contains an array of 8 elements. The next three statements call the method to place values 10, 20, and 30 in the queue, respectively. Within the for loop, the dequeue() method is called to remove each item from the queue. These items are then displayed on the screen.

```java
class Queue
{
    private static final int DEFAULT_SIZE = 8;
```

```
private int size;
private int front;
private int back;
private int[] values;
public Queue()
{
    this(DEFAULT_SIZE);
}
public Queue(int size)
{
    this.size = size;
    values = new int[size];
    front = 0;
    back = 0;
}
public boolean isFull()
{
    if( (back+1) % size == front)
    {
        return true;
    }
    else
    {
        return false;
    }
}
public boolean isEmpty()
{
    if(back == front)
    {
        return true;
    }
    else
    {
        return false;
    }
}
public void enqueue(int x)
{
    if(!isFull())
    {
        back = (back+1) % size;
        values[back] = x;
    }
```

```
    }
    public int dequeue()
    {
        if(!isEmpty())
        {
            front = (front+1) % size;
            return values[front];
        }
        return 0;
    }
}
public class queueArrayDemo{
    public static void main( String args[]){
        Queue queue = new Queue(8);
        queue.enqueue(10);
        queue.enqueue(20);
        queue.enqueue(30);
        for(int i=0; i<3; i++)
        {
            System.out.println(queue.dequeue());
        }
    }
}
```

Quiz

1. What is a queue?

2. What is the relationship between a queue and its underlying array?

3. Explain how the index of the front and back of the queue is calculated.

4. What is the purpose of the enqueue process?

5. What is the purpose of the dequeue process?

6. Why is the isFull() member method called?

7. Why is the isEmpty() member method called?

8. What happens to the data stored on the array when the data is removed from the queue?

9. What is the purpose of setting the default size of the queue?

10. Why does the C++ version of the queue delete the underlying array from memory using the destructor and the Java version of the queue does not?

CHAPTER 6

What Is a Linked List?

Sports fans probably don't realize that the coach uses a linked list all the time during the game when switching players. In fact, the coach probably doesn't realize it either. Many teams have three strings of players. For example, in football, there's the starting quarterback, a backup quarterback, and a third string quarterback. The coach has a list of their numbers. If the starter takes a hard hit, the coach looks at the list for the number of the next quarterback. When the backup quarterback can't do the job, the coach looks at the list again and chooses either the previous quarterback (the starter) or the next quarterback (third string).

As you probably surmised, the list the coach uses is a linked list because it links quarterbacks to the order in which they are called upon to play in the game. A linked list is a list of elements that point to the current data (current quarterback), the previous data (quarterback who just left the game), and the next data (quarterback who hasn't entered the game). In this chapter, you'll learn about single linked lists and doubly linked lists and how linked lists work. In the next two chapters, you'll learn common uses for linked lists.

A Linked List

A linked list is a data structure that makes it easy to rearrange data without having to move data in memory. Sound a little confusing? If so, picture a classroom of students who are seated in no particular order. A unique number identifies each seat, as shown in Figure 6-1. We've also included the relative height of each student, which we'll use in the next exercise.

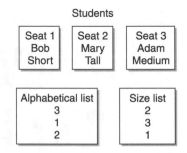

Figure 6-1   Students are seated in a classroom in random order.

Let's say that a teacher needs to place students names in alphabetical order so she can easily find a name on the list. One option is to have students change their seats so that Adam sits in seat 1, Bob sits in seat 2, and Mary in seat 3. However, this can be chaotic if there are a lot of students in the class.

Another option is to leave students seated and make a list of seat numbers that corresponds to the alphabetical order of students. The list would look something like this: 3, 1, and 2, as shown in Figure 6-1. The student in seat 3 is the first student who appears in alphabetical order, followed by the student seated in seat 1, and so on. Notice how this option doesn't disrupt the class.

Suppose you want to rearrange students in size order. There's a pretty good chance that you won't move students about the classroom. Instead, you'd probably create another list of seat numbers that reflect each student's height. Here's the list: 1, 3, and 2, which is illustrated in Figure 6-1. The list can be read from bottom to top for the shortest to tallest or vice versa for tallest to shortest.

Once the list is created, the teacher can simply go down the list to see which seat contains the next student. To quiz students in alphabetical order, the teacher would use the alphabetical list to see that the student sitting in seat 3 is alphabetically first, followed by seat 1. The teacher can be tricky and call on the previous student by looking at the list to determine the student's seat.

Programmers call this sort of list a linked list because each item on the list is linked to the previous item and the next item. That is, the seat of the current student is linked to the seat of the previous student and to the seat of the next student by the list.

The Real World and Linked Lists

It is very important to keep the real world in mind as you learn how to use a linked list; otherwise, you'll fall into the trap of thinking that a linked list is an abstract concept that has little use in the real world. Actually, linked lists play a critical role in applications that help companies and governments manage data dynamically.

There are two versions of a linked list, a single link and a double link. A single link list enables a program to move through the list in one direction, which is usually from the front of the list moving to the end of the list. A doubly linked list enables the program to move through the list in both directions. We'll focus on the doubly linked list for most of the examples in this chapter and then discuss the single link list toward the end of the chapter.

Although we've mentioned that an entry in a linked list contains data and pointers to the previous and next entries in the list, this is an oversimplification. The data we're talking about is typically a set of data such as customer information. Customer information could be a customer ID, customer first name, customer last name, customer street address, customer city, customer state, customer ZIP, and so on. Programmers call this a record. This means that an entry in a linked list may contain several data elements. In our example, however, we'll store only a single value of an integer so that we can focus on the principle of how a linked list works. In reality, you can add as many additional attributes to each node as you need.

Programmers choose linked lists over an array because linked lists can grow or shrink in size during runtime. Another entry can be placed at the end of the last entry on the linked list simply by assigning reference to the new entry in the last entry on the linked list.

Likewise, the last entry can be removed from the linked list by simply removing reference to it in the next element of the second-to-last entry on the linked list. This is more efficient than using an array and resizing at runtime.

If you change the size of the array, the operating system tries to increase the array by using memory alongside the array. If this location is unavailable, then the operating system finds another location large enough to hold elements of the array and new array elements. Elements of the array are then copied to the new location.

If you change the size of a linked list, the operating system changes references to the previous item and the next item on the list, which is fewer steps than changing the size of an array.

The Structure of a Linked List

Each entry in a linked list is called a *node*. Think of a node as an entry that has three subentries. One subentry contains the data, which may be one attribute or many attributes. Another points to the previous node, and the last points to the next node. When you enter a new item on a linked list, you allocate the new node and then set the pointers to previous and next nodes.

Programmers create a node in C++ by using either a structure or a class object; our example uses a structure. As you'll recall from your C++ programming course, a structure is a user-defined data type. The following example is a structure used to define a node. Figure 6-2 shows a node.

```
typedef struct Node
{
   struct Node(int data)
   {
      this->data = data;
      previous = NULL;
      next = NULL;
   }
   int data;
   struct Node* previous;
   struct Node* next;
} NODE;
```

The structure might look a bit strange even if you are familiar with structures because this example uses a pointer to the structure itself as two of its attributes. We'll clear up any confusion by taking apart this example. The structure is called Node.

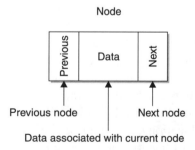

Figure 6-2   A node contains reference to the next node and the previous node in the linked list and contains data that is associated with the current node.

The name of the structure creates an instance of the structure similar to how you use a constructor to create an instance of a class and data type.

For now, let's skip the second definition of the structure and turn our attention to the last three statements within the structure. The first statement declares an integer that stores the current data of the node. The next two statements declare pointers to the previous and next nodes in the linked list.

The constructor initializes elements of the node when an instance of the node is created. This works in a similar manner as a class constructor. As you'll see in "LinkedList Constructor Destructor," you provide the current data to the structure when you create a new node. This data is assigned to data in the argument list. The value of data is then assigned to the data element of the instance of the structure. Also, reference to the previous and next nodes are initialized to NULL, which tells the program that there are no other elements of the linked list. The NULL is replaced with reference to a node when a new node is added to the linked list.

Single Linked List vs. Doubly Linked List

Programmers call this a doubly linked list or bidirectional (Figure 6-3) because each node contains reference to the previous and next node on the linked list. This enables the programmer to traverse the linked list in both directions by referencing the previous and next nodes. The node can be transformed into a single linked list (Figure 6-3) by only having one pointer in the structure that contains the address of the next node. Typically, a node in a single linked list references the next node and not the previous node, although nothing stops you from creating a backward reference by using only the previous node reference.

The following example is nearly the same as the previous example except this is a single direction node. You'll notice that reference to the previous node is missing. This means a programmer can only move down the linked list and not in both directions.

```
 typedef struct Node
{
    struct Node(int data)
    {
       this->data = data;
       next = NULL;
    }
    int data;
    struct Node* next;
} NODE;
```

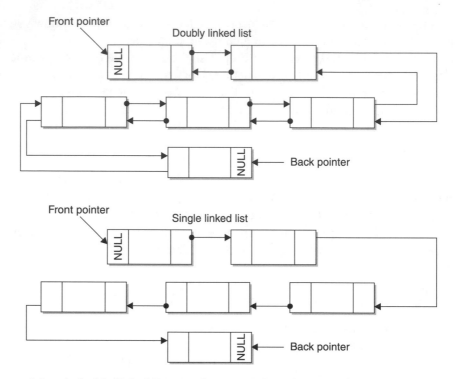

Figure 6-3 A doubly linked list contains next and previous members, and a single linked list contains only a next member.

The Linked List Class

Programmers use a LinkedList class to create and manage a linked list. C++ programmers define their own LinkedList class while Java programmers use the LinkedList collection class. You'll learn about the LinkedList collection class in the "Linked Lists Using Java" section of this chapter. For now, we'll focus on defining a LinkedList class in C++.

The LinkedList class definition consists of two data members and six function members, as shown in the example in this section. The two data members are pointers to instances of the Node structure that was defined previously in this chapter. The first pointer, front, references the first node on the linked list. The second pointer, back, references the last node on the linked list.

The six member functions manipulate the linked list. The first member function is the constructor of the LinkedList class and is called when an instance of the class is declared. Following the constructor is the destructor. When you return memory to the operating system by using the delete operator, the destructor is called. If you don't call the `delete` operator, then the destructor never gets called and the application causes a memory leak.

The `appendNode()` member function places a new node at the end of the linked list. The `appendNode()` requires an integer representing the current data of the node.

The next two member functions display the contents of the linked list. The `displayNodes()` method displays the linked list in natural order (first to last). The `displayNodesReverse()` member function displays the linked list in reverse order.

The last member function is `destroyList()` and is called to remove the instance of the `LinkedList` from memory.

The `LinkedList` class specification is defined in the header file, and the implementation is defined in the source file. We'll take a closer look at the implementation of these member functions in the next few sections of this chapter.

```
class LinkedList
{
   private:
      NODE* front;
      NODE* back;
   public:
      LinkedList();
 ~LinkedList();
      void appendNode(int);
      void displayNodes();
      void displayNodesReverse();
      void destroyList();
};
```

LinkedList Constructor Destructor

The `LinkedList` constructor is a member function that is called when an instance of the `LinkedList` is declared. The purpose of the constructor in the linked list example is to initialize the `front` and `back` pointers as shown in the following definition. Both the `front` and `back` pointers are assigned a NULL value, which is used by the `appendNode()` member function to determine if the linked list is empty. You'll see how this is done in the next section.

```
LinkedList()
{
   front = NULL;
```

```
    back = NULL;
}
```

The destructor is a member function called when the instance of the
`LinkedList` class is deleted using the delete operator. In the example shown next,
the destructor contains one statement that calls the `destroyList()` member
function.

The `destroyList()` member function deletes the contents of the linked list
but does not delete the linked list itself. That is, it removes all the nodes from the
linked list. You'll see how this is done later in this chapter. The `destroyList()`
also resets the front and back pointers to NULL, signifying the linked list is empty of
nodes. The destructor is responsible for deallocating all the memory that was allocated for the linked list. In this case, it would be all the nodes.

You might be wondering why we defined two member functions to perform basically the same task. We do so to enable the programmer to empty the linked list. This
way you can reset the contents of the linked list without destroying the instance of
the `LinkedList` class.

```
~LinkedList()
{
    destroyList();
}
```

Appending a Node to a Linked List

The `appendNode()` member function places a new node at the end of the linked list.
There are several steps that must be performed in order to add the node to the list. These
are shown in the following definition of the `appendNode()` member function:

```
void appendNode(int data)
{
  NODE* n = new NODE(data);
  if(back == NULL)
  {
     back = n;
     front = n;
  }
  else
  {
     back->next = n;
     n->previous = back;
     back = n;
  }
}
```

The appendNode() member function requires one argument called data, which is the current data for the node. The argument is passed to the instance of the NODE structure. As you'll recall from previous sections of this chapter, the value passed to the NODE structure is assigned to the data element of the node.

The first statement in the appendNode() member function declares an instance of the NODE structure by using the new operator, which returns a pointer to the instance, which in turn is assigned to a pointer variable called n.

Once the new node is created, the appendNode() member function positions the new node in the linked list. First, it determines if the linked list is empty by comparing the back node to NULL. As you'll recall, the back node is assigned a NULL when an instance of the LinkedList class is declared and when the destroyList() member function removes all the nodes from the list.

If the linked list is empty, then the new node is assigned to both the back and front pointers. This means that the linked list contains one node after the appendNode() member function is called, which is the new node.

However, if there is at least one node on the linked list, then a little shifting of pointers must be performed. The else statement contains three statements that perform this shifting. The first statement assigns the pointer to the new node to the next pointer of the last node on the linked list. The back pointer is then assigned to the previous pointer of the new node. The new node is then assigned to the back pointer, making the new node the first node on the linked list.

This can be a little confusing, so take a look at Figure 6-4. Figure 6-4 shows nodes of the linked list. Assume that the linked list has two nodes before the new node is appended to the list. This is represented in the top block.

The first step assigns the memory address of the new node to the next member of the back node, which is shown in the second block of memory in Figure 6-4.

The second step assigns the memory address of the back node to the previous member of the new node. This links both nodes.

The third step replaces the memory address of the back node on the linked list with the memory address of the new node. This places the new node at the beginning of the linked list.

Display the Linked List

The displayNodes() member function displays each node of the linked list, beginning with the node at the front of the list and ending with the node at the back of the list. This is shown in the next example:

```
void displayNodes()
{
    cout << "Nodes:";
```

```
NODE* temp = front;
while(temp != NULL)
{
    cout << " " << temp->data;
    temp = temp->next;
}
}
```

The displayNodes() member function begins by displaying the word "Nodes:" on the screen and then declares a pointer to a node, which is initialized with the node that appears at the back of the linked list.

Before attempting to display data assigned to the node, displayNodes() determines if there is a node at the back of the linked list. It does so by determining if the node pointed to by the temp pointer is NULL. If so, the linked list is empty and

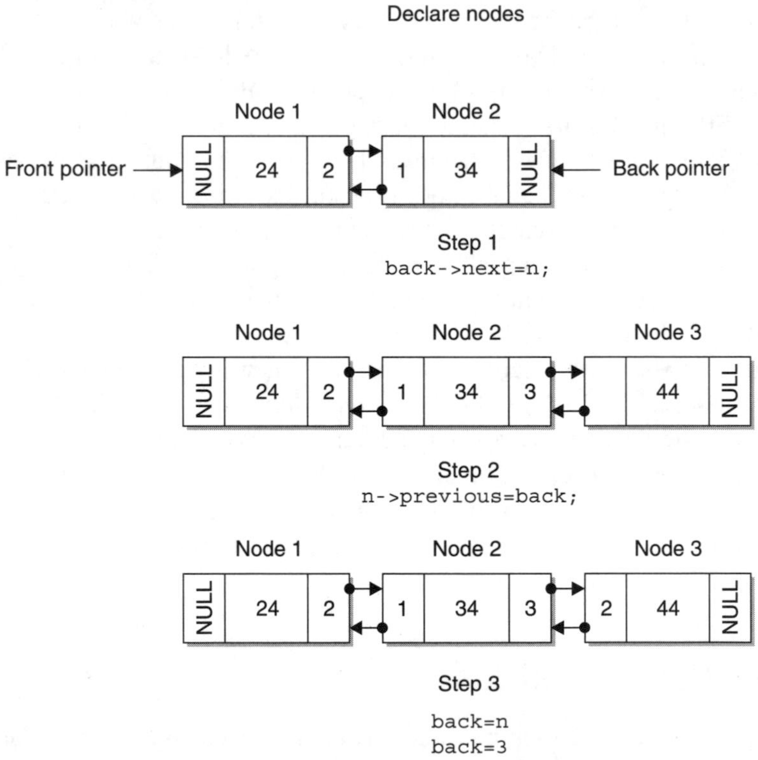

Figure 6-4 The appendNode() member function changes what nodes are pointed to in the linked list.

there is nothing to display. If not, the member function proceeds and displays the data assigned to the node located at the back of the linked list.

A space is then displayed, followed by the data assigned the node. The displayNode() member function uses the node's next member to assign the pointer to the next node to the temp pointer. The process continues by first determining if the node isn't NULL before displaying the data assigned to the node.

This process ends after the node at the back of the linked list is displayed because the next member of the node at the back of the list is NULL.

Transverse the Linked List

The displayNodesReverse() member function displays the contents of a linked list in reverse order, beginning with the node at the back of the linked list and continuing until the first node is displayed. The following example shows the how this is done:

```
void displayNodesReverse()
{
   cout << "Nodes in reverse order:";
   NODE* temp = back;
   while(temp != NULL)
   {
      cout << " " <<  temp->data;
      temp = temp->previous;
   }
}
```

You'll notice that the displayNodesReverse() member function is nearly the same as the displayNodes() member function described in the previous section. However, there are two important differences between the two member functions. The displayNodesReverse() member function assigns the pointer to the node at the back of the list to the temp pointer, causing the node at the back of the linked list to be displayed first. The displayNodes() member function assigns the back pointer to the temp pointer, causing the last node on the linked list to be displayed.

The other difference between the displayNodesReverse() member function and the displayNodes() member function is that in the displayNodesReverse() member function the previous member of the node is used to determine the next node to display. This enables nodes to be displayed in reverse order. Figure 6-5 illustrates how the linked list is transversed.

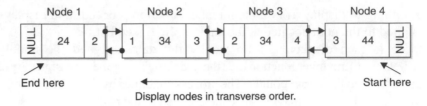
Figure 6-5   The previous member of each node transverses the linked list.

Destroying a Linked List

The destroyList() member function removes nodes from the linked list without removing the linked list itself, as shown in the following example. Each node is declared dynamically using the new operator, as you learned previously in this chapter. This enables you to remove the node by using the delete operator.

```
void destroyList()
{
   NODE* temp = back;
   while(temp != NULL)
   {
      NODE* temp2 = temp;
      temp = temp->previous;
      delete temp2;
   }
   back = NULL;
   front = NULL;
}
```

The destroyList() member function begins by declaring a temporary pointer that is assigned the pointer to the node that is at the back of the linked list. However, before the node is removed, the member function determines if there is a node at the back of the linked list by testing whether the temp pointer is NULL. If so, then the destroyList() member function assumes there are no nodes on the linked list. If the temp pointer isn't NULL, then the member function proceeds to delete the node.

Another temporary node is declared and assigned reference to the node pointed to by the temp node. This is done because the temp pointer is assigned the next node that is to be deleted from the linked list in the next statement.

The pointer to the next node is in the next member of the temp node, which is then assigned to the temp pointer. This means that temp2 points to the node at the back of the linked list and temp now points to the node that is immediately previous to the node at the back of the linked list. The node pointed to by temp2 is then deleted, as illustrated in Figure 6-6.

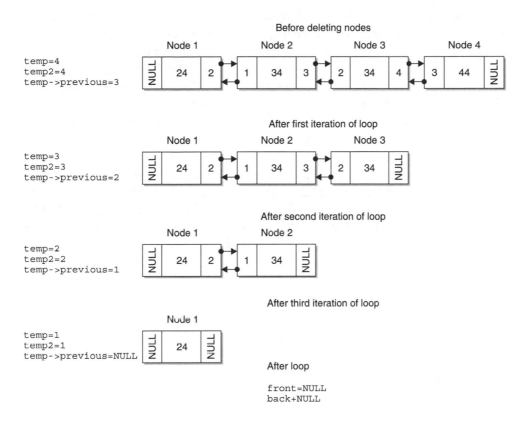

Figure 6-6 The destroyList() member function removes nodes beginning with the last node on the linked list and works its way to the beginning of the linked list.

This process continues until all the nodes are removed from the linked list. The final step in the destroyList() member function is to assign NULL values to the front and back of the linked list, which indicates that the linked list is empty of any nodes.

Linked Lists Using C++

Now that you know the parts of a linked list and how to create and manipulate the linked list using a class, we'll put those parts together and create a real-world C++ application that uses a linked list.

Professional programmers organized a linked list C++ application into three files. The first file is the header file that contains the definition of the NODE structure and the LinkedList class definition. The second file is a source code file containing the implementation of member functions of the LinkedList class. The last file is the application file that contains code that creates and uses the LinkedList class.

Let's begin with the header file. LinkedList.h, shown in the code in this section, is the header file for the C++ linked list example. This file contains two components, the definition of the NODE structure and the definition of the LinkedList class, which programmers called a class specification.

You'll notice that both components were discussed in detail previously in this chapter. You'll also notice that the LinkedList class definition does not contain the implementation of member functions. Instead, it contains prototypes of member functions that are implemented in the source file. Keeping the specifications and implementation in separate header and source files is common practice. Parts of the program that use the class only care about the interface functions defined in the header file; they don't care about the implementation. This also allows you to precompile your source code into library modules so the users of this class need only the headers and modules.

```cpp
//LinkedList.h
typedef struct Node
{
   struct Node(int data)
   {
      this->data = data;
      previous = NULL;
      next = NULL;
   }
   int data;
   struct Node* previous;
   struct Node* next;
} NODE;
class LinkedList
{
   private:
      NODE* front;
      NODE* back;
   public:
      LinkedList();
 ~LinkedList();
      void appendNode(int);
      void displayNodes();
      void displayNodesReverse();
      void destroyList();
};
```

Definitions of member functions for the LinkedList class are contained in the
LinkedList.cpp file as shown in the next code in this section. The file begins
with a preprocessor statement that tells the preprocessor to reference the contents of
the LinkedList.h file during preprocessing. The LinkedList.h file contains the LinkedList class definition and the NODE structure definition, both of
which are required to resolve statements in the LinkedList.cpp that refer to the
class and node.

Each member function definition is this example is practically the same definition as those discussed in the last several sections of this chapter. The only exception
is that reference is made to the LinkedList class in the name of each member
function definition. This associates each definition with the LinkedList class for
the compiler.

```cpp
//LinkedList.cpp
#include "LinkedList.h"
LinkedList::LinkedList()
{
   front = NULL;
   back = NULL;
}
LinkedList::~LinkedList()
{
   destroyList();
}
void LinkedList::appendNode(int data)
{
   NODE* n = new NODE(data);
   if(back == NULL)
   {
      back = n;
      front = n;
   }
   else
   {
      back->next = n;
      n->previous = back;
      back = n;
   }
}
void LinkedList::displayNodes()
{
   cout << "Nodes:";
   NODE* temp = front;
```

```
   while(temp != NULL)
   {
      cout << " " << temp->data;
      temp = temp->next;
   }
}
void LinkedList::displayNodesReverse()
{
   cout << "Nodes in reverse order:";
   NODE* temp = back;
   while(temp != NULL)
   {
      cout << " " <<  temp->data;
      temp = temp->previous;
   }
}
void LinkedList::destroyList()
{
   NODE* temp = back;
   while(temp != NULL)
   {
      NODE* temp2 = temp;
      temp = temp->previous;
      delete temp2;
   }
   back = NULL;
   front = NULL;
}
```

The last file is the C++ application that uses the linked list. We call the file LinkedListDemo.cpp, which is shown next. It is amazing that the application itself is so small when compared to all the code used to define the NODE structure and the LinkedList class.

```
//LinkedListDemo.cpp
#include <iostream>
using namespace std;
void main(){
   LinkedList * list = new LinkedList();
   list->appendNode(10);
   list->appendNode(20);
   list->appendNode(30);
   list->displayNodes();
```

```
list->displayNodesReverse();
delete list;}
```

The application begins by declaring an instance of the LinkedList class. As you recall from earlier in this chapter, the constructor initializes the front and back pointers.

The instance is declared using the new operator. The new operator returns a reference to the memory location of the instance. The same statement declares a pointer to reference a LinkedList. You call this pointer list and assign it the reference to the instance of the LinkedList class.

Next, the appendNode() member function is called three times. The appendNode() member function appends a new node at the back of the linked list and assigns the value passed to the appendNode() member function to the data member of the node.

The last two statements in this example display the data member of each node on the linked list. First, the displayNodes() member function is called to display nodes in natural order, starting with the front of the linked list and ending with the node at the back of the linked list.

Next, the displayNodesReverse() member function is called to do the same as the displayNodes() member function, except it starts with the back node and ends with the front node. The delete operator is then called to delete the instances of the LinkedList class from memory.

Here is the output of the code example:

10

20

30

30

20

10

Linked Lists Using Java

A linked list is implemented differently in Java than it is in C++ because Java has a LinkedList class defined as part of the Java collection framework, which is found in the java.util package.

The Java `LinkedList` class performs the same basic operations that we defined in the C++ `LinkedList` class. In addition, the Java `LinkedList` class has other features used to manipulate nodes in the linked list. You'll learn about these in the next two chapters, where the `LinkedList` class is used to implement other kinds of data structures. For now, we'll show you how to implement a linked list using Java.

The best thing about using the Java `LinkedList` class is that you simply declare an instance of the `LinkedList` class and call member methods as required by your program to manipulate the linked list.

The code example in this section is the Java version of the C++ application described previously in this chapter. You'll notice that both programs are similar, although the Java application has some subtle differences.

The first statement in the Java program is the same statement as is in the C++ program. It declares an instance of the `LinkedList` class. The next three statements call the `add()` member method of the `LinkedList` class to create a new node at the end of the linked list.

The `add()` member method is similar to the `appendNode()` member function used in the C++ application. However, you probably noticed that the parameter passed to the `add()` method is somewhat different from the parameter passed to the `appendNode()` member function. The parameter to the `appendNode()` member function is an integer, which is a primitive data type. However, the `add()` member method requires an object and not a primitive data type.

As you'll remember from your Java programming class, Java has a wrapper class for primitive data types. A wrapper class definition contains a data member that is of the corresponding primitive data type and defines member methods to manipulate the data type.

This example declares an instance of the `Integer` wrapper class using the `new` operator as the parameter to the `add()` member method. You pass to the constructor of the `Integer` class the integer that you want placed in the new node. The instance of the `Integer` class is an object, which is what the `add()` member method expects to receive. All the Java collections require a data type that inherits from the object. This is somewhat similar to the void pointer in C++. You're not allowed to store primitive data types in the collections as you can in C++.

Once three nodes are appended to the linked list, the program then displays the contents of the linked list by using two `for` loops. The first `for` loop displays the linked list in natural order. This has the same effect as if you called the `displayNodes()` member function in the C++ program. The second `for` loop displays the linked list in reverse order, which is identical to calling the `displayNodesReverse()` member function in the C++ program.

Both `for` loops call the `size()` member method of the `LinkedList` class to determine the number of nodes that are contained in the linked list. The data member of each node is retrieved by calling the `get()` method of the `LinkedList` class. The `get()` method requires one parameter, which is the number of the node on the list. In this example, the number is the integer value of the `for` loop.

The `get()` member method returns an object that must be type cast to an instance of the `Integer` class.

```
(Integer)list.get(i);
```

The node is then assigned to an `Integer` object and displayed on the screen. This is similar behavior with all the Java collection classes. With JDK 1.5, type safe collections will be introduced that are similar to template classes in C++, and you'll have an option to specify the type of object in a collection so all this type casting will not be necessary. It will also allow the compiler to do the type checking, leading to fewer errors. This generic object reference has the same pitfall as the void pointer in C++: it can lead to errors.

The only difference between both `for` loops is the expression used to determine the direction of the loop. Otherwise, both loops are identical.

Here is the output of the following example:

10

20

30

30

20

10

```
import java.util.LinkedList;
public class LinkedListDemo {
  public static void main(String[] args) throws IOException
  {
    LinkedList list = new LinkedList();
    list.add(new Integer(10));
    list.add(new Integer(20));
    list.add(new Integer(30));
    for(int i=0; i<list.size(); i++)
    {
```

```
        Integer temp = (Integer)list.get(i);
        System.out.println(temp);
    }
    for(int i=list.size()-1; i>=0; i--)
    {
        Integer temp = (Integer)list.get(i);
        System.out.println(temp);
    }   }
}
```

Quiz

1. What is a linked list?

2. What is the benefit of using a linked list?

3. What is a node?

4. What are the elements of a node?

5. What advantage does a linked list have over an array?

6. Can a node reference more than one data element?

7. In Java, why can't you pass a primitive data type to the add() method of the LinkedList class?

8. How can a node be inserted in the middle of a linked list?

9. What is a doubly linked list?

10. What is a single linked list?

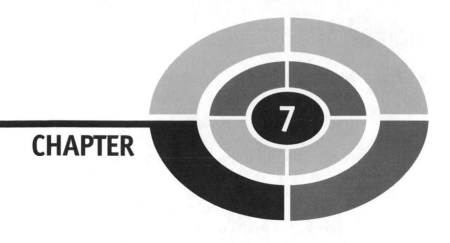

Stacks Using Linked Lists

Football fans know that piling on after the whistle will penalize the team (although advertisers love it because it gives broadcasters time to run a few commercials while the officials pull players off the pile). If you are not football fan, "piling on" is the un-official football term for players jumping on other players during a tackle. If you are a programmer, "piling on" is the unofficial computer term for a stack. You learned about stacks back in Chapter 4 when you discovered how to use an array to create your own stack. However, using arrays presents a problem: you cannot adjust the size of the stack when the program runs. The solution? Use a linked list to create a stack. You learned about linked lists in general in the last chapter. In this chapter, you'll learn how to use a linked list to create a stack.

A Stack

As you'll recall from Chapter 4, a stack is a data structure that organizes data similar to how you organize dishes in a stack on your kitchen counter. The newest dish is on top and the oldest is on the bottom of the stack.

When accessing dishes, the last disk on the stack is the first dish removed from the stack. If you want the third dish, you must remove the first two dishes from the top of the stack first so that the third dish becomes the top of the stack and you can remove it. There is no way to remove a dish from anywhere other than the top of the stack. You'd need to use a different kind of data structure (or stacking system) if you wanted to randomly access dishes.

A stack is useful whenever you need to store and retrieve data in last in, first out order. For example, your computer processes instructions using a stack in which the next instruction to execute is at the top of the stack.

LinkedList Class

Although we discuss data as being stacked like a stack of dishes, it isn't physically stacked at all. Instead, data is linked together sequentially in a list, where the last data always appears at the front of the list. Data is removed only from the front of the list.

You create this sequential list by using a linked list. In Chapter 6, you learned that a linked list contains entries called nodes. A node has three subentries, data and two pointers. The data subentry is the data stored on the stack. Pointers point to the previous node and the next node (Figure 7-1). When you enter a new item on a linked list, you allocate the new node and then set the pointers to the previous and next nodes.

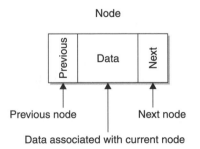

Figure 7-1   A node contains references to the previous node and the next node in the linked list and contains data that is associated with the current node.

A node is defined in C++ by using a structure, which is a user-defined data type. The following structure defines a node:

```
typedef struct Node
{
    struct Node(int data)
    {
        this->data = data;
        previous = NULL;
        next = NULL;
    }
    int data;
    struct Node* previous;
    struct Node* next;
} NODE;
```

The structure is called Node. The name of the structure creates an instance of the structure similar to the way a constructor creates an instance of a class and data type. Let's skip the second definition of the structure and look at the last three statements within the structure because statements at the beginning of the structure actually create an instance of the structure and don't define the structure. The first statement declares an integer that stores the current data of the node. The next two statements declare pointers to the previous and next nodes in the linked list.

The constructor initializes elements of the node when the node is created, which is similar to the way constructors work in a class definition. You provide the current data to the structure when you create a new node. This data is assigned to data in the argument list, which is then assigned to the `data` element of the instance of the structure. The `previous` and `next` nodes are initialized to NULL , which indicates there are no other elements of the linked list. The NULL is replaced with a reference to a node when a new node is added to the linked list.

As you'll recall from Chapter 6, a `LinkedList` class is defined to create and manage a linked list. There are two data members and six function members defined in the `LinkedList` class. Data members are pointers to instances of the Node structure. The first pointer is called `front`, and it references the first node on the linked list. The second pointer is called `back`, and it references the last node on the linked list.

Both the `front` and `back` pointers are declared in the protected access specifier area of the class definition because the `LinkedList` class is inherited by the `StackLinkedList` class, which you'll learn about in the "The StackLinkedList Class" section of this chapter. The `StackLinkedList` class uses the `front` and `back` pointers.

The six member functions manipulate the linked list. These function members are the constructor, destructor, `appendNode()`, `displayNodes()`, `displayReverseNodes()`, and `destroyNodes()`. You learned about them in Chapter 6.

Here is the `LinkedList` class definition. You'll notice that this is nearly the same as the `LinkedList` class definition you saw in Chapter 6, but there is a subtle difference. In Chapter 6, the `front` and `back` pointers were declared in the private access specifier area of the class definition. Here they are defined in the protected access specifier area because the `StackLinkedList` class will use them:

```
class LinkedList
{
    protected:
        NODE* front;
        NODE* back;
    public:
        LinkedList();
        ~LinkedList();
        void appendNode(int);
        void displayNodes();
        void displayNodesReverse();
        void destroyList();
};
```

The StackLinkedList Class

An efficient programmer does not repeat code if possible and instead inherits attributes and behaviors of another class, defining a `LinkedList` class to create and manipulate a linked list. An efficient programmer might also define a `StackLinkedList` class to create and manipulate a stack-linked list. The `StackLinkedList` class inherits attributes and behaviors of the `LinkedList` class and then defines other behaviors that are necessary to work with a stack-linked list.

In addition to the attributes and behaviors defined in the `LinkedList` class, the `StackLinkedList` class requires five behaviors defined as member functions: a constructor and destructor, `push()`, `pop()`, and `isEmpty()`. The `StackLinkedList` class definition is shown here:

```
class StackLinkedList : public LinkedList
{
    public:
        StackLinkedList();
        virtual ~StackLinkedList();
        void push(int);
```

```
        int pop();
        bool isEmpty();
};
```

StackLinkedList Constructor and Destructor

The constructor and destructor of the StackLinkedList class may be confusing
the first time you look at them because both are empty and there aren't any instructions specified in the body of the constructor and destructor, as shown here:

```
StackLinkedList()
{
}

~StackLinkedList()
{
}
```

   The constructor is empty because the constructor of the LinkedList class is
called before the constructor of the StackLinkedList class. You'll recall that the
StackLinkedList class inherits the LinkedList class. The LinkedList
class constructor initializes the front and back pointers of the linked list to NULL.
Therefore, there is nothing else for the StackLinkedList class constructor to do.

   Likewise, the destructor of the LinkedList class is called before the destructor
of the StackLinkedList class. The LinkedList class constructor deletes
all memory that is associated with the nodes of the linked list. Therefore, the destructor of the StackLinkedList class also has nothing to do.

Pushing a Node onto a Stack-Linked List

In Chapter 4, you learned that data is placed at the top of the stack and removed from
the top of the stack. Programmers call this *pushing* data onto the stack and *popping*
data off the stack. The same steps occur when using a linked list for the stack, but instead of placing data at the next available index in an array, it is placed at the back of
the linked list.

   You'll need to define a push() member function for the StackLinkedList
class that is called whenever data is added to the stack. Remember that you are really
adding a node to the linked list and not simply data. Data is contained *in* the node.

   To add a node to the stack, you use the same steps you use to add a node to a linked
list. This means that the appendNode() member function of the LinkedList
class can be used to place a new node on the stack. Therefore, all you need is to call

the appendNode() member function from the push() member function. Because appendNode() is public, you could just call appendNode directly to push a node onto the stack, but putting a push() function in the stack class makes this more intuitive to somebody using this class. This also helps hide the underlying implementation so using the class is a little more straightforward.

As you'll recall from Chapter 6, the appendNode() member function requires one argument, which is the data that is assigned to the new node. You must define the push() member function to accept the same data as its argument in order to pass this data to the appendNode() member function. This is illustrated in the following example. The push() member function requires an integer passed as an argument. The integer is then passed to the appendNode() member function within the body of the push() function definition.

```
void push(int x)
{
    appendNode(x);
}
```

Popping a Node from a Stack-Linked List

You'll also need to define a member function to pop a node from the stack. In this example, we'll call it pop(). Because you're using the linked list as the stack, the pop() member function must remove the node from the back of the linked list.

Unfortunately, you cannot simply call a member function of the LinkedList class to pop the node off the stack because the LinkedList class doesn't define a member function that removes a node from the linked list. If you had a member function in the base class for removeBack(), you could call that to pop a node off the list. In this case, you'll need to define a pop() function in the StackLinkedList class to do this. This will give you a last in, first out access to the stack.

Here is the definition of the pop() member function. Refer to the picture of the stacked linked list in Figure 7-2 as you read to help you understand how the pop() member function works.

```
int pop()
{
    if (isEmpty())
    {
        return -1;
    }
    int retVal = back->data;
    NODE * temp = back;
```

```
if (back->previous == NULL)
{
   back = NULL;
   front = NULL;
}
else
{
   back = back->previous;
   back->next = NULL;
}
delete temp;
return retVal;
}
```

First, you must determine if there is anything on the stack by calling the
isEmpty() member function. We'll show you how this member function works
later in this section. For now, understand that the isEmpty() member function returns a Boolean true if the stack is empty, or a Boolean false if it is not. You can
see in Figure 7-2 that the stack has two nodes on the stack, so it is not empty. Therefore, the return statement in the if statement is not executed.

The pop() member function refers to the back attribute of the LinkedList
class. It is important to remember that the back attribute refers to the top of the
stack. Nodes will be removed from the back of the linked list to do a pop operation.
Therefore, the value of front is Node 2.

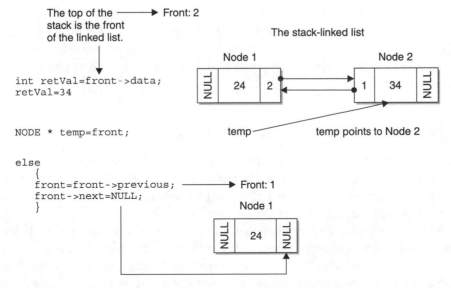

Figure 7-2   The pop() member function removes the node at the top of the stack,
which is the node at the front of the linked list.

The value of Node 2 is assigned to the `retVal` variable, which is the value returned by the `pop()` member function if there is a node on the stack. This pops the value from the stack.

Next, the address of the `back` node, which is Node 2, is assigned to a temporary pointer. The node that the temporary pointer points to is removed from memory with the `delete` operator at the end of the `pop()` member function.

Next, you determine if the node at the back of the stack was the only node on the linked list. You make this determination by seeing if the previous attribute of the node is NULL. If the previous pointer on the back of the list is NULL, this indicates that there's only one node in the linked list.

Be careful when analyzing the `pop()` member function. Remember that the back of the linked list is the top of the stack and that the bottom of the stack is the top of the linked list.

If the `pop()` member function is removing the only node on the stack, then the `front` and `back` attributes of the `LinkedList` class are set to NULL, indicating there are no nodes left on the linked list after the `pop()` is executed.

However, if there is at least one node on the stack, statements within the `else` statement are executed, as in Figure 7-2. The first statement within the `else` statement assigns the previous attribute of the `back` attribute as the new back. In Figure 7-2, the `previous` attribute is 1. This tells you that Node 1 comes before Node 2. You then assign Node 1 as the new back of the stack.

Remember that there isn't a next node on the stack because you are always working with the back of the linked list. Therefore, you need to assign NULL to the next attribute of the `back` node, which is Node 1. This makes Node 1 at the top of the stack.

The next to last statement removes the node from memory using the `delete` operator. The temporary pointer points to the memory address of the node that was removed from the stack. The last statement returns the value of the node that was removed from the stack.

Determine If the Stack Is Empty

The `pop()` member function must determine if the stack is empty, or it will attempt to remove a node that isn't on the stack. The `pop()` member function determines if the stack is empty by calling the `isEmpty()` member function, which you must define as part of the `StackLinkedList` class.

The `isEmpty()` member function is a simple function, as shown next. It determines if the stack is empty by seeing if the value of the `front` attribute of the `LinkedList` class is NULL. If so, then a Boolean `true` is returned; otherwise, a Boolean `false` is returned. If the stack is empty, both `front` and `back` are equal to NULL but you only need to check one of them.

```
bool isEmpty()
{
   if(front == NULL)
   {
      return true;
   }
   else
   {
      return false;
   }
}
```

StackLinked List Using C++

Now that you have an understanding of components, you need to create a stack-linked list. In this section, we'll focus on assembling them into a working C++ application. Some programmers organize components of a stack-linked list into five files: `LinkedList.h`, `LinkedList.cpp`, `StackLinkedList.h`, `StackLinkedList.cpp`, and `StackLinkedListDemo.cpp`. All these files are joined together at compile time to create the executable.

The `LinkedList.h` file is the header file that contains the definition of the Node structure and the definition of the `LinkedList` class. The `LinkedList.cpp` is a source code file that contains the implementation of member functions of the `LinkedList` class, both of which you learned about in Chapter 6.

The `StackLinkedList.h` file is the header that contains the definition of the `StackLinkedList` class. The `StackLinkedList.cpp` is the source code file that contains the implementation of member functions of the `StackLinkedList` class.

The `StackLinkedListDemo.cpp` contains the application. It is here where an instance of the `StackLinkedList` class is declared and member functions are called.

LinkedList Header File and LinkedList Functions

The `LinkedList.h` file and the `LinkedList.cpp` file are shown in the following code. These should look familiar to you because they are the same files described in Chapter 6. However, there is one exception. The `front` and `back` attributes defined in the `LinkedList` class in the `LinkedList.h` file are defined within the protected access specifier section of the class definition. They appeared within the private access specifier in the sample file in Chapter 6. The `StackLinkedList` class needs access to these variables, so you protect them so they're visible to the subclass.

Refer to Chapter 6 for a complete explanation of these files and member functions.

```
//LinkedList.h
typedef struct Node
{
    struct Node(int data)
    {
        this->data = data;
        previous = NULL;
        next = NULL;
    }
    int data;
    struct Node* previous;
    struct Node* next;
} NODE;
class LinkedList
{
    protected:
        NODE* front;
        NODE* back;
    public:
        LinkedList();
        ~LinkedList();
        void appendNode(int);
        void displayNodes();
        void displayNodesReverse();
        void destroyList();
};


//LinkedList.cpp
#include "LinkedList.h"
LinkedList::LinkedList()
{
    front = NULL;
    back = NULL;
}
LinkedList::~LinkedList()
{
    destroyList();
}
void LinkedList::appendNode(int data)
```

```
{
   NODE* n = new NODE(data);
   if(back == NULL)
   {
      back = n;
      front = n;
   }
   else
   {
      back->next = n;
      n->previous = back;
      back = n;
   }
}
void LinkedList::displayNodes()
{
   cout << "Nodes:";
   NODE* temp = front;
   while(tcmp !- NULL)
   {
      cout << " " << temp->data;
      temp = temp->next;
   }
}
void LinkedList::displayNodesReverse()
{
   cout << "Nodes in reverse order:";
   NODE* temp = back;
   while(temp != NULL)
   {
      cout << " " <<  temp->data;
      temp = temp->previous;
   }
}
void LinkedList::destroyList()
{
   NODE* temp = back;
   while(temp != NULL)
   {
      NODE* temp2 = temp;
      temp = temp->previous;
      delete temp2;
```

```
    }
    back = NULL;
    front = NULL;
}
```

StackLinkedList Header File and StackLinkedList Source File

The `StackLinkedList.h` file contains the definition of the `StackLinkedList` class, as shown next. Below the `StackLinkedList.h` file is the `StackLinkedList.cpp` file that contains the definitions of member functions.

The class definition and each member function were explained in the "The StackLinkedList Class" section of this chapter.

```
//StackLinkedList.h
 class StackLinkedList : public LinkedList
{
    public:
        StackLinkedList();
        virtual ~StackLinkedList();
        void push(int);
        int pop();
        bool isEmpty();
};

//StackLinkedList.cpp
StackLinkedList.h
StackLinkedList::StackLinkedList()
{
}
StackLinkedList::~StackLinkedList()
{
}
void StackLinkedList::push(int x)
{
    appendNode(x);
}
int StackLinkedList::pop()
{
    if(isEmpty())
    {
```

```
      return -1;
  }
  int retVal = back->data;
  NODE* temp = back;
  if(back->previous == NULL)
  {
    back = NULL;
    front = NULL;
  }
  else
  {
    back = back->previous;
    back->next = NULL;
  }
  delete temp;
  return retVal;
}
bool StackLinkedList::isEmpty()
{
  if(front == NULL)
  {
    return true;
  }
  else
  {
    return false;
  }
}
```

StackLinkedList Application

The StackLinkedListDemo.cpp file contains the actual stack application, as shown in the following code listing. The application begins by declaring an instance of the StackLinkedList class. Remember that this statement also indirectly calls the constructor of the LinkedList class, which is inherited by the StackLinkedList class.

The application then calls the push() member function to push the values 10, 20, and 30 onto the stack. The displayNodes() member function is then called to display the values on the stack. The displayNodes() member function is a member of the LinkedList class and is described in detailed in Chapter 6.

Before calling pop()

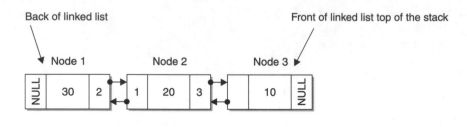

After calling pop()

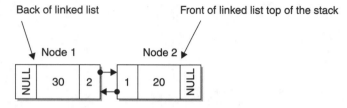

Figure 7-3   Before the pop() member function is called, there are three nodes on the stack. Two nodes remain after pop() is called.

The pop() member function is then called to remove the last node on the stack, which is then displayed on the screen (see Figure 7-3). The program then calls the delete operator to remove the stack from memory.

Here's the output of this program:

Nodes: 10 20 30 10

```
//StackLinkedListDemo.cpp
#include <iostream>
using namespace std;
void main(){
    StackLinkedList* stack = new StackLinkedList();
    stack->push(10);
    stack->push(20);
    stack->push(30);
    stack->displayNodes();
    cout << stack->pop() << endl;
    delete stack;
}
```

StackLinked List Using Java

Java's version of the stack-linked list is less complex than the C++ version because Java programmers use the Stack class defined in the java.util package. The Stack class contains the push(), pop(), and empty() member methods similar to those that you define in the C++ version of the stack-linked list. Understanding the basics of the C++ version helps you also understand the internal implementation of the stack, which in turn helps you make better choices when you select from data structures that have already been written, such as the Stack class in Java.

The following Java application is comparable to the C++ application that is discussed throughout this chapter. The application begins by declaring an instance of the Stack class and then calls the push() member method to place three values on the stack. The push() member method expects an object rather than an integer. Therefore, integers are passed to the constructor of the Integer wrapper class, as discussed in detail in the "Linked Lists Using Java" section of Chapter 6.

After the stack is loaded with data, the Java application determines if there is any data stored on the stack by calling the empty() member method of the Stack class. The empty() member method performs the same functionality as the isEmpty() member function in the C++ application.

The empty() member method returns a Boolean true if the stack is empty; otherwise, a Boolean false is returned. The program uses the not operator (!) to reverse the logic. That is, if the empty() member method returns false, then statements within the 0 loop execute.

The first statement within the while loop calls the pop() member method, which returns an Integer wrapper class object. The pop() method returns an object, so this must be typecast to an integer. The value is displayed using the System.out.println() method. Here's what is displayed when you run this application:

30

20

10

```java
import java.util.*;
public class StackLinkedListDemo {
   public static void main(String[] args)
   {
```

```
Stack stack = new Stack();
stack.push(new Integer(10));
stack.push(new Integer(20));
stack.push(new Integer(30));
while(!stack.empty())
{
   Integer temp = (Integer)stack.pop();
   System.out.println(temp);
}
   }
}
```

Quiz

1. What is a stack-linked list?

2. How does a stack-linked list differ from a linked list?

3. What is the benefit of using a stack-linked list?

4. Where is the front of the stack in a stack-linked list?

5. What is the maximum number of nodes that you can have on a stack-linked list?

6. Can a node on a stack-linked list have more than one `data` element?

7. Why does the `StackLinkedList` class inherit the `LinkedList` class?

8. Why is the constructor of the `StackLinkedList` class empty?

9. Why is the destructor of the `StackLinkedList` class empty?

10. What happens when you push a new node onto a stack?

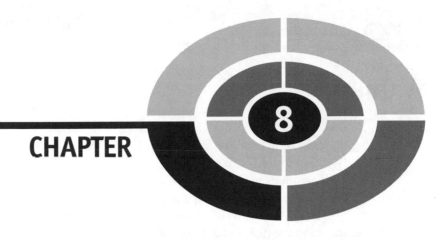

CHAPTER

8

Queues Using Linked Lists

Did you ever get ready to queue up to buy tickets for a hot concert, only to stand in the parking lot because there wasn't room at the ticket counter to accommodate all the fans? This is a common scenario, but you may not realize that programmers experience a similar problem storing data using queues: there is not enough room on the queue for all the data (just like the problem with all the fans) that must be processed. Box office staff still wrestle with this problem, but programmers have arrived with a solution: they use a linked list to create a queue. In this chapter, you'll learn how and when to use a linked list to queue data.

A Queue

In Chapter 5, you learned that a queue is a sequential organization of data where data is accessible on a first in, first out (fifo) basis, which is similar to the line that you stand in to buy concert tickets.

The queue in Chapter 5 was created using an array to store data. As you'll recall, the array is separate from the queue. Data is assigned to elements of the array. The queue itself consists of two variables called `front` and `back`. Each points to the array element that is at the front of the queue or at the back of the queue. When data is removed from the front of the queue, the program changes the value of the `front` variable to point to the next array element. However, the data removed from the queue remains assigned to the array. That is, data isn't removed from memory.

There is a serious problem with using arrays to store data for queues: you must know the size of the array when you write the program. An array can store only a specific maximum number of elements at any point in time, similar to an architect designing a specific space for a box office that can accommodate a maximum number of fans at any point in time.

However, there is a difference between exceeding the number of array elements and overflowing the space around the box office: unlike the stadium, there is no parking lot for fans to gather in while waiting to get in the queue to purchase tickets inside a computer.

Programmers work around the size issue by using a linked list instead of an array when creating a queue. As you learned in previous chapters, a linked list can grow and shrink at runtime based on the needs of the application.

The Linked List Queue

Conceptually, a linked list queue is the same as a queue built using an array. Both store data. Both place data at the front of the queue and remove data from the front of the queue. However, in an array queue, data is stored in an array element. In a linked list queue, data is stored in a node of a linked list. The linked list queue consists of three major components: the node, the `LinkedList` class definition, and the `QueueLinkedList` class definition. Collectively, they are assembled to organized data into a queue.

As you'll recall from Chapter 6, a node is created in C++ as a user-defined data type structure that contains three elements. These are the data and pointers to the previous node and the next node on the linked list (Figure 8-1). The next code snippet is the user-

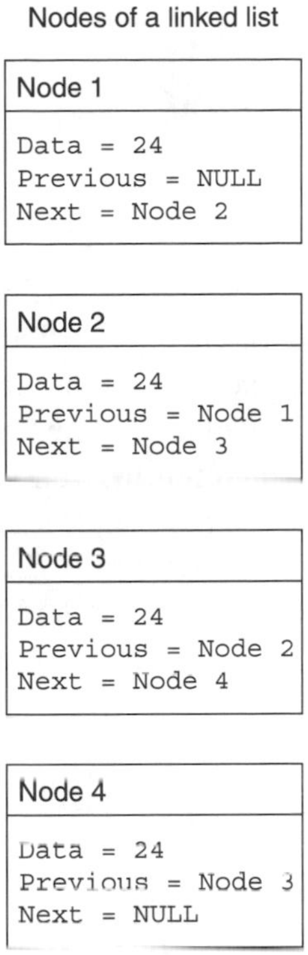

Nodes of a linked list

```
Node 1

Data = 24
Previous = NULL
Next = Node 2
```

```
Node 2

Data = 24
Previous = Node 1
Next = Node 3
```

```
Node 3

Data = 24
Previous = Node 2
Next = Node 4
```

```
Node 4

Data = 24
Previous = Node 3
Next = NULL
```

Figure 8-1   Each node points to the previous node and the next node.

defined data type structure node that we used in Chapter 6. You'll be using the following user-defined data type structure in this chapter to create the linked list queue.

The name of the user-defined data structure is called Node in this example and is used within the LinkedList class definition to declare instances of the node. The last three statements in the structure declare an integer that stores the current data and declares two pointers to reference the previous node and the next node on the linked list.

Each time a node is created, the user-defined structure is passed data for the node. Pointers to the previous node and to the next node are assigned NULL, which indicates there isn't a previous node or next node. NULL is replaced with reference to a node once the new node is added to the linked list.

```
typedef struct Node
{
    struct Node(int data)
    {
        this->data = data;
        previous = NULL;
```

Data Structures Demystified

```
        next = NULL;
    }
    int data;
    struct Node* previous;
    struct Node* next;
} NODE;
```

The LinkedList class creates and manages the linked list. As you'll remember from Chapter 6, the LinkedList class identifies the node that is the front of the linked list and the node that is at the back of the linked list.

In addition, the LinkedList class defines member functions that manage the linked list. These are the same member functions described in Chapter 6, a constructor and destructor, appendNode(), displayNodes(), displayNodesReverse(), and destroyList().Here is the LinkedList class definition that you'll use to create the linked list queue:

```
class LinkedList
{
    protected:
        NODE* front;
        NODE* back;
    public:
        LinkedList();
        ~LinkedList();
        void appendNode(int);
        void displayNodes();
        void displayNodesReverse();
        void destroyList();
};
```

Programmers usually place the node structure and the LinkedList class definition in the same header file, LinkedList.h. Placing the code needed to create a linked list in one file like this helps keep it organized. Programmers then use the preprocessor directive #include to include LinkedList.h in any program that uses a linked list.

The last component of the linked list queue is the QueueLinkedList class definition. The QueueLinkedList class inherits the LinkedList class and then defines member functions that are specifically designed to manage a queue.

You might wonder why you don't simply define one class that combines the LinkedList class and the QueueLinkedList class. Intuitively, this seems to be a good idea because everything needed to create a linked list queue is contained in one file. However, doing so repeats code, which is something programmers avoid if possible.

For example, definitions of a node and the LinkedList class would be located in two places. If you needed to upgrade either definition, you'd need to remember all the places where they are defined in your code. A better approach is to place each definition in its own file (for example, LinkedList.h, QueueLinkedList.h) so code won't be repeated.

Here is the definition of the QueueLinkedList class that you'll use to create a queue. Programmers save this definition in a file called QueueLinkedList.h. The QueueLinkedList class has five member functions: a constructor and destructor, enqueue(), dequeue(), and isEmpty()

```
//QueueLinkedList.h
#include "LinkedList.h"
class QueueLinkedList : public LinkedList
{
    public:
        QueueLinkedList();
        virtual  QueueLinkedList();
        void enqueue(int);
        int dequeue();
        bool isEmpty();
};
```

The constructor and destructor of the QueueLinkedList class are empty, as shown in the next code snippet. The constructor typically initializes data members of an instance of the class. In the case of the linked list queue, initialization is performed by the constructor of the LinkedList class, which is called before the constructor of the QueueLinkedList class. This means there isn't anything for the constructor of the QueueLinkedList class to do.

The destructor typically frees memory used by an instance of a class. The linked list used for the queue is removed by the destructor of the LinkedList class, which is also called before the destructor of the QueueLinkedList class. Therefore, there isn't anything for the destructor of the QueueLinkedList to do either.

```
QueueLinkedList::QueueLinkedList()
{
}
QueueLinkedList::~QueueLinkedList()
{
}
```

Enqueue

The `enqueue()` member function of the `QueueLinkedList` class is called whenever a new node is placed on the queue. As you see from the function definition in the next code snippet, the `enqueue()` member function is sparse because it contains only one statement, which calls the `appendNode()` member function of the `LinkedList` class.

You don't have to include additional statements in the `enqueue()` member function because placing a node on the queue is the same process as appending a node to the linked list. Each new node is placed at the back of the linked list. Therefore, the `appendNode()` member function is all you need.

You may wonder why the new node is being placed on the back of the queue, but it's just because you're reusing the same code in the `LinkedList` class. The new node will be placed on the back of the queue like a line at the grocery store. Nodes will be pulled off the front.

The `enqueue()` member function has one argument, which is the data that is being assigned to the new node. In this example, the node is used to store an integer. However, you can store any type of data in a node. In fact, the data can be a pointer to a set of data such as student information. To change this example from integer data to another type of data, you'd need to change the data element in the Node structure to reflect the type of data you want to store in the node.

Data received by the `enqueue()` member function is passed to the `appendNode()` member function. Figure 8-2 illustrates how the `appendNode()` member function places a new node at the back of the linked list. At the top of the illustration is a linked list that contains two nodes. The `appendNode()` is then called to add a new node to the back of this linked list.

The first step in this process assigns a reference to the new node to the next member of the front node. The front node is Node 2 and is assigned the reference Node 3 as the value of the next node in the linked list. This makes Node 3 the back of the linked list.

The second step assigns reference to Node 2 as the value of the previous node in Node 3. This means the program looks at the value of the previous node of Node 3 to know which node comes before Node 3 in the linked list.

The last step is to assign Node 3 as the new value of the `back` data member of the `LinkedList` class.

```
void enqueue(int x)
{
    appendNode(x);
}
```

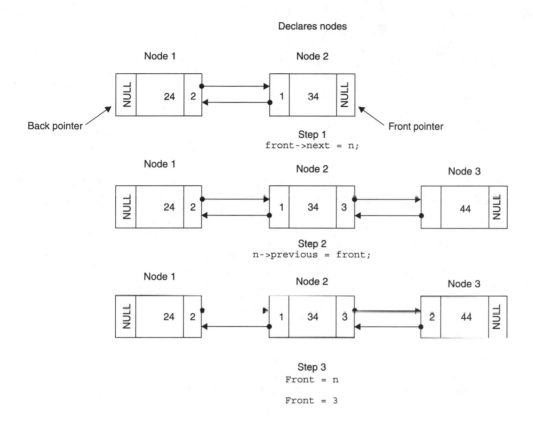

Figure 8-2   A new node is added to the queue at the back of the linked list.

Dequeue

The dequeue() member function of the QueueLinkedList class removes a node from the front of the queue. Unfortunately, there aren't any member functions in the LinkedList class that remove a node from the back of the linked list. Therefore, the dequeue() member function must do the job.

The dequeue() function begins by determining if there are any nodes on the queue by calling the isEmpty(). The isEmpty() member function returns a Boolean true if the queue is empty, in which case the dequeue() returns a −1. A Boolean false is returned if there is at least one node on the queue.

Figure 8-3 shows how the dequeue() member function works. You'll notice there are three nodes on the queue, so the isEmpty() member function returns a Boolean false, causing the program to remove the front node from the queue.

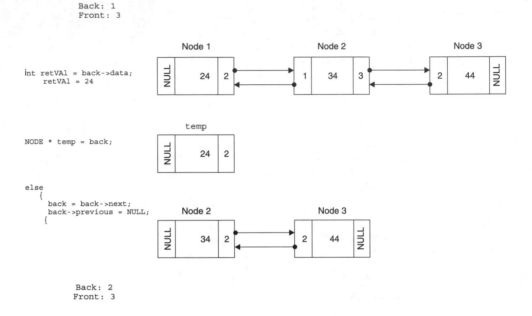

Back: 1
Front: 3

```
int retVAl = back->data;
    retVAl = 24
```

Node 1   Node 2   Node 3

NULL 24 2 →← 1 34 3 →← 2 44 NULL

temp

```
NODE * temp = back;
```

NULL 24 2

```
else
    {
       back = back->next;
       back->previous = NULL;
    {
```

Node 2   Node 3

NULL 34 2 →← 2 44 NULL

Back: 2
Front: 3

Figure 8-3   Node 1 is removed from the back of the queue by the dequeue()
member function.

The removal process starts by assigning the data of the node at the front of the queue
to a variable called retVal. The value of the retVal is returned by the dequeue()
member function in the last statement of the function.

Next, reference to the front node is assigned to the temp variable pointer. The
delete operator later in the function uses the temp variable to remove the back
node from memory.

Next, the function determines if there is another node on the queue by examining the
value of the next member of the front node. If the value of the next member is NULL,
there aren't any other nodes on the queue. In this case, the front and back members
of the LinkedList class are set to NULL, indicating that the queue is empty.

However, if the next member of the front node is not NULL, the value of the next
member of the front node is assigned to the front member of the LinkedList class.
In this example, Node 2 is the next node following Node 1. Node 2 becomes the new
front of the queue.

Notice that the `previous` member of Node 2 is set to Node 1. However, Node 1 no longer exists. Therefore, the `previous` member must be set to NULL because there isn't a previous node. Node 2 is the front of the queue.

The temp node is then deleted from memory. Remember that the temp node is a pointer that points to Node 1, and Node 1 no longer exists in memory. The final statement returns the value of the `retVal` variable, which is the data that was stored in Node 1.

```
int dequeue()
{
    if(isEmpty())
    {
        return -1;
    }
    int retVal = front->data;
    NODE* temp = front;
    if(front->next == NULL)
    {
        back = NULL;
        front = NULL;
    }
    else
    {
        front = front->next;
        front->previous = NULL;
    }
    delete temp;
    return retVal;
}
```

The `isEmpty()` member function determines if there are any nodes on the queue, which is called by the `dequeue()` member function. The `isEmpty()` member function examines the value of the `front` data member of the `LinkedList` class. If the value of `front` is NULL, then the queue is empty; otherwise, the queue has at least one node.

The `isEmpty()` member function returns a Boolean `true` if the value of `front` is NULL, otherwise a Boolean `false` is returned as shown in the definition of the `isEmpty()` here:

```
bool isEmpty()
{
    if(front == NULL)
```

```
    {
        return true;
    }
    else
    {
        return false;
    }
}
```

Linked List Queue Using C++

Now that you understand how to create a queue using a linked list, let's assemble all the pieces and build a working queue in C++. Programmers organize an application into several files, each containing a distinct component of the application.

In the case of the demo queue application illustrated next, there are five distinct components: the driver file (QueueLinkedListDemo.cpp), the header file that contains the definition of the node and the LinkedList class (LinkedList.h), the file that contains the implementation of member functions of the LinkedList class (LinkedList.cpp), the header file that contains the definition of the QueueLinkedList class (QueueLinkedList.h), and the file that contains the implementation of member functions of the QueueLinkedList class (QueueLinkedList.cpp).

The application is called QueueLinkedListDemo, and it uses a linked list to create a queue, as shown in the next code. The application begins by declaring an instance of the QueueLinkedList class using the new operator. It then declares a pointer to an instance of the QueueLinkedList. The pointer is called queue, which is assigned a reference to the instance created by the new operator.

The enqueue() member function is then called three times, each time another node is placed on the queue. The queue shown in Figure 8-4 depicts the queue after the last time the enqueue() method is called.

The dequeue() member function is then called to remove the first node from the queue and display its data member on the screen. Figure 8-5 shows the queue after the dequeue() member function is called.

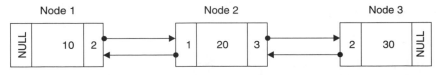

Figure 8-4   The queue after all three values are placed on the queue.

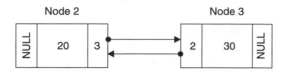

Figure 8-5   The queue after the `dequeue()` member function is called

The last statement in the program removes the queue from memory.

Each of the remaining components of the application was discussed in the previous section.

```cpp
//QueueLinkedListDemo.cpp
#include <iostream>
using namespace std;
void main(){
    QueueLinkedList* queue = new QueueLinkedList();
    queue->enqueue(10);
    queue->enqueue(20);
    queue->enqueue(30);
    cout << queue->dequeue() << endl;
    delete queue;
}

//LinkedList.h
typedef struct Node
{
    struct Node(int data)
    {
        this->data = data;
        previous = NULL;
        next = NULL;
    }
    int data;
    struct Node* previous;
    struct Node* next;
} NODE;
class LinkedList
{
    protected:
        NODE* front;
        NODE* back;
    public:
        LinkedList();
        ~LinkedList();
```

```cpp
        void appendNode(int);
        void displayNodes();
        void displayNodesReverse();
        void destroyList();
};

//LinkedList.cpp
#include "LinkedList.h"
LinkedList::LinkedList()
{
   front = NULL;
   back = NULL;
}
LinkedList::~LinkedList()
{
   destroyList();
}

void LinkedList::appendNode(int data)
{
   NODE* n = new NODE(data);
   if(front == NULL)
   {
      back = n;
      front = n;
   }
   else
   {
      back->next = n;
      n->previous = back;
      back = n;
   }
}

void LinkedList::displayNodes()
{
   cout << "Nodes:";
   NODE* temp = front;
   while(temp != NULL)
   {
      cout << " " << temp->data;
      temp = temp->next;
   }
}
```

```cpp
void LinkedList::displayNodesReverse()
{
    cout << "Nodes in reverse order:";
    NODE* temp = back;
    while(temp != NULL)
    {
        cout << " " <<  temp->data;
        temp = temp->previous;
    }
}

void LinkedList::destroyList()
{
    NODE* temp = back;
    while(temp != NULL)
    {
        NODE* temp2 = temp;
        temp = temp->previous;
        delete temp2;
    }
    back = NULL;
    front = NULL;
}

//QueueLinkedList.h
#include "LinkedList.h"
class QueueLinkedList : public LinkedList
{
    public:
        QueueLinkedList();
        virtual ~QueueLinkedList();
        void enqueue(int);
        int dequeue();
        bool isEmpty();
};

//QueueLinkedList.cpp
#include "QueueLinkedList.h"
QueueLinkedList::CQueueLinkedList()
{
}
QueueLinkedList::~CQueueLinkedList()
{
}
void QueueLinkedList::enqueue(int x)
{
```

```
      appendNode(x);
}

int QueueLinkedList::dequeue()
{
    if(isEmpty())
    {
        return -1;
    }
    int retVal = front->data;
    NODE* temp = front;
    if(front->next == NULL)
    {
        back = NULL;
        front = NULL;
    }
    else
    {
        front = front->next;
        front->previous = NULL;
    }
    delete temp;
    return retVal;
}

bool QueueLinkedList::isEmpty()
{
    if(front == NULL)
    {
        return true;
    }
    else
    {
        return false;
    }
}
```

Linked List Queue Using Java

You learned in your Java programming class that Java has several Java collection classes that create and manipulate data structures, and you learned in Chapter 6 that the LinkedList class is one of those collection classes.

However, Java does not have a `QueueLinkedList` class. Therefore, you need to define your own `QueueLinkedList` class to create a queue that is formed using a linked list. The good news is that the `QueueLinkedList` class contains only three member methods, and each has a simple definition.

The `QueueLinkedList` class requires that you define a constructor, an `enqueue()` member method, and a `dequeue()` member method. The constructor initializes the linked list, and the `enqueue()` and `dequeue()` member methods place data on the queue and remove data from the queue.

The `QueueLinkedList` class inherits the `LinkedList` collection class and uses member methods of the `LinkedList` class to create and manipulate the queue. This simplifies the task of defining member methods for the `QueueLinkedList` class.

The purpose of the constructor is to create and initialize the linked list. The `LinkedList` class constructor performs these tasks, which means the `QueueLinkedList` class constructor needs to call the `LinkedList` class constructor. This is done by entering the `super()` statement in the `QueueLinkedList` constructor definition as shown next:

```
public QueueLinkedList()
    {
        super();
    }
```

The definition of the `enqueue()` member method places data at the back of the queue. Fortunately, the `LinkedList` class defines the `addLast()` member method, which does just that. Therefore, the `enqueue()` member method must simply call the `addLast()` member method to place data at the end of the linked list.

The next code snippet is the definition of the `enqueue()` member method. The `enqueue()` member method requires one argument, which is the data that is placed on the queue. We use an integer in this example, but you can use data of any data type.

The data is assigned to a wrapper class and then passed to the `addLast()` member method. As you'll recall from your Java class, a wrapper class is a class that has member methods defined to manipulate a primitive data type. The `Integer()` wrapper class is used in this example because we are using an integer. Java also has wrapper classes for other primitive data types.

You must use a wrapper class because the `addLast()` member method expects to receive an object and not a primitive data type. Therefore, you need to pass the primitive data type (variable x in this example) to the constructor of the wrapper class. The constructor assigns the value of the primitive data type to a data member of the wrapper class.

Notice in the parameter of the `addLast()` member method that the `new` operator declares the instance of the wrapper class (`Integer`) and returns a reference to the instance, which is passed to the `addLast()` member method.

```
public void enqueue(int x)
   {
       addLast(new Integer(x));
   }
```

The definition of the `dequeue()` member method is a little more complicated than the other member methods of the `QueueLinkedList` class. The purpose of the `dequeue()` member method is to remove data from the front of the queue, so the first task the `dequeue()` member method performs is to determine if there is any data on the queue. It does this by calling the `size()` member method of the `LinkedList` class. This is similar to calling the `isEmpty()` member method of the `QueueLinkedList` class in a C++ program.

The `size()` member method returns a zero if the linked list is empty. The `dequeue()` member method then returns the zero to the statement that called the `dequeue()` member method. A nonzero value is returned by the `size()` member method if there is data on the linked list.

If there is data on the linked list, the `dequeue()` member method removes the data from the first node on the linked list and assigns it to a variable called `temp`. The `temp` variable refers to an instance of the `Integer` wrapper class. However, the `removeFirst()` member method returns the value of the node, which is an integer in this example. Therefore, the value returned by the `removeFirst()` member method must be cast as an instance of the Integer wrapper class (`Integer`) before it is assigned to the `temp` variable.

You do this because in the next statement, you call the `intValue()` member method of the `Integer` wrapper class to retrieve the data member of the wrapper class, which is the value that is returned by the `dequeue()` member method.

Here is the definition of the `dequeue()` member method:

```
public int dequeue()
   {
       if(size() == 0)
       {
          return 0;
       }
       Integer temp = (Integer)removeFirst();
       return temp.intValue();
   }
```

Now that you understand how to define the `QueueLinkedList` class, let's use a queue in a Java application. The next piece of code is the complete Java applica-

tion. It begins with the definition of the `QueueLinkedList` class, which you learned about in this section.

At the end of the application is the `main()` method. The first statement in the `main()` method declares an instance of the `QueueLinkedList()` class called queue. This is the same statement that is used in the C++ version of this application.

The `enqueue()` member method is called three times, placing the values 10, 20, and 30 on the queue. The result is a queue that looks like Figure 8-4. The application then removes the first data element from the queue and displays it on the screen by calling the `dequeue()` member method. The value returned by the `dequeue()` method is then displayed on the screen by calling the `System.out.println()` method.

Here's what is displayed on the screen.

10

Next, the application places three more values on the queue by calling the `enqueue()` member method, which places 40, 50, and 60 on the queue. Figure 8-6 shows the queue.

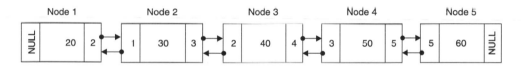

Figure 8-6   The queue after all values are placed on the queue

The last step in the application is to display each node on the linked list. Here's the output of the following program:

20

30

40

50

60

```
import java.util.*;
class QueueLinkedList extends LinkedList
{
    public QueueLinkedList()
    {
        super();
```

```java
        }
    public void enqueue(int x)
    {
        addLast(new Integer(x));
    }
    public int dequeue()
    {
        if(size() == 0)
        {
            return 0;
        }
        Integer temp = (Integer)removeFirst();
        return temp.intValue();
    }
}
public class QueueLinkedListDemo {
    public static void main(String[] args)
    {
        QueueLinkedList queue = new QueueLinkedList();
        queue.enqueue(10);
        queue.enqueue(20);
        queue.enqueue(30);
        System.out.println(queue.dequeue());
        queue.enqueue(40);
        queue.enqueue(50);
        queue.enqueue(60);
        while(queue.size() > 0)
        {
            System.out.println(queue.dequeue());
        }
    }
}
```

Quiz

1. What is a queue linked list?

2. How does a queue linked list differ from an array queue?

3. What is the benefit of using a queue linked list?

4. Where are new nodes added to the queue?

5. Which node is removed from the queue when the dequeue() member method is called?

6. Can a node on a queue linked list have more than one data element?

7. What form of access is used to add and remove nodes from a queue?

8. Why is the constructor of the QueueLinkedList class empty?

9. Why does the QueueLinkedList class inherit the LinkedList class?

10. What happens when dequeue() is called?

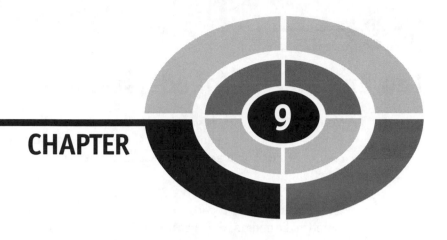

Stacks and Queues: Insert, Delete, Peek, Find

When you began learning about programming, you probably started with a bare-bones computer and then, once you learned how to program, you probably traded up for a system that had all the bells and whistles. Learning how to use the LinkedList class works in a similar way. The LinkedList class has basic functionality that is useful when working with stacks and queues. However, it lacks powerful features that are required to build industrial-strength applications. Now it is time to learn how to use those features and upgrade the LinkedList class. We'll teach you how to do that in this chapter by introducing insert, peek, delete, and find functionality to the LinkedList class and showing you how to use them in your stack and queue applications.

Sometimes you may not know the index of the node that you want to remove from the linked list. In that case, you need to define another function that removes a node based on the data of the node, not the node's index. You can call this function deleteNode(). The deleteNode() differs from the removeNodeAt() function by the way the function identifies the node to remove from the linked list. The removeNodeAt() function locates the node to remove by using the node's index value. The deleteNode() locates the node to remove by using the value of the data of the node, which is passed to the deleteNode() function.

So far in this book, you've accessed nodes on a linked list in sequential order. However, nodes are accessed randomly in some real-world applications. The next new function that you'll define for the LinkedList class enables you to access a specific node. This function is called findNode(), and it is used when you know the data contained in the node but you don't know the position of the node on the linked list. To locate the node, you provide the function with the data stored in the node. The findNode() function returns the index of the node.

The original LinkedList class is capable of appending a new node to the linked list. There will be situations when you'll want to insert a new mode somewhere in the middle of the linked list. To do this, you need to define the insertNodeAt() function. The insertNodeAt() function will require two parameters. The first parameter is the index of the node that will be moved in the linked list to make room for the new node. This becomes the index of the new node. The second parameter is the data that will be assigned to the new node. The insertNodeAt() function creates the new node and adjusts references within the linked list to link the new node to other nodes in the linked list.

Another major enhancement to the LinkedList class is to retrieve data that is stored at a specific node. Previously, two display functions were the only functions that you could use to see the data in the linked list (these function didn't return anything, they just count all the nodes). Both functions print out all the data stored in a linked list. Call the new function peek(). The peek() function requires that you pass it the index of the node that contains the data you want to retrieve. It then returns the data stored at that node.

The last enhancement that you'll make to the LinkedList class is to define a function that returns the number of nodes contained on the linked list. Call this function getSize() and use it whenever you need to determine the size of the linked list.

The following example is the revised LinkedList.h file that contains the definitions of the node structure and the enhanced LinkedList class. Notice that the size data member and the removeNode() member function are placed within the protected access specifier area of the class definition. This is because neither is directly used by the application. Instead, they are used by member functions of the LinkedList class and by member functions that inherit from the LinkedList class.

All the other member functions are placed in the public access specifier area of the `LinkedList` class definition and are available for direct use by the application. You'll learn how each new member function works in forthcoming sections of this chapter.

```
//LinkedList.h
typedef struct Node
{
   struct Node(int data)
   {
      this->data = data;
      previous = NULL;
      next = NULL;
   }
   int data;
   struct Node* previous;
   struct Node* next;
} NODE;
class LinkedList
{
   protected:
      NODE* front;
      NODE* back;
      int size;
      void removeNode(NODE* node);
   public:
      LinkedList();
      virtual ~LinkedList();
      void appendNode(int);
      void displayNodes();
      void displayNodesReverse();
      void destroyList();
      void removeNodeAt(int);
      int findNode(int);
      void deleteNode(int);
      void insertNodeAt(int,int);
      int peek(int);
      int getSize();
};
```

removeNode(), removeNodeAt(), and deleteRemove()

Removing a node from a linked list is a tricky operation. First, you must disconnect the node from the linked list. However, doing so breaks the link. There is no longer anything connecting the previous node and the next node because the node you removed was the link between them. This means that after removing a node, you must link together the previous node and the next node.

You can enhance the `LinkedList` class to include three member functions that remove a node from a linked list and then connect the previous node and next node to each other. These functions are `removeNode()`, `removeNodeAt()`, and `deleteNode()`.

The `removeNode()` function is passed a reference to the node that is to be removed from the linked list and is called by the `removeNodeAt()` function and the `deleteNode()` function. You cannot call the `removeNode()` function directly from the application because it is a protected member of the class.

The `removeNodeAt()` function uses the index of a node to locate the node that is to be removed. Once the node is found, its reference is passed to the `removeNode()` function. Similarly, the `deleteNode()` uses the data value of a node to locate the node. Once found, the `deleteNode()` retrieves the reference of the node, which is then passed to the `removeNode()` function.

For examples in this section, you'll use the linked list, shown in Figure 9-1, which has five nodes, NodeA through NodeE, respectively. Each node holds a position in the linked list, and each position is identified by an index value. Index values begin with zero and are shown above the name of each node in Figure 9-1.

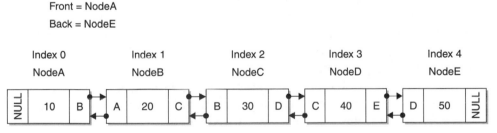

Front = NodeA

Back = NodeE

| Index 0 | Index 1 | Index 2 | Index 3 | Index 4 |
| NodeA | NodeB | NodeC | NodeD | NodeE |

| NULL | 10 | B | A | 20 | C | B | 30 | D | C | 40 | E | D | 50 | NULL |

Figure 9-1   A linked list containing five nodes with each node identified by an index value

Begin by defining the `removeNode()` function, which is illustrated in the next code listing. Reference to the node being removed is passed to the `removeNode()` function. The `removeNode()` function must determine which of four processes to use to remove the node.

The first process is for the `removeNode()` to determine if the node is the only node on the linked list. It makes this determination by evaluating if the previous and the next node are NULL. If so, the node being deleted is the only node on the list. The node is then removed by assigning NULL to the back and front data members of the `LinkedList` class. As you'll recall from previous chapters, functions that retrieve data from a linked list always examine the front and back data members to determine if each is NULL. If so, then the function knows the linked list does not contain any nodes.

If the node is *not* the only node on the linked list, the removeNode() function must next determine if the node being removed is at the front of the linked list. It determines this by examining the previous member of the node. If the node is at the front of the linked list, then the previous member is NULL, and the removeNode() function takes the following steps to remove the node:

1. The node pointed to by the deleted node's next member is assigned to the front data member of the LinkedList class. This makes it the front of the linked list.

2. The previous member of the node that is now at the front of the linked list is assigned a NULL value, indicating there is no previous node because you removed its previous node. Here's how this is done. It might look a little confusing, but it's easy to understand if you take apart this statement:

   ```
   node->next->previous = NULL;
   ```

3. Say that you're removing Node D. The next node is Node E. Now substitute the numbers for the terms in this statement:

   ```
   Node D->Node E->previous = NULL;
   ```

It's clear that the previous member belongs to Node E.

In the third process, the removeNode() function determines if the node being removed is at the back of the linked list. It does this by comparing the value of the next member of the node to NULL. If the next member is NULL, then the node being removed is the last node on the linked list.

The value of the previous member of the node is then assigned to the back member of the LinkedList class. This moves the previous node to the back of the list and in effect removes the node that is passed to the removeNode() function from the linked list.

The value of the next member of the previous node is then set to NULL, indicating there isn't another node because it is at the back of the list. The statement that performs this operator might seem confusing, but replacing references to node and previous with the node number should clear up any confusion. Here's the statement:

```
node->previous->next = NULL;
```

Say that you're removing NodeC. The previous node is NodeB. Now substitute the numbers for the terms in this statement:

```
NodeC->NodeB->next = NULL;
```

If the node being deleted isn't the only node on the linked list and isn't the node at the front or back of the linked list, the only other possibility is that the node is somewhere in the middle of the linked list.

The fourth process is to remove a node in the middle of the linked list and then link together the previous and next nodes. I'll illustrate this with an example because this operation can be confusing.

Say that you're removing NodeC. The previous node is NodeB and the next node is NodeD. First, link NodeB to NodeD by using the following statement:

```
node->previous->next = node->next;
```

Replace node, previous, and next with the name of the actual node to better understand this operation:

```
NodeC->NodeB->next = NodeC->NodeD;
```

Now that NodeB is linked to NodeD, you need to link NodeD to NodeB:

```
node->next->previous = node->previous;
```

Again, replace the node, shown next, and previous with names of nodes to see how this operation works:

```
NodeC->NodeD->previous = NodeC->NodeB;
```

Both NodeB and NodeD are linked to each other, and NodeC is removed from the linked list.

Although the node passed to the `removeNode()` function is no longer on the linked list, it remains in memory. Therefore, you need to remove the node from memory by calling `delete`. The final step is to adjust the value of the size member of the `LinkedList` class to reflect one less node on the linked list. You do this by decrementing the value of the size.

Figure 9-2 shows the linked list after the `removeNode()` function executes. Notice that NodeC is no longer on the linked list, and the index values are adjusted to reflect the new number of nodes on the linked list.

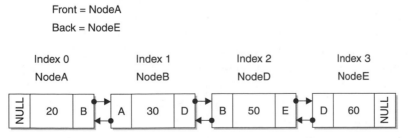

Figure 9-2   The linked list after NodeC is removed

```
void removeNode(NODE* node)
{
      if(node->previous == NULL && node->next == NULL)
      {
            back = NULL;
            front = NULL;
      }
      else if(node->previous == NULL)
      {
            front = node->next;
            node->next->previous = NULL;
      }
      else if(node->next == NULL)
      {
            back = node->previous;
            node->previous->next = NULL;
      }
      else
      {
            node->previous->next = node->next;
            node->next->previous = node->previous;
      }

      delete node;
      size--;
}
```

removeNodeAt()

The removeNodeAt() function removes a node by using the node's index rather than the reference to the node in memory. Remember, the index is the position of the node on the linked list. Say you want to remove the third node of the linked list. You simply pass the index 2 to the removeNodeAt() function, and removeNode() performs the operation internally. You can't call removeNode() directly, partly because it's protected, but also because outside this class you don't have any knowledge of the actual pointer values. Remember that the index begins with zero. Therefore, you don't need to know the actual reference of the node you want removed. This is illustrated in the next code.

The first step in the removeNodeAt() function is to determine if the index is valid. To do that, the removeNodeAt() function determines if the index is less than zero or greater than one less than the size of the linked list. It uses the value of the size member of the LinkedList class to determine the size of the linked list. If either is true, then the index is invalid and no attempt is made to remove the node.

However, if both are false, the removeNodeAt() function begins the process of removing the node from the list. This process has two steps. First, the index locates a reference to the corresponding node, and second, the removeNode() function is called and passed the reference.

The removeNodeAt() function begins searching for reference to the node by declaring a temporary pointer to a node called temp_node and assigning it the reference to the node at the front of the linked list. Next, a for loop iterates through each node on the linked list until the node represented by the index is found. During each iteration, the temp_node is assigned the node referenced by the next member of the current temp_node.

When the index is reached, the value of the temp_node is reference to the node that corresponds to the index that is passed to the removeNodeAt() function. The removeNode() function is called and passed the temp_node.

```
void removeNodeAt(int index)
{
      if(index < 0 || index > size-1)
      {
            rcturn,
      }

      NODE* temp_node = front;

      for(int i=0; i<index; i++)
      {
            temp_node = temp_node->next;
      }

      removeNode(temp_node);
}
```

deleteNode()

The deleteNode() function uses data stored in a node to find and remove a corresponding node from the linked list. The deleteNode() function then searches the linked list to locate and remove the node.

Here's how this process works. First, a temporary node called temp_node is declared and assigned reference to the node that is located at the front of the linked list. If the temp_node is not NULL, then the list is not empty and the function determines if the data matches the data member of the current node.

If it does, the temp_node is passed to the removeNode() function, and the function is completed. If the data doesn't match, the next node is assigned to the temp_ node, and the process continues until either the node containing the data is found or the `deleteNode()` function reaches the end of the linked list.

```
void deleteNode(int data)
{
        NODE* temp_node = front;

        while(temp_node != NULL)
        {
                if(temp_node->data == data)
                {
                        removeNode(temp_node);
                        return;
                }
                else
                {
                        temp_node = temp_node->next;
                }
        }
}
```

findNode()

Let's say that you need to access a particular node on a linked list, but you don't know the reference to the node or the position the node has on the linked list, although you do know the data is stored in the node. You can locate the node by calling the `findNode()` function.

The `findNode()` function requires that you pass it the data stored in the node. It then uses the data to locate the node and return to you the index of the node, as shown in the following example.

The process of finding a node begins when you declare an index variable that will eventually be assigned the index of the node if the node is found. A temporary node is also declared and assigned a reference to the node at the front of the linked list.

As long as the temp_node isn't NULL, the `findNode()` function iterates through the linked list. With each iteration, the data member of the current node is compared to the data passed as an argument to the `findNode()` function.

If both are equal, then the current value of the index is returned, which is the index of the node. If they are not equal, then the value of the next member of the current node is assigned to temp_node and the index is incremented. A –1 is returned if the data isn't found in the linked list because the value –1 can never be a valid return value.

```
int findNode(int data)
{
      int index = 0;
      NODE* temp_node = front;

      while(temp_node != NULL)
      {
            if(temp_node->data == data)
            {
                  return index;
            }
            else
            {
                  temp_node = temp_node->next;
                  index++;
            }
      }

      return -1;
}
int findNode(int data)
```

insertNodeAt()

The insertNodeAt() function places a new node at a specific location in the linked list. Previously in this chapter, you learned that each position in a linked list is identified by an index. The first location has the index value of 0, the second location is index 1, and so on. You use the index to specify the location within the linked list where you want to insert the new node.

The insertNodeAt() function requires two arguments, the location where the node will be inserted within the linked list, and the data that will be stored in the node. The following example shows how the new node is placed within the linked list.

The first step is for the insertNodeAt() function to determine if the index passed to the function is valid. It does so by determining if the index is less than zero or greater than the size of the linked list (this information is contained in the size member of the LinkedList class). If the index is invalid, then the insertNodeAt() terminates and returns to the statement that called it. There's a subtle difference in the index checking here compared to removeNodeAt(). If the index were equal to size, this would append a node onto the linked list. The index is out of range by 1, but that's okay because you're going to add a new node onto the linked list, whereas removeNodeAt() needs a valid index so it checks (size −1), which is the last node in the linked list.

Once the `insertNodeAt()` knows that that index is valid, it proceeds to create the new node and then insert the node in the linked list. This process begins by creating an instance of the node structure and assigning it the data passed to the function as an argument. The instance is then assigned to the `new_node` pointer.

Next, it must be determined if there are any nodes in the linked list. You do this by evaluating the value of the size member of the `LinkedList` class. If the value is zero, then the linked list is empty and the new node will become the only node in the list.

You place the new node in the list by assigning the `new_node` pointer to both the front member of the `LinkedList` class and to the back member of the `LinkedList` class. The previous and next members of the node are already set to NULL by default, so you don't have to do anything to the new node.

```
front = new_node;
back = new_node;
```

If the linked list has one or more nodes, then the `insertNodeAt()` function determines if the new node is to be inserted into the first position in the linked list by evaluating the value of the index passed to the function. If the index value is zero, then the new node will become the first node on the linked list.

Here's how this is done. The `new_node` is assigned to the previous member of the node assigned to the front member of the `LinkedList` class. Next, the next member of new_node is assigned the node assigned to the front member of the `LinkedList` class. Finally, the new_node is assigned the front member.

```
front->previous = new_node;
new_node->next = front;
front = new_node;
```

If the new node isn't going to become the first node on the linked list, the `insertNodeAt()` function decides if the node will become the last node on the linked list by comparing the index to the size member of the `LinkedList` class. If these values are equal, then the new node is placed at the back of the linked list. Remember that `index` 0 is the front of the list and index (`size` −1) is the back of the list.

Here's how this is done. The `new_node` is assigned to the next member of the node that is currently the back of the linked list. Next, the node at the back is assigned to the previous member of the `new_node`. Finally, the new_node is assigned to the back member of the `LinkedList` class.

```
back->next = new_node;
new_node->previous = back;
back = new_node;
```

At this point, if the new node hasn't been inserted in either the front or back of the linked list, then the `insertNodeAt()` function assumes that the new node is to be inserted into the middle of the linked list.

This process begins by declaring a pointer called temp and assigning it the node at the front of the linked list. Next, the function finds the node at the index. This node will be moved to the right. However, it's not set to the node previous, it's set to the index position and the node in that position is moved to the right. It does this by using a `for` loop. For each iteration, the node assigned to the next member of the temp node is assigned to the temp node. This sounds confusing, but will become clearer if you examine what is happening.

Say there are five nodes on the linked list, as shown in Figure 9-1. The front node is NodeA, and the initial value of temp is NodeA. Say you want to insert NodeN at index 2.

Before the first iteration, front = NodeE. During the first iteration, here's what happens:

```
temp = temp->next
temp = NodeA->NodeB
temp = NodeB
```

After the first iteration, temp is assigned NodeB and the value of *i* is 1, which is less than the value of the index, so another iteration executes. Here's what happens:

```
temp = temp->next
temp = NodeB->NodeC
temp = NodeC
```

The temp pointer now points to NodeC, and the value of *i* is 2, which is equal to the value of the index, so there are no additional iterations and the temp pointer points to NodeC.

Now that you're at the desired location within the linked list, it is time to switch pointers around to insert the new node into the list. Here's how to do it:

```
new_node->next = temp;
new_node->previous = temp->previous;
temp->previous->next = new_node;
temp->previous = new_node;
```

Confused? If so, you're not alone, because what is happening isn't intuitive. I'll clarify the code by substituting nodes for pointers.

```
new_node->next = NodeC;
new_node->previous = NodeC->NodeB;
NodeC->NodeB->next = new_node;
NodeC->previous = new_node;
```

Figure 9-3 shows the linked list after the new node is inserted into index 2 position of the list. I've called the new node NodeN.

Front = NodeA
Back = NodeE

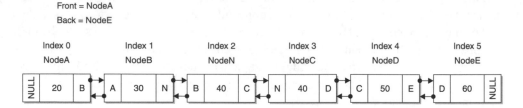

Figure 9-3   A new node called NodeN is placed in index position 2 within the linked list.

The final step is to increment the size member of the LinkedList class to reflect the new node. Following is the complete definition of the insertNodeAt() function:

```
void insertNodeAt(int index, int data)
{
      if(index < 0 || index > size)
      {
            return;
      }

      NODE* new_node = new NODE(data);

      if(size == 0)
      {
            front = new_node;
            back = new_node;
      }
      else if(index == 0)
      {
            front->previous = new_node;
            new_node->next = front;
            front = new_node;
      }
      else if(index == size)
      {
            back->next = new_node;
            new_node->previous = back;
            back = new_node;
      }
      else
      {
            NODE* temp = front;
```

```
for(int i=0; i<index; i++)
{
        temp = temp->next;
}

new_node->next = temp;
new_node->previous = temp->previous;

temp->previous->next = new_node;
temp->previous = new_node;
}

size++;
}
```

peek()

The peek() function retrieves data stored in a node specified by the index passed to the peek() function. The peek() function requires one argument, which is the index of the position within the linked list that contains the data you want to retrieve. The data is then returned by the peek() function. In the following example, you'll store and retrieve an integer, but you can also store and retrieve any kind of data by simply changing the data type in the node definition.

Let's take a closer look and see how the peek() function works. It begins by validating the index using the same validation procedures as discussed in the removeNodeAt() function section of this chapter, except peek() checks that the index is valid. If the index is invalid, then a zero is returned by the function.

If the index is valid, then a pointer called temp is declared and assigned the node that is at the front of the linked list. The peek() function then proceeds to step through the linked list, stopping at the node you're interested in. This search process is the same as in the insertNodeAt() function section.

When the peek() function exits the for loop, the temp pointer points to the node that contains the data that must be returned by peek(). You then point to the data member of the node in the return statement to return the data to the statement that called the peek() function.

Here is the complete definition of the peek() function:

```
int peek(int index)
    {
    if(index < 0 || index > size-1)
    {
        return 0;
    }
```

```
        NODE* temp = front;

        for(int i=0; i<index; i++)
        {
                temp = temp->next;
        }

        return temp->data;
}
```

getSize()

The getSize() function retrieves the value of the size member of the LinkedList class. You'll notice that the getSize() function contains one statement that simply returns the value of the size member.

You might be wondering why you need the getSize() function since you could make the size member accessible to the application by placing it in the public access specifier of the LinkedList class.

As you'll recall from your programming classes, most data members of a class should be only accessible by a function member within the class or by a derived class. This way, you always control access to the data and thereby protect the data from inadvertent changes caused by the application. Allowing it to be changed externally by a user of this class could lead to errors.

```
int getSize()
{
   return size;
}
```

Enhanced LinkedList Class Using C++

You've seen how enhancements to the LinkedList class individually work; now we'll take a look at the entire application. I've divided the following application into three files: the demo.cpp file, the LinkedList.h file, and the LinkedList. file. All three files are shown in the following code listing. You can use the LinkedList.h file and the LinkedList.cpp file, along with the specific files for queues and stacks that you learned about in Chapter 7 and Chapter 8.

The demo.cpp file contains the C++ application that uses the enhanced LinkedList class to create and manipulate a linked list. The LinkedList.h file contains definitions of the node and of the LinkedList class. The

LinkedList.cpp file contains the definitions of member functions of the LinkedList class. All three files are shown next.

The demo.cpp file is where all the action takes place. As you'll see in the following example, the application begins by declaring an instance of the LinkedList class and then assigning the instance to a reference call list.

Next, the appendNode() function is called five times. The appendNode() function is an original member function of the LinkedList class and appends a new node to the linked list. The linked list shown at the top of Figure 9-4 is the linked list after the last appendNode() function is called.

Before the node at index 3 is removed by removeNodeAt(3)

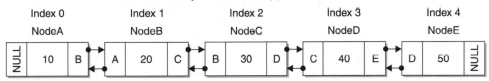

After the node at index 3 is removed by removeNodeAt(3)

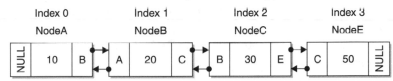

After the node that contains 20 as its data is removed by delete(20)

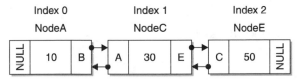

Figure 9-4   The top is the linked list before the node is removed, the middle is after removeNodeAt(3) is called, and the bottom is after deleteNode(2) is called.

Once the linked list is created, the application calls the removeNodeAt(3) function to remove the node located at index 3. The middle linked list in Figure 9-4 shows the status of the linked list after the removeNodeAt(3) function executes.

The application then calls the findNode(20) function to locate the index of the node that contains 20 as its data element. Based on the linked list shown at the bottom of Figure 9-4, the findNode(20) function returns the index value 1.

The deleteNode(20) function is then called and removes the node from the linked list that has 20 as the value of its data element. The linked list shown at the bottom of Figure 9-4 illustrates the linked list after the deleteNode(20) function is called.

A new node is then inserted into the linked list by calling the `insertNodeAt(1, 35)` function. This function inserts a new node at index 1 in the linked list and assigns 35 to the data element of the node. Figure 9-5 is the linked list after the `insertNodeAt(1, 35)` function is called.

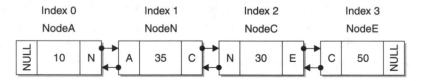

Figure 9-5   The linked list after the `insertNodeAt(1)` is called

The `peek(3)` function is called to retrieve the value of the node in the third index position of the linked list. Based on the linked list shown in Figure 9-5, the `peek(3)` function returns 50 as the data value of the node in index position 3.

The last function called is `getSize()`, which returns the size of the linked list. As seen in Figure 9-5, the linked list has four nodes; therefore, the `getSize()` function returns the value 4.

The last statement in the demo application uses the `delete` operator to remove the instance of the `LinkedList` class from memory.

```cpp
//demo.cpp
#include <iostream>
using namespace std;
void main(){
    LinkedList* list = new LinkedList();
    list->appendNode(10);
    list->appendNode(20);
    list->appendNode(30);
    list->appendNode(40);
    list->appendNode(50);
    list->removeNodeAt(3);
    int index = list->findNode(20);
    list->deleteNode(20);
    list->insertNodeAt(1, 35);
    int data = list->peek(3);
    int size = list->getSize();
    delete list;
}
```

```cpp
//LinkedList.h
typedef struct Node{
    struct Node(int data)
    {
        this->data = data;
        previous = NULL;
        next = NULL;
    }
    int data;
    struct Node* previous;
    struct Node* next;
} NODE,
class LinkedList
{
    protected:
        NODE* front;
        NODE* back;
        int size;
        void removeNode(NODE* node);
    public:
        LinkedList();
        virtual ~LinkedList();
        void appendNode(int);
        void displayNodes();
        void displayNodesReverse();
        void destroyList();
        void removeNodeAt(int);
        int findNode(int);
        void deleteNode(int);
        void insertNodeAt(int,int);
        int peek(int);
        int getSize();
};

//LinkedList.cpp
#include "LinkedList.h"
CLinkedList::CLinkedList()
{
        front = NULL;
        back = NULL;
        size = 0;
}
```

```
CLinkedList::~CLinkedList()
{
      destroyList();
}

void CLinkedList::appendNode(int data)
{
      NODE* n = new NODE(data);

      if(back == NULL)
      {
            back = n;
            front = n;
      }
      else
      {
            back->next = n;
            n->previous = back;
            back = n;
      }

      size++;
}

void CLinkedList::displayNodes()
{
      cout << "Elements: ";
      NODE* temp = front;
      while(temp != NULL)
      {
            cout << temp->data << " ";
            temp = temp->next;
      }

      cout << endl;

}

void CLinkedList::displayNodesReverse()
{
      cout << "Elements: ";
      NODE* temp = back;
      while(temp != NULL)
```

```
      {
            cout << temp->data << " ";
            temp = temp->previous;
      }

      cout << endl;
}

void CLinkedList::destroyList()
{
      NODE* temp = back;
      while(temp != NULL)
      {
            NODE* temp2 = temp;
            temp = temp->previous;
            delete temp2;
      }

      back = NULL;
      front = NULL;
}

void CLinkedList::removeNode(NODE* node)
{
      if(node->previous == NULL && node->next == NULL)
      {
            back = NULL;
            front = NULL;
      }
      else if(node->previous == NULL)
      {
            front = node->next;
            node->next->previous = NULL;
      }
      else if(node->next == NULL)
      {
            back = node->previous;
            node->previous->next = NULL;
      }
      else
      {
            node->previous->next = node->next;
            node->next->previous = node->previous;
```

```
        }

        delete node;
        size--;
}

void CLinkedList::removeNodeAt(int index)
{
        if(index < 0 || index > size-1)
        {
                return;
        }

        NODE* temp_node = front;

        for(int i=0; i<index; i++)
        {
                temp_node = temp_node->next;
        }

        removeNode(temp_node);
}

int CLinkedList::findNode(int data)
{
        int index = 0;
        NODE* temp_node = front;

        while(temp_node != NULL)
        {
                if(temp_node->data == data)
                {
                        // return the index of the node
                        return index;
                }
                else
                {
                        temp_node = temp_node->next;
                        index++;
                }
        }

        return -1;
```

```
}

void CLinkedList::deleteNode(int data)
{
      NODE* temp_node = front;

      while(temp_node != NULL)
      {
            if(temp_node->data == data)
            {
                  removeNode(temp_node);
                  return;
            }
            else
            {
                  temp_node = temp_node->next;
            }
      }
}

void CLinkedList::insertNodeAt(int index, int data)
{
      if(index < 0 || index > size)
      {
            return;
      }

      NODE* new_node = new NODE(data);

      if(size == 0)
      {
            front = new_node;
            back = new_node;
      }
      else if(index == 0)
      {
            front->previous = new_node;
            new_node->next = front;
            front = new_node;
      }
      else if(index == size)
      {
            back->next = new_node;
            new_node->previous = back;
```

```
                back = new_node;
        }
        else
        {
                NODE* temp = front;

                for(int i=0; i<index; i++)
                {
                        temp = temp->next;
                }

                new_node->next = temp;
                new_node->previous = temp->previous;

                temp->previous->next = new_node;
                temp->previous = new_node;
        }

        size++;
}

int CLinkedList::peek(int index)
{
        if(index < 0 || index > size-1)
        {
                return 0;
        }

        NODE* temp = front;

        for(int i=0; i<index; i++)
        {
                temp = temp->next;
        }

        return temp->data;

}

int CLinkedList::getSize()
{
        return size;
}
```

Enhanced LinkedList Class Using Java

As you've seen throughout this book, the LinkedList class is defined in the java.util package and defines member methods that are similar in functionality to member functions that were defined in the C++ example of this chapter.

Following is the Java version of the C++ application described in the previous section. Both versions produce the same results. However, I've defined a printList() method in the Java example that displays the linked list at various times during the application.

Let's walk through the Java version of the application to see how it works. The application begins similar to the way the C++ begins in that it declares an instance of the LinkedList class and assigns it to a reference called list. The add() method is then called fives times to add nodes to the linked list. This is similar to the appendNode() function in the C++ version of the application. The linked list is then displayed on-screen by calling the printList() method defined later in the application. Here's what is displayed on-screen:

```
Initial List:
10
20
30
40
50
```

Next, the remove() method is called and is passed the index of the node that we want removed from the linked list. This is similar to the removeNodeAt() function in the C++ version. Again, we call the printList() method to show the results of calling the remove(3) method. Here's the display:

```
Removed index 3:
10
20
30
50
```

The indexOf() method is called next to return the index of the node that contains 20 as its data value. This is the same as the findNode() in the C++ version. The indexOf() method requires an object rather than the data. In this example, the data is an integer, therefore we need to declare an instance of the Integer wrapper class and initialize the instance with the value 20. The declaration occurs within the parameter of the indexOf() method. The indexOf() method returns the index value that is assigned to the index integer. If you pass in your own class, you may need to implement a Comparator so the Java collection can determine equality on the different Objects. The Comparator is similar to overloading the `quality` operator in C++. The value of the index variable is then displayed on-screen as follows:

```
Index of value 20: 1
```

Once again the `remove()` method is called. However, this time the `remove()` method is passed data instead of an index. This causes the `remove()` method to remove the node from the linked list that contains 20 as its data value. This is similar to the `deleteNode()` method shown in the C++ version. The `printList()` method is called again to show how the linked list looks after the `remove()` method is called. Here's what is displayed on-screen:

```
Removed value 20:
10
30
50
```

Next, the application inserts a new node at index position 1 and assigns the new node 35 as its value. Java doesn't have an `insertNodeAt()` method like the one you created in the C++ version. However, the `add()` method provides the same functionality as long as you specify the index position at which you want to insert the new node and provide it the data to store in the node. The `printList()` method is called once again. Here's the linked list following the execution of the `add()` method:

```
Added 35 at index 1:
10
35
30
50
```

The `LinkedList` class in Java doesn't have a `peek()` method, but the `get()` method is used for the same purpose. In this example, the `get()` method is passed the index value 3 and returns the data stored in the node located at the third index position on the linked list. Next, `get()` returns an object, which is cast to an integer. The data variable is then displayed on-screen. Here's what appears on the display:

```
Value at index 3: 50
```

The application then calls the `size()` method, which returns the size of the linked list similar to the `getSize()` function defined in the C++ example. The `size()` method returns an integer that is assigned the size variable, which is then displayed on-screen. Here's what is displayed:

```
Size of linked list: 4

import java.io.*;
import java.util.*;
public class demo
{
    public static void main(String[] args)
    {
        LinkedList list = new LinkedList();
        list.add(new Integer(10));
        list.add(new Integer(20));
        list.add(new Integer(30));
        list.add(new Integer(40));
        list.add(new Integer(50));
        printList("Initial List", list);
        list.remove(3);
        printList("Removed index 3", list);
        int index = list.indexOf(new Integer(20));
        System.out.println("\nIndex of value 20: " + index);
        list.remove(new Integer(20));
        printList("Removed value 20", list);
        list.add(1, new Integer(35));
        printList("Added 35 at index 1", list);
        Integer data = (Integer)list.get(3);
        System.out.println("\nValue at index 3: " + data);
        int size = list.size();
        System.out.println("\nSize of linked list: " + size);
    }
    public static void printList(String header, LinkedList list)
    {
        System.out.println("\n" + header + ":");
        for(int i=0; i<list.size(); i++)
        {
            Integer temp = (Integer)list.get(i);
            System.out.println(temp);
        }
    }
}
```

Quiz

1. What is a linked list index?

2. What is the value of the first linked list index?

3. What is the difference between the `removeNode()` and `deleteNode()` functions?

4. What is the return value of the `findNode()` function?

5. What is the difference between the `insertNodeAt()` and the `appendNode()` functions?

6. What happens if an invalid index value is passed to a function?

7. Can a linked list store data other than integers?

8. Why would you define a `getSize()` function instead of having the application access the size of the linked list directly?

9. Can the `insertNodeAt()` function place a node at the front or back of a linked list?

10. Why is it important to enhance the functionality of the `LinkedList` class?

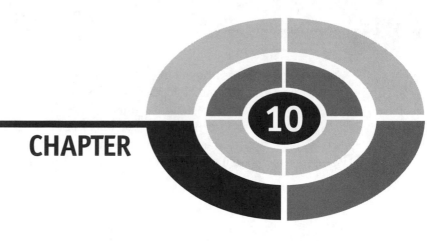

What Is a Tree?

If you are going to our school (Columbia University), you travel down the road a bit before seeing a fork in the road. You then have two choices: bear left and you'll be on campus; bear right and you'll be lost. What does this have to do with a tree data structure? Everything. A tree data structure is similar to the road because it provides you with a series of forks in the road that lead you down a path to reach a decision. In this chapter, you'll learn about the concept of trees, and we'll show you how to build your own tree data structure.

A Tree

When you read the word "tree" in the title of this chapter, you probably imagined your favorite tree covered with a full coat of green leaves. However, this doesn't truly represent the tree that we'll be talking about. Instead, envision a tree barren of leaves, where all you can see are branches stretched in all directions. Each stem terminates with only two branches, similar to a fork in the road. Those branches lead to other stems and other forks.

This type of tree is a binary tree. *Binary* means two, as you learned when you studied the binary numbering systems in your first computer course. The binary numbering system consists of two digits, zero and one.

A *binary tree* is a tree where each stem has not more than two branches (see Figure 10-1). Typically, the stem has two branches, but there can be situations when the stem has one branch or simply terminates, resulting in no additional branches.

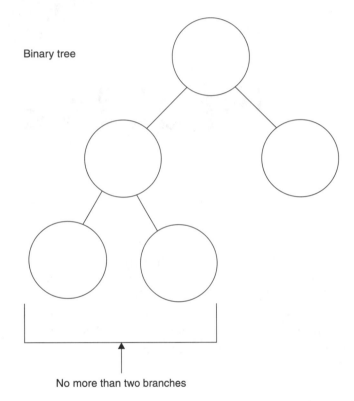

Figure 10-1 A binary tree is a tree where each stem has no more than two branches.

Why Use a Binary Tree?

Programmers use a binary tree as a model to create a data structure to encode logic used to make complex decisions. Here's how this works. Let's say that a stem consists of a set of program instructions. At the end of the stem, the program evaluates a binary expression. You'll recall that a binary expression evaluates to either a Boolean `true` or `false`. Based on the evaluation, the program proceeds down one of two branches. Each branch has its own set of program instructions.

The basic concept of a binary tree isn't new to you because it uses Boolean logic that you learned to implement using an `if` statement in your program. An `if` statement evaluates an expression that results in a Boolean value. Depending on the Boolean value, the `if` statement executes one of two sets of instructions. However, a binary tree is much more than an `if` statement, as you'll learn in this chapter.

Parts of a Binary Tree

Although we introduced the concept of a binary tree with terms commonly used when referring to a tree, programmers established different terms to refer to parts of a binary tree. Let's take a moment to become familiar with those terms.

"Node" is the term used to describe a termination point. There are three kinds of termination points in a binary tree (see Figure 10-2): the starting node, the ending node, and the branch node. The starting node is called the *root node*, which is the top-level node in the tree. The stem leading from the root node leads to the branch node.

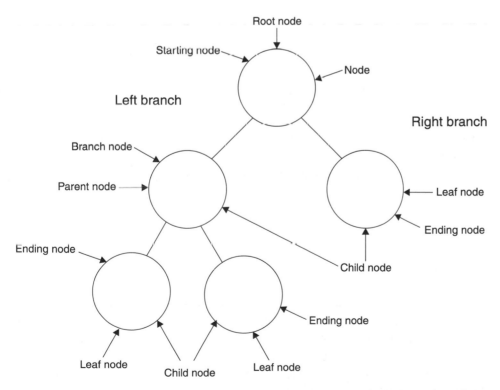

Figure 10-2   A binary tree is comprised of several nodes, each of which are related to other nodes on the tree.

The branch node is the fork in the road that links the root node to two branches. Each branch terminates with a child node. Programmers call these the *left branch* and the *right branch*.

As you can see, a binary tree defines a strong parent-child relationship among nodes. A parent-child relationship is relative to a node. All nodes except the root node have a parent node. However, some nodes have no children, while other nodes have one or two child nodes. Programmers determine the parent-child relationship by selecting a node, which is called the current node. The node that spawns the current node is called the current node's *parent node*. The node or nodes spawned by the current node is called the *child node*.

The child node is also referred to as the left node or the right node, depending on which direction the node branches from the *current node*. If the current node doesn't have any child nodes, then the current node is referred to as the *leaf node*. A leaf node is located at the bottom of the tree. If you look at your favorite tree, you'll notice that the end of nearly every branch is either another branch (child node) or a leaf, and that's why programmers call a node with no child nodes a leaf node.

Depth and Size

A binary tree is described by using two measurements: tree depth and tree size (see Figure 10-3). Tree depth is the number of levels in the tree. A new level is created each time a current node branches to a child node. For example, one level is created when the root node branches into child nodes.

The size of a tree is the number of nodes in the tree. For example, the first level in Figure 10-3 has one node, which is the root node. The second level has up to two nodes, which are the child nodes of the root. The third level may have up to four nodes. Programmers estimate the size of a tree by using the following formula.

$$\text{size} \approx 2^{\,\text{depth}}$$

Let's say the binary tree has five levels, which is a depth of 5. Here's how you estimate the size of the tree:

$$32 \approx 2^{\,5}$$

The size is an approximation because the tree may or may not be balanced. A balanced tree is a binary tree where each current node has two child nodes. An unbalanced tree is a binary tree where one or more current nodes have fewer than two child nodes. This formula gives you a rough idea of how well balanced the tree is. Binary trees are usually used for very large data sets. The formula is not terribly accurate for the small tree shown in Figure 10-3.

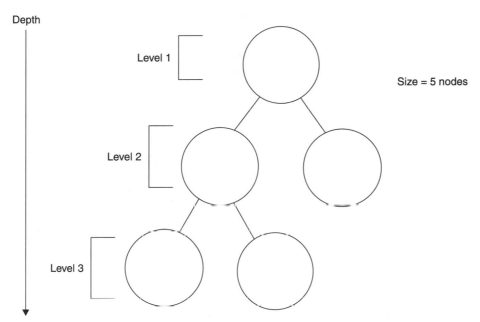

Figure 10-3   The number of levels in a tree defines a tree's depth, and the number of
nodes defines the size of the tree

Why Use a Binary Tree?

Programmers use a binary tree to quickly look up data stored at each node on the binary tree. Let's say that you need to find a student ID in a list of a million student IDs. What is the maximum number of comparisons that you'll need to make before finding the student ID?

You could make a maximum of a million comparisons if you sequentially searched the list of a million student IDs. More than a million comparisons are necessary if you randomly selected student IDs from the list and then replaced those that didn't match back into the list.

However, you'd need to make a maximum of only 20 comparisons if student IDs were stored in a binary tree. This is because of the way data is organized in a binary tree. Data stored on the left node is less than data stored on all the right nodes at any current node.

This might sound a little confusing, but an example will make this concept clear. Suppose you had a list of five student IDs: 101, 102, 103, 104, and 105. These student IDs are stored in a binary tree so that the center student ID is the root node, the student ID that is less than the current node is stored on the left child node, and the student ID that is more than the current node is stored on the right child node, as shown in Figure 10-4.

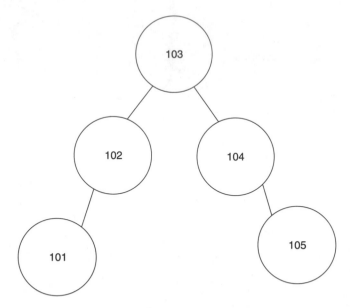

Figure 10-4   The left child node is always less than the parent node, and the right child node is always greater than the parent node.

The same pattern is applied to each child node. Thus, student ID 101 is the left child of the node that contains student ID 102 because student ID 101 is less than student ID 102. Likewise, student ID 105 is the right node of student ID 104 because student ID is greater than student ID 105.

Let's say you want to locate student ID 101 on the binary tree. First, you compare the value of the root node to student ID 101. There's no match. Because student ID 101 is less than student ID 103, your next comparison uses the left child node. This eliminates the need to compare all the nodes to the right of the node that contains student ID 103. You can ignore half the student IDs because you know that student ID 101 isn't the right node or a child of the right node.

After comparing student ID 101 to student ID 102, you notice two things. First, they don't match. Second, student ID 102 is greater than student ID 101. This means you compare the left child node to student ID 101. You ignore the right child node and subsequent child nodes because they are greater than student ID 101. There aren't any right child nodes of student ID 102 in this example. The next comparison results in a match. So, in a large binary tree, each time you do a comparison, you eliminate another half of the remaining nodes from the search. If you had 1 million nodes in the tree, you would divide 1 million by 2 about 20 times to reduce it down to one node (2 ^ 20 is about 1 million). This way, you can find the node you're looking for by doing about 20 comparisons.

Programmers think of every node as the root node and all subsequent nodes as its own subtree. They approach nodes in this way because functions that deal with trees are recursive. A function works on a child node and performs the same functionality as if the child node is the root node of the entire tree. That is, the value of the child node is compared to the value of its left node and right node to determine which branch of the tree to pursue.

The Key

Each node of a tree contains a key that is associated with a value similar to the relationship between a primary key of a database and a row within a table of the database. A key is a value that is compared to search criteria. If the index and the search criteria match, then the application retrieves data stored in the row that corresponds to the key. The data is referred to as the value of the node, as shown in Figure 10-5.

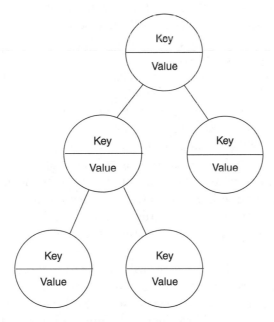

Figure 10-5   Each node has an index and a value; the index uniquely identifies the node and retrieves the value of a node.

Any data type can be used as the key. We use a string as the key in examples in this chapter, but we could have chosen any data type. Unlike the primary key of a database, the key to the tree doesn't have to be in natural order. That is, the key doesn't have to be in alphabetical order or numerical order. In a typical tree implementation,

Data Structures Demystified

you would define a comparator to tell the tree how to order the nodes. In our case, we'll use the natural ordering sequence of a string so we can keep our focus on the internal workings of the tree.

Creating a Binary Tree

Let's create a binary tree by first defining a structure. Call the structure Metadata because it describes data that is used in the binary tree, and "metadata" refers to data that describes other data, such as how an employee ID can be used to get the employees name. Metadata typically refers to name/value pairs, or in our case, key/value pairs.

Each instance of the data structure is a node on the binary tree and contains four data elements. The first two data elements are the key and the value. In this example, both the key and value are char arrays. The size of these arrays is determined by the #define preprocessing directive at the top of this example. You set the array size by using the preprocessing directive because you can easily change its value in one place within the application without having to locate every place in the code where the array sizes are used.

The other two data elements of the metadata structure are pointers called left and right. Each of these points to a metadata structure. In other words, they point to the next node on the left and on the right of the current node. This enables the application to do two things. First, the application can move to the next level of the tree. It can also access both the key and the value of nodes at the next level.

You might become confused when looking at the example of the structure definition because the structure uses itself to initialize data elements of the structure. Here's what's happening. A key and related value are passed to the metadata structure when an instance of the metadata structure is declared, that is, when a new node is inserted into the binary tree. Both of these are passed as char pointers because they are arrays.

The application copies the key and the value to the data elements of the instance of the metadata structure by using the strcpy() function. The strcpy() function copies the second parameter to the first parameter. Notice the this operator is used in this example. As you'll recall from your programming course, the this operator tells the compiler that you want to refer to the data element of this instance of the structure instead of the parameter that was passed in.

The last two data elements to be initialized are the left and right pointers. Both of these are set to NULL because the new node doesn't have a child node when the new node is created. Later in this chapter, you'll define a function that adds a child node and replaces the NULL with reference to an actual node.

```
#include <string.h>
#define SIZE_KEY 32
#define SIZE_VALUE 256
typedef struct Metadata
{
    struct Metadata(char* key, char* value)
    {
        strcpy(this->key, key);
        strcpy(this->value, value);
        left = NULL;
        right = NULL;
    }
    char key[SIZE_KEY];
    char value[SIZE_VALUE];
    struct Metadata* left;
    struct Metadata* right;
} METADATA;
```

In addition to defining a structure, you'll also define the `BinarySearchTree` class. The `BinarySearchTree` class defines data members and member functions that create and manipulate a node. As illustrated in the code that follows, the class definition is organized into two areas, the private access specifier and the public access specifier. As you'll recall from your object-oriented programming class, the application can only access data and member functions defined within the public access specifier; members defined within the private access specifier area of the class definition can only be accessed by member functions of the class. The private access specifier section of the `BinarySearchTree` class defines two data members, `size` and `root`. The `size` is an integer that stores the number of nodes on the tree. The `root` is a pointer to an instance of the metadata structure. In other words, `root` is the first node on the tree.

The private access specifier also contains nine member functions:

```
addNode()
            getNode()
            removeAllNodes()
            processNodesInOrder()
            getTreeDepth()
      containsNode()
       removeNode()
            removeRootNode()
      moveLeftMostNode()
```

These functions are used by functions defined in the public access specifier of the class definition to manipulate nodes on the tree. You'll learn how each of these functions works later in this chapter.

The public access specifier contains the constructor and destructor for the class and several member functions that enable the application to create and remove nodes and manipulate nodes on the tree. Here is a list of those member functions. You'll learn how they work later in this chapter.

```
BinarySearchTree();
            ~BinarySearchTree()
            add()
            remove()
      removeAll()
            get()
            contains()
            displayInOrder()
            getSize()
            getDepth()


class BinarySearchTree
{
   private:
      int size;
      METADATA* root;
      bool addNode(METADATA** current_node, METADATA* new_node);
      bool getNode(METADATA* current_node, char* key, char* value);
      void removeAllNodes(METADATA* node);
      void processNodesInOrder(METADATA* node);
      int getTreeDepth(METADATA* node);
      bool containsNode(METADATA* node, char* key);
      bool removeNode(METADATA** node, char* key);
      void removeRootNode(METADATA** node);
      void moveLeftMostNode(METADATA** node, METADATA* root);
   public:
      BinarySearchTree();
      virtual ~BinarySearchTree();
      bool add(char* key, char* value);
      bool remove(char* key);
      void removeAll();
      bool get(char* key, char* value);
      bool contains(char* key);
      void displayInOrder();
      int getSize();
      int getDepth();
};
```

Constructor and Destructor

The constructor of the `BinarySearchTree` class initializes the root data member of the `BinarySearchTree` class with a NULL value. As you'll recall from the previous section, `root` is a pointer to an instance of the metadata structure and points to the root node for the binary search tree once a node is added to the tree.

The constructor also initializes the `size` data member to zero. This means there are no nodes on the tree. The `size` data member is incremented each time a new node is inserted into the tree and decremented when a node is removed from the tree. You'll see how these steps are done later in this chapter.

The destructor removes all the nodes from the tree and releases memory used by those nodes. The destructor doesn't directly remove the nodes. Instead, it calls the `removeAll()` member function that actually handles deleting nodes and releasing memory.

The following are definitions of the constructor and the destructor for the `BinarySearchTree` class:

```
BinarySearchTree()
{
    root = NULL;
    size = 0;
}
 ~BinarySearchTree()
{
    removeAll();
}
```

add() and addNode()

You add a new node to the tree by calling the `add()` member function of the `BinarySearchTree` class as shown in the next code snippet. The `add()` function requires two arguments, a pointer to the key of the new node and another pointer to the node's value. In this example, we call these key and value.

Before the node is added to the tree, the `add()` function validates both the key and the value with two tests. First, it makes sure that the key and the value don't have a NULL value. Next, it tests to be sure that neither the key nor the value is larger than the array size allocated for the key. It does so by comparing the length of the key and the length of the value to the corresponding value defined in the `#define` preprocessor directive. If any of these tests fail, then the `add()` function returns a Boolean `false` to the statement in the application that calls the `add()` function.

If the key and value are valid, then the add() function proceeds to create the new node. First, it declares an instance of the metadata structure and passes the key and value to the instance. Previously in this chapter you learned that the key and value become the initial values for corresponding data elements in the metadata structure.

The final step in the process of adding a new node to the tree is to call the addNode() function. The addNode() function is defined within the private access specifier in the BinarySearchTree class and is responsible for placing the new node into the tree.

```
bool add(char* key, char* value)
{
   if(key == NULL || value == NULL || strlen(key) > SIZE_KEY-1
           || strlen(value) > SIZE_VALUE-1)
   {
      return false;
   }
   METADATA* new_node = new METADATA(key, value);
   return addNode(&root, new_node);
}
```

The addNode() function shown in the next code requires two arguments. The first argument is a pointer to a pointer that points to the current node. The other argument is a pointer to the new node. The process of adding a new node to the tree begins by the addNode() function determining if the new node passed to is NULL. When the value of current_node is NULL, then you've reached a leaf node on the tree. This is where the addition takes place. All nodes are added as leaf nodes. If this is the first node being added to the tree, then the leaf node also happens to be the root node. The new node is assigned to the pointer field of current_node, and the size data member is incremented. This adds the new node to the tree. The addNode() function then returns a Boolean true, indicating that the operation is successful. You need to pass a pointer to a pointer as the first argument because you're going to alter the data in that node. What you're really passing is the address of the pointer field in the parent node. By passing the address of the pointer, you can change the pointer value in the parent. The pointer in the parent is changed to point to this new child node that's being added.

If the current node isn't NULL, the next step is to find where in the tree the node is to be added. This process is tricky because the new node must be located in a position where it will be either less than or greater than its parent node.

Here's how it works. The addNode() function compares the key of the current node to the key of the new node using the strcmp() function. If the return value of the strcmp() function is less than zero, then the key of the new node is less than the key of the current node. Then addNode() is called again recursively, but this time reference to the left node of the current node is passed as the first argument to the addNode() function. As you'll recall, the first argument is considered by the addNode() function as the current node. In this case, the left node of the current node is considered the current node. The second argument is the new node. Notice that the addNode() function is recursively called until the addNode() function finds a place for the new node. The first call to addNode() passes the first argument as the root node of the tree. Each subsequent call passes a root node of a subtree. Remember that each node in the tree can be considered a root node for all the nodes below it. The same rules apply at every node—all the nodes on the left are less than and all the nodes on the right are greater than.

If the key of the new node is greater than the key of the current node, then a similar process occurs except the current node's right node is used instead of the left node when addNode() is subsequently called.

This recursive process continues until the first argument to addNode() points to NULL, which indicates a leaf node where the addition takes place.

If the key of the new node equals an existing node, then the new node is deleted and the addNode() function returns a Boolean false. This is because all keys must be unique: duplicate keys are not permitted on the tree.

```
bool addNode(METADATA** current_node, METADATA* new_node)
{
    if(*current_node == NULL)
    {
        *current_node = new_node;
        size++;
        return true;
    }
    else
    {
        if(strcmp(new_node->key, (*current_node)->key) < 0)
        {
            return addNode(&((*current_node)->left), new_node);
        }
        else if(strcmp(new_node->key, (*current_node)->key) > 0)
        {
            return addNode(&((*current_node)->right), new_node);
        }
        else
        {
            delete new_node;
            return false;
        }
    }
}
```

remove(), removeNode(), and removeRootNode()

Removing a node from the tree is a multiple-step process that begins when the application calls the remove() member function as shown in the next code snippet The remove() function requires the key of the node being removed. It then calls the removeNode() member function. The removeNode() function is a private member of the BinarySearchTree class and therefore cannot be called directly by the application.

The removeNode() function requires two parameters. The first is a reference to the current node being evaluated, which is where the search begins. You begin the search by passing the root node of the tree, then subsequent calls will pass the root of a subtree. You always have to think about the tree as being a set of subtrees—each node is a root for all the nodes below it. The second parameter is the key received by the remove() function.

```
bool remove(char* key)
{
    return removeNode(&root, key);
}
```

The removeNode() function shown in the next code snippet uses the value passed by the remove() function to locate the node that is being deleted. Before the search begins, the removeNode() determines if a root node passed to it by the remove() function is NULL. This may be the root node of the tree if this is the first call to the function, or it may be the root of a subtree. If it's NULL, then the Boolean value false is returned because the node to remove was not found.

If the root node isn't NULL, the search continues. The objective of the removeNode() function is to find a key of a node in the tree that matches the key passed by the remove() function. Once found, reference to the node that contains the key is passed to the removeRootNode(), which actually removes the node from the tree. The removeRootNode() may be removing the root node of the tree or a root of a subtree.

The search begins by comparing the key of the root node passed by the remove() function to the key passed by the remove() function. If the keys match, then the root node is passed to the removeRootNode() function where the node is removed. The size data member is decremented to reflect that a node has been removed from the tree. A Boolean true is then returned by the removeNode() function.

If there isn't a match, then the removeNode() function determines if the key of the root node is less than the key passed by the remove() function. If so, then the removeNode() function compares the key of the left node to that of the key passed by the remove() function. The removeNode() function is called recursively until a match is found, at which time the removeRootNode() function is called and passed the reference to the matching node.

If the key is greater than the key of the root node, then the key of the right node of the root node is compared to the key. Again, the removeNode() function is called recursively until there is a match, at which time the removeRootNode() function is called and passed a reference to the matching node.

```
bool removeNode(METADATA** node, char* key)
{
    if(*node != NULL)
    {
        if (strcmp(key, (*node)->key) == 0)
        {
            removeRootNode(node);
            size--;
            return true;
        }
        else if(strcmp(key, (*node)->key) < 0)
        {
            return removeNode(&((*node)->left), key);
        }
        else
        {
            return removeNode(&((*node)->right), key);
        }
    }
    else
    {
        return false;
    }
}
```

The removeRootNode() member function is the function that actually removes a node from the tree. The term "root node" can sometimes be confusing because you intuitively assume that the root node is the first node on the tree. In reality, any node can be a root node for all the nodes below it in the tree. Even if the node is a leaf node, it's still a root node of the subtree. It just so happens that this subtree contains only one node. Therefore, we use the term root node in the name of this function.

The removeRootNode() function requires one argument, which is a pointer to a pointer for the node being removed. The removal process begins by declaring a pointer to the metadata structure. We call this pointer temp in the code example shown next.

Before removing the node, the `removeRootNode()` function determines if the node has a right child and left child node. If both the left and right child nodes are NULL, then no children exist and the `delete` operator is called to release the memory associated with this node. Then the pointer field in the parent node is set to NULL because this child node was removed. Note that if this were the only node in the tree, this call would set the root node of the tree to NULL, which makes sense because the tree would be empty.

If one child isn't NULL, then the right child is compared to NULL. This would be the case if the node being deleted doesn't have a right child. In this case, you change the pointer field in the parent to the node on the left of the one being deleted. The root node is assigned to the `temp` pointer to remember the location of the node that is being removed from the tree. Next, reference to the left node is assigned to the parent node. The `delete` operator then removes the node referenced by the `temp` pointer to release the memory associated with the node being deleted.

If the right node isn't NULL, then the `removeRootNode()` determines if the left node is NULL. This follows similar logic to the previous example, except the node being deleted doesn't have a left child, so the pointer in the parent node is set to the node on the right of the one being deleted. The reference to the root node is assigned to the `temp` pointer. Reference to the right node is then assigned to the parent node. The `delete` operator then releases the memory associated with the node being removed.

The last—and most complex—scenario is if the node being removed has both a left child and right child node. In this case, the `removeRootNode()` calls the `moveLeftMostNode()` function and passes it the address of the right node.

```
void removeRootNode(METADATA** root)
{
    METADATA* temp;
    if((*root)->left == NULL && (*root)->right == NULL)
    {
        delete(*root);
        *root = NULL;
    }
    else if((*root)->right == NULL)
    {
        temp = *root;
        *root = (*root)->left;
        delete(temp);
    }
    else if((*root)->left == NULL)
    {
        temp = *root;
        *root = (*root)->right;
```

```
      delete(temp);
   }
   else
   {
      moveLeftMostNode(&((*root)->right), *root);
   }
}
```

The objective of the `moveLeftMostNode()` function is to find the node that will replace the current root node of the subtree. To achieve this goal, you must move once to the right and then go down the tree as far left as possible until you find the smallest node on the right. The move to the right occurs when the `moveLeftMostNode()` is called the first time. You then move left subsequent calls to the function. Once the smallest value on the right is found, the node containing the smallest value becomes the new root node.

Let's see how this works by walking through the following definition of the `moveLeftMostNode()` function. This function requires two arguments, the current node being evaluated and the node that will be replaced. Remember, this function will copy the key and value from the smallest node on the right subtree to the node that's being removed. This replaces the node that's being removed with one of the leaf nodes, and then the leaf node is deleted.

If reference to the node being moved is not NULL and the left pointer of the node being moved is NULL, then you've found the node that will be moved up to the position of the one that's to be removed. A pointer is declared and assigned to the node being moved. Next, the key and the value of the node are copied to the key and value of the root node. The root node in this case is the node that's being removed from the tree. Because you're moving the leftmost child of the right subtree, this leftmost child may have nodes to the right of it. The pointer value in the parent of the node that is being moved is set to the right pointer in the one that's being moved. This keeps these subnodes intact. Finally, the `delete` operator removes the node.

If you haven't found the leftmost node of the right subtree, then `moveLeftMostNode()` is called again. This time, the left child node is passed as the node to be moved to the root position. The root position is the node that is being removed.

```
void moveLeftMostNode(METADATA** node, METADATA* root)
{
   if(*node != NULL && (*node)->left == NULL)
   {
      METADATA* temp = *node;
      strcpy(root->key, (*node)->key);
      strcpy(root->value, (*node)->value);
      *node = (*node)->right;
```

```
      delete(temp);
   }
   else
   {
      moveLeftMostNode(&((*node)->left), root);
   }
}
```

removeAll() and removeAllNodes()

The previous section showed you several functions that remove one node from the tree. There are occasions when you'll need to clear the entire tree of nodes. To do this, you'll need to call the `removeAll()` function.

The `removeAll()` function is shown in the next code snippet and performs two operations. First, it calls the `removeAllNodes()` function, which is defined in the private access specifier section of the `BinarySearchTree` class. This is the function that actually removes all the nodes from the tree. The second operation is to reset the `root` and `size` data members of the `BinarySearchTree` class. The `root` data member is set to NULL, indicating there aren't any nodes on the tree. The `size` data member is set to zero, indicating that the tree is empty. The `removeAll()` function is also called by the destructor.

```
void removeAll()
{
   removeAllNodes(root);
   root = NULL;
   size = 0;
}
```

The `removeAllNodes()` function, shown next, requires one argument, which is a reference to the root node. As long as the root node isn't NULL, the `removeAllNodes()` function calls itself each time, passing it first the left child node and then the right child node as the root node. The ordering of these calls is important. Remember that the root node is either the root node of the tree or the root of a subtree. You must remove all the child nodes before removing the parent. You recurse the left tree, recurse the right tree, then, when it returns to the caller, it's safe to delete the current node (root node) because all the children have been deleted. As with all recursive functions, you have to define a stopping point. In this case, if you are at a leaf node, the left and right pointers would be NULL and the calls to `removeAllNodes()` would return (they would not continue the recursion) because the node would be NULL.

A message is displayed on the screen stating the key and the value of the node that is being removed from the tree. The `delete` operator is then used to remove the node.

```
void removeAllNodes(METADATA* node)
{
   if(node != NULL)
   {
      removeAllNodes(node->left);
      removeAllNodes(node->right);
      cout << "Removing node - key: " << node->key << "\t"
         << node->value << endl;
      delete node;
   }
}
```

get() and getNode()

The `get()` member function of the `BinarySearchTree` class is called within the application whenever you want to retrieve the value of a node. To retrieve a value, you must provide the `get()` function with the search key and with the variable that will store the value once the key is found.

Here's how this works. As illustrated in the next code snippet, you pass the `get()` function two arguments. The first argument is a reference to the search key. In this example, the key is a string. Therefore, you pass the `get()` function a pointer to a `char`, which you'll recall from your programming class actually points to the first character of the string. The second argument is also a `char` pointer. This points to the first element of a character array that the `get()` function uses to store the value of the node that is associated with the search key.

Let's say that the search key is student ID "1234" and the value associated with the key is "Bob Smith." You pass the `get()` function "1234" and the `get()` function copies "Bob Smith" to the value `char` array if the search key "1234" is found in a node of the tree. You then use the value `char` array throughout your application.

The `get()` function is defined in the public access specifier section of the `BinarySearchTree` class and is therefore accessible to an application. However, the `get()` function simply calls the `getNode()` member function, which is defined in the private access specifier section of the class. The `getNode()` function returns a Boolean `true` if the search key is found; otherwise, a Boolean `false` is returned. The return value also becomes the return value of the `get()` function.

```
bool get(char* key, char* value)
{
```

```
    return getNode(root, key, value);
}
```

The getNode() function is where all the action occurs. Here the search is conducted and the value of the node is copied to the value array. As illustrated next, the getNode() function requires three arguments. The first argument is a reference to the root node. The root node is the starting point of the search and is usually the uppermost node of the tree, but it can be any node. The second argument is a reference to the search key, which is a char pointer in this example. The third argument is a reference to the variable that stores the value of the node that contains the search key. Both the search key and the value variable are the same as those passed to the get() function.

The getNode() begins processing by validating the root node. If the root node is NULL, then the value argument is set to an empty string (it sets the first character to NULL) and a Boolean false is returned by the getNode() function to indicate that the key was not found in the tree.

If the root node isn't NULL, then the search continues. The getNode() function is called recursively. Each time it is called, it compares the search key with the key of the root node. If they match, then the value of the root node is copied to the value variable and a Boolean true is returned by the function.

If the search key doesn't match the key of the root node, then the getNode() function determines if the search key is less than or greater than the key of the root node. Depending on the results of this comparison, the getNode() function calls itself and uses either the left child or the right child of the root node as the root node argument of the getNode() function. This process continues until either the search key matches the key of the root node or the root node is NULL, indicating the key doesn't exist in the tree. This type of search is where the power of binary trees comes into play. Notice that each time the function is called, by doing one comparison on the key, you eliminate half the remaining nodes from the search, so you're able to find the key very quickly even in a large data set.

```
bool getNode(METADATA* node, char* key, char* value)
{
    if(node == NULL)
    {
        value[0] = '\0';
        return false;
    }
    else
    {
        if(strcmp(key, node->key) == 0)
        {
```

```
            strcpy(value, node->value);
            return true;
    }
    else if(strcmp(key, node->key) < 0)
    {
            return gctNode(node->left, key, value);
    }
    else
    {
            return getNode(node->right, key, value);
    }
    }
}
```

contains() and containsNode()

Previously in this chapter, you learned that a key in a tree must be unique. You cannot have two keys with the same key value. Don't confuse key value with the value stored in a node. A key value is the value of the key itself.

Before adding a new node to the tree, you should determine if the key of the new node already exists in the tree. It is possible to construct a binary tree that allows duplicate keys, but this is not a common implementation and goes beyond the scope of this chapter. In this case, you've defined a rule for the tree that states all the keys must be unique.

You determine if the key already exists in the tree by calling the contains() member function of the BinarySearchTree class, which is illustrated next. The contains() function requires one argument, a reference to the key. It returns a Boolean true if the key exists; otherwise, a Boolean false is returned.

You'll notice that the contains() function is a simple function in that it has one statement. This statement calls the containsNode() member function. The containsNode() function searches the tree for the key and returns a Boolean true if the key is found; otherwise, a Boolean false is returned, which is then used as the return value of the contains() function.

The contains() function is defined in the public access specifier section of the BinarySearchTree class. The containsNode() function is defined in the private access specifier section of the same class.

```
bool contains(char* key)
{
    return containsNode(root, key);
}
```

The containsNode() member function, as shown next, requires two arguments. The first argument is a reference to the root node. Any node can be the root node, but typically the first node of the tree is the root node because you want the search for the key to begin at the top of the tree. The second argument is reference to the key, which is the same key that is passed to the contains() function.

The process begins by determining if the root pointer is NULL. If the pointer is NULL, then the key doesn't exist and a Boolean false is returned; otherwise, the key is compared and the search continues.

First, the containsNode() function compares the key to the key of the root node. If there is a match, then a Boolean true is returned and the search ends. If they are different, then the containsNode() determines if the key is less than the key of the root node. If so, then the containsNode() calls itself and uses the left child node of the root node as the new root node.

If the key isn't less than the key of the root node, then the containsNode() determines if the key is greater than the key of the root node. If so, then the containsNode() calls itself using the right child node of the root node as the new root node.

The containsNode() is called recursively until either the key is found or until the value of the root node is NULL, indicating that you've reached the end of the tree without finding the key.

```
bool containsNode(METADATA* node, char* key)
{
    if(node == NULL)
    {
        return false;
    }
    else
    {
        if(strcmp(key, node->key) == 0)
        {
            return true;
        }
        else if(strcmp(key, node->key) < 0)
        {
            return containsNode(node->left, key);
        }
        else
        {
            return containsNode(node->right, key);
```

```
      }
    }
}
```

displayInOrder() and processNodesInOrder()

You can display the contents of the tree by calling the `displayInOrder()` member function of the `BinarySearchTree` class. As the name implies, the `displayInOrder()` function is a public function that displays the key and the value of all the left nodes followed by all the right nodes for each node in the tree.

As shown next, the `displayInOrder()` function has one statement that calls the `processNodesInOrder()` member function of the `BinarySearchTree` class. The `processNodesInOrder()` function is defined in the private access specifier section of the class and is therefore unavailable to the application.

You must pass the `processNodesInOrder()` function one argument, which is a reference to the root node. The root node is typically the first node of the tree, but you can start displaying the contents of the tree from any node by passing it as the argument to the `processNodesInOrder()` function.

```
void displayInOrder()
{
    processNodesInOrder(root);
}
```

The definition of the `processNodesInOrder()` member function is illustrated next. You'll notice that this is a recursive function and is called multiple times in order to print nodes contained on the left and right branches of the tree.

Processing begins by determining if the root node is NULL. If so, you're at the end of tree. If it is not NULL, then the `processNodesInOrder()` is called again and passed the left child of the root node. The key and value of the node is then displayed on the screen.

This continues until keys and values of all the left nodes appear on the screen. A similar process is followed to display the right children of the root node. For any given node, all the left nodes will be printed first, then the node itself is printed, then all the right nodes.

```
void processNodesInOrder(METADATA* node)
{
    if(node != NULL)
    {
        processNodesInOrder(node->left);
```

```
        cout << "key: " << node->key << "\tvalue: " << node->value << endl;
        processNodesInOrder(node->right);
    }
}
```

getSize(), getDepth(), and getTreeDepth()

Previously in this chapter, you learned that a tree is measured by its number of nodes and levels. The number of nodes in a tree is called the size of the tree, and the number of levels is the depth of the tree. We've defined member functions that you can use to determine the size and the depth of a tree.

The first of these functions is called the getSize() member function, which is shown next. This function simply returns the value of the size data member of the BinarySearchTree class. Functions that add and remove nodes adjust the value of the size data member so the size data member always reflects the current number of nodes in a tree.

```
int getSize()
{
    return size;
}
```

The getDepth() member function determines the number of levels in the tree. This function calls the getTreeDepth() member function and passes it reference to the root node that is used as the starting level when calculating the depth of the tree. It returns an integer that represents the number of levels of the tree.

The getDepth() function and the getSize() function are both defined in the public access specifier section of the BinarySearchTree class. The getTreeDepth() function is defined in the private access specifier.

```
int getDepth()
{
    return getTreeDepth(root);
}
```

The getTreeDepth() function is shown next and performs all the calculations to determine the total number of levels in a tree. The getTreeDepth() function requires one argument, which is a reference to the root node. This should be the first node in the tree, although you can use any node. If you do use a node other than the top node, the function calculates levels from that node to the end of the tree. Levels previous to this node are not considered in the calculation.

The process starts by determining if the tree is empty. If so, then the root node is NULL and a zero is returned. If the root node isn't NULL, then the getTreeDepth() function drills down each level of the tree by recursively calling itself. You get a NULL parameter when you reach a leaf node. This doesn't mean the tree is empty, it just means you reached a leaf node. Then the recursive calls return, incrementing the count value through each recursion to add up the levels.

Each time the getTreeDepth() function is called, the left child node and the right child node are passed to the getTreeDepth() function and the function returns an integer representing the level, which is assigned to either the depth_left variable or the depth_right variable.

The depth_left and the depth_right variables are compared. If the value of the depth_left variable is greater than the depth_right variable, the depth_left variable is incremented and returned by the getTreeDepth() function; otherwise, the depth_right variable is incremented and returned.

```cpp
int getTreeDepth(METADATA* node)
{
    int depth_left;
    int depth_right;
    if(node == NULL)
    {
        return 0;
    }
    else
    {
        depth_left = getTreeDepth(node->left);
        depth_right = getTreeDepth(node->right);
        if(depth_left > depth_right)
        {
            return depth_left + 1;
        }
        else
        {
            return depth_right + 1;
        }
    }
}
```

Binary Tree Using C++

Now that you've learned the pieces of the BinarySearchTree class, let's assemble them into a working application. You'll organize the application into three files, BinaryTreeDemo.cpp, BinarySearchTree.h, and BinarySearchTree.cpp. BinaryTreeDemo.cpp is the application file that contains the code that creates and manipulates the tree. BinarySearchTree.h contains the definition of the structure used to build a node and the definition of the BinarySearchTree class. BinarySearchTree.cpp contains the definition of member functions of the BinarySearchTree class. All these files are listed in the next code snippet.

Previously in this chapter, we discussed the structure used to create a node and the BinarySearchTree class definition. In addition, each member function was discussed in the preceding section of this chapter.

All that remains is for you to take a close look at how the application creates and manipulates a tree. To do this, you'll explore the BinaryTreeDemo application, which creates a tree and stores two nodes: IDs (keys) and first names (values). It then manipulates these nodes. Here is the application:

```cpp
//BinaryTreeDemo.cpp
#include <iostream.h>
#include <time.h>
#include <stdlib.h>
#include <string.h>
#include <stdio.h>
#include "BinarySearchTree.h"
void main()
{
    BinarySearchTree* tree = new BinarySearchTree();
    char key[SIZE_KEY];
    char value[SIZE_VALUE];
    int i;
    cout << "Adding three keys and values into the tree." << endl;
    for(i=0; i<3; i++)
    {
        if (i==0)
        {
            strcpy(key,"345");
            strcpy(value,"Bob");
        }
        if (i==1)
        {
            strcpy(key,"123");
            strcpy(value,"Mary");
        }
        if (i==2)
        {
            strcpy(key,"999");
            strcpy(value,"Sue");
```

```
    }
    if (!tree->contains(key))
    {
       cout << "Adding node - key: " << key << " value: " << value
       << endl;
       tree->add(key, value);
    }
    else
    {
       cout << "Generated duplicate key: " << key << endl;
    }
}
cout << "\nIn order traversal of tree:" << endl;
tree->displayInOrder();
cout << "\nDepth of tree before removing nodes: " << tree->getDepth()
     << endl;
cout << "Size of tree before removing nodes: " << tree->getSize()
     << endl;
cout << "\nRetrieving one value from the tree:" << endl;
if(tree->get("123", value))
{
   cout << " Value: " << value << endl;
}
cout << "\nRemoving one node from the tree:" << endl;
if(tree->contains("123"))
{
   tree->remove("123");
}
cout << "\nIn order traversal of tree:" << endl;
tree->displayInOrder();
cout << "\nDepth of tree after removing nodes: " << tree->getDepth()
     << endl;
cout << "Size of tree after removing nodes: " << tree->getSize()
     << endl;
cout << "\nDestroying the tree:" << endl;
delete tree;
}
```

The application begins by declaring an instance of the `BinarySearchTree` class and assigns it to a reference called `tree`. Next, two `char` arrays are declared and an `int` is declared. The `char` arrays are called `key` and `value`, and the size of these arrays is established by using the macro defined in the `BinarySearchTree.h` file. The arrays store an ID and a first name that is assigned to a node on the tree. The `int` controls the `for` loop.

The for loop then adds each ID and first name to the tree. For each iteration, the strcpy() function is called to copy a string that contains either an ID or a first name to the key and value array. You use an if statement to determine which set of ID and first name to copy to the arrays.

Once the set of strings is copied to the arrays, the application calls the contains() member function to determine if the key already exists in the tree. Remember that each key must be unique. The contains() function returns a Boolean true if the key is contained in the tree. You reverse the logic with the not operator so that a Boolean true is treated as a Boolean false. This means that statements within the if statement will not execute if the key already exists in the tree.

If the key doesn't exist, then the application displays the key and value on the screen before calling the add() member function to place the key and value on the tree, as shown here:

```
Adding three keys and values into the tree.
Adding node - key: 345 value: Bob
Adding node - key: 123 value: Mary
Adding node - key: 999 value: Sue
```

Figure 10-6 illustrates keys and values organized on the tree.

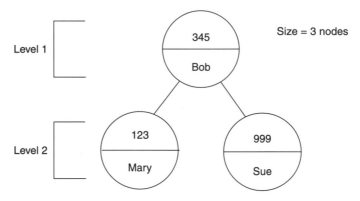

Figure 10-6 Regardless of the order in which data is added to the tree, the left child node is less than the parent node and the right child node is greater than the parent node.

If the key does exist, then a message is displayed on the screen telling everyone that the key is a duplicate key.

After all three IDs and first names are placed on the tree, the application manipulates nodes on the tree. The first manipulation is to call the displayInOrder() member function that displays keys and values of each node, as shown next:

```
In order traversal of tree:
key: 123 value: Mary
key: 345 value: Bob
key: 999 value: Sue
```

Next, the application displays the depth and the size of the tree by calling the getDepth() and getSize() member functions. The result is displayed on the screen, as shown here:

```
Depth of tree before removing nodes    2
Size of tree before removing nodes    3
```

Remember that the depth of a tree is the number of levels on the tree. In this example, there are two levels. The first level contains the root node, and the second level contains the left child node and the right child node.

Next, the application retrieves the value associated with key 123 by calling the get() member function. The get() member function returns a Boolean value true if the key is found; otherwise, a Boolean false is returned. If the key is found, then the value is displayed on the screen, as shown here. Remember that the first name associated with the key 123 is assigned to the value array by the get() function.

```
Retrieving one value from the tree:
Value    Mary
```

Next, the application removes the node that contains the key 123. First, the contains() function is called to determine if the tree contains a key that has the value 123. If so, a Boolean true is returned; otherwise, a Boolean false is returned. Because there is a node containing 123 as a key, the remove() member function is called and passed the string 123 to remove the node.

The displayInOrder() function is called once again to display the tree after the node is removed. Here's what is displayed on the screen. Notice that the node containing 123 no longer exists in the tree (see Figure 10-7).

```
Removing one node from the tree:
In order traversal of tree:
key: 345 value: Bob
key: 999 value: Sue
```

Finally, the application calls the getDepth() and getSize() functions to display the depth and size of the tree after the node is removed. Here's what is displayed:

```
Depth of tree after removing nodes    2
Size of tree after removing nodes    2
```

The application finishes removing the tree by calling the delete operator. Remember that the destructor of the BinarySearchTree class calls the

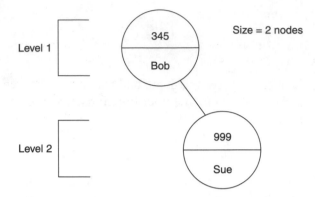

Figure 10-7   The left child node is removed from the tree; the tree still has a depth of two levels.

`removeAllNodes()` member function that displays keys and values of nodes that are removed. Here's what is displayed:

```
Removing node - key: 345     Bob
Removing node - key: 999     Sue
```

```
// BinarySearchTree.h"
#include <string.h>
#define SIZE_KEY   32
#define SIZE_VALUE      256
typedef struct Metadata
{
   struct Metadata(char* key, char* value)
   {
     strcpy(this->key, key);
     strcpy(this->value, value);
     left = NULL;
     right = NULL;
   }
   char key[SIZE_KEY];
   char value[SIZE_VALUE];
   struct Metadata* left;
   struct Metadata* right;
} METADATA;
class BinarySearchTree
{
   private:
     int size;
     METADATA* root;
```

```cpp
        bool addNode(METADATA** current_node, METADATA* new_node);
        bool getNode(METADATA* current_node, char* key, char* value);
        void removeAllNodes(METADATA* node);
        void processNodesInOrder(METADATA* node);
        int getTreeDepth(METADATA* node);
        bool containsNode(METADATA* node, char* key);
        bool removeNode(METADATA** node, char* key);
        void removeRootNode(METADATA** node);
        void moveLeftMostNode(METADATA** node, METADATA* root);
    public:
        BinarySearchTree();
        virtual ~BinarySearchTree();
        bool add(char* key, char* value);
        bool remove(char* key);
        void removeAll();
        bool get(char* key, char* value);
        bool contains(char* key);
        void displayInOrder();
        int getSize();
        int getDepth();
};

// BinarySearchTree.cpp
#include <iostream.h>
#include "BinarySearchTree.h"
BinarySearchTree::BinarySearchTree()
{
    root = NULL;
    size = 0;
}
BinarySearchTree::~BinarySearchTree()
{
    removeAll();
}
bool BinarySearchTree::add(char* key, char* value)
{
    if(key == NULL || value == NULL || strlen(key) > SIZE_KEY-1
            || strlen(value) > SIZE_VALUE-1)
    {
        return false;
    }
    METADATA* new_node = new METADATA(key, value);
    return addNode(&root, new_node);
}
```

```cpp
bool BinarySearchTree::addNode(METADATA** current_node, METADATA* new_node)
{
    if(*current_node == NULL)
    {
        *current_node = new_node;
        size++;
        return true;
    }
    else
    {
        if(strcmp(new_node->key, (*current_node)->key) < 0)
        {
            return addNode(&((*current_node)->left), new_node);
        }
        else if(strcmp(new_node->key, (*current_node)->key) > 0)
        {
            return addNode(&((*current_node)->right), new_node);
        }
        else
        {
            delete new_node;
            return false;
        }
    }
}
bool BinarySearchTree::remove(char* key)
{
    return removeNode(&root, key);
}
function
bool BinarySearchTree::removeNode(METADATA** node, char* key)
{
    if(*node != NULL)
    {
        if (strcmp(key, (*node)->key) == 0)
        {
            removeRootNode(node);
            size--;
            return true;
        }
        else if(strcmp(key, (*node)->key) < 0)
        {
            return removeNode(&((*node)->left), key);
        }
```

```
        else
        {
            return removeNode(&((*node)->right), key);
        }
    }
    else
    {
        return false;
    }
}
void BinarySearchTree::removeRootNode(METADATA** root)
{
    METADATA* temp;
    if((*root)->left == NULL && (*root)->right == NULL)
    {
        delete(*root);
        *root = NULL;
    }
    else if((*root)->right == NULL)
    {
        temp = *root;
        *root = (*root)->left;
        delete(temp);
    }
    else if((*root)->left == NULL)
    {
        temp = *root;
        *root = (*root)->right;
        delete(temp);
    }
    else
    {
        moveLeftMostNode(&((*root)->right), *root);
    }
}
void BinarySearchTree::moveLeftMostNode(METADATA** node, METADATA* root)
{
    if(*node != NULL && (*node)->left == NULL)
    {
        METADATA* temp = *node;
        strcpy(root->key, (*node)->key);
        strcpy(root->value, (*node)->value);
        *node = (*node)->right;
        delete(temp);
```

```
    }
    else
    {
        moveLeftMostNode(&((*node)->left), root);
    }
}
void BinarySearchTree::removeAll()
{
    removeAllNodes(root);
    root = NULL;
    size = 0;
}
void BinarySearchTree::removeAllNodes(METADATA* node)
{
    if(node != NULL)
    {
        removeAllNodes(node->left);
        removeAllNodes(node->right);
        cout << "Removing node - key: " << node->key << "\t" << node->value
            << endl;
        delete node;
    }
}
bool BinarySearchTree::get(char* key, char* value)
{
    return getNode(root, key, value);
}
bool BinarySearchTree::getNode(METADATA* node, char* key, char* value)
{
    if(node == NULL)
    {
        value[0] = '\0';
        return false;
    }
    else
    {
        if(strcmp(key, node->key) == 0)
        {
            strcpy(value, node->value);
            return true;
        }
        else if(strcmp(key, node->key) < 0)
        {
            return getNode(node->left, key, value);
```

```
        }
        else
        {
            return getNode(node->right, key, value);
        }
    }
}
bool BinarySearchTree::contains(char* key)
{
    return containsNode(root, key);
}
bool BinarySearchTree::containsNode(METADATA* node, char* key)
{
    if(node == NULL)
    {
        return false;
    }
    else
    {
        if(strcmp(key, node->key) == 0)
        {
            return true;
        }
        else if(strcmp(key, node->key) < 0)
        {
            return containsNode(node->left, key);
        }
        else
        {
            return containsNode(node->right, key);
        }
    }
}
void BinarySearchTree::displayInOrder()
{
    processNodesInOrder(root);
}
void BinarySearchTree::processNodesInOrder(METADATA* node)
{
    if(node != NULL)
    {
        processNodesInOrder(node->left);
        cout << "key: " << node->key << "\tvalue: " << node->value << endl;
        processNodesInOrder(node->right);
```

```
   }
}
int BinarySearchTree::getSize()
{
   return size;
}
int BinarySearchTree::getDepth()
{
   return getTreeDepth(root);
}
int BinarySearchTree::getTreeDepth(METADATA* node)
{
   int depth_left;
   int depth_right;
   if(node == NULL)
   {
      return 0;
   }
   else
   {
      depth_left = getTreeDepth(node->left);
      depth_right = getTreeDepth(node->right);
      if(depth_left > depth_right)
      {
         return depth_left + 1;
      }
      else
      {
         return depth_right + 1;
      }
   }
}
```

Binary Tree Using Java

A tree data structure can also be incorporated into a Java application by using the
`TreeMap` collection class that is defined in the `java.util` package. The `TreeMap`
class has many member methods that are comparable to member functions that you defined in the C++ `BinarySearchTree` class. However, the `TreeMap` class is missing two methods that you used in the C++ application, the `displayInOrder()` and

getTreeDepth() member functions. You can define your own displayInOrder() method to display keys and values stored in nodes of the tree, but there isn't any way of calculating the depth of a tree in Java. This is an implementation detail that's hidden from the end user.

At the end of this section is the Java equivalent of the C++ application presented previously in this chapter. The Java application creates a tree and places the same three keys and values on the tree and then manipulates those values the same way as the C++ application manipulated those values.

Let's see how the Java application works. It begins by declaring an instance of the TreeMap class and assigning it to the tree reference. The TreeMap class is similar to the BinarySearchTree class defined in the C++ version of this application.

The application then declares two strings to store the key and value of a node. These are initialized to NULL. The application also declares an integer to control the for loop. The for loop assigns strings to the key and value variables and then adds each key and value to the tree.

Similar to the C++ version of the application, the Java version calls the containsKey() method that is a member of the TreeMap class. This method returns a Boolean true if the key already exists in the tree; otherwise, a Boolean false is returned. As with the C++ version, the not operator is used to reverse the logic of the value returned by the containsKey().

The put() member method of the TreeMap class places the key and value on the tree. The put() method is similar to the add() member function that you defined in the C++ version of this application. Each time a new key and value is added to the tree, the key and value are displayed on the screen, as shown here:

```
Adding three keys and values into the tree.
Adding node - key: 345 value: Bob
Adding node - key: 123 value: Mary
Adding node - key: 999 value: Sue
```

Next, the displayInOrder() method is called to display the contents of the tree on the screen. The displayInOrder() method is defined at the bottom of the Java listing. Here's how it works. First the keySet() method is called to copy the contents of the tree to a key set. Think of a key set as a two-column table where one column contains keys and the other corresponding values. Each row is a node of the tree.

Next, an instance of the Iterator class is created. As you'll remember from your Java programming course, the Iterator class has member methods that enable you to move through a list such as a key set. In this example, the Iterator class returns the key of each row in the key set. The key is then passed to the get() member method of the TreeMap class to retrieve the value associated with the key. Both the key and the value are then displayed on the screen, as shown next.

```
In order traversal of tree:
key: 123 value: Mary
key: 345 value: Bob
key: 999 value: Sue
```

After the contents of the tree is displayed on the screen, the application displays the size of the tree by calling the `size()` member method of the `TreeMap` class. Here's what is displayed on the screen. Remember that the size is the number of nodes on the tree.

```
Size of tree before removing nodes 3
```

The application then calls the `get()` member method to retrieve the value associated with the key 123. If the value isn't NULL, then the application displays the key and the value on the screen, as shown here:

```
Retrieving a value from the tree:
Found key: 999 value: Mary
```

Next, the application removes the node whose key is 123 by first calling the `containsKey()` member method of the `TreeMap` class to determine if there is a node that has 123 as a key. If so, the `remove()` member method is called and passed the key 123 to remove the node. A message is displayed on the screen, as shown here, to indicate that the node is being removed:

```
Removing a node from the tree:
Removing key    999
```

To show the result of the node being removed, you call the `displayInOrder()` method to display the contents of the tree and call the `size()` member method to display the size of the tree. Here's what is displayed on the screen when these methods are called:

```
In order traversal of tree:
key: 345 value: Bob
key: 999 value: Sue

Size of tree after removing nodes    2
```

Here is the program that creates and manipulates the tree in Java:

```
import java.lang.*;
import java.text.*;
import java.util.*;
public class BinarySearchTreeDemo
{
    public static void main(String[] args)
    {
```

```
TreeMap tree = new TreeMap();
String key = null;
String value = null;
int i;
System.out.println("Adding three keys and values into the tree.");
for(i=0; i<3; i++)
{
   if (i==0)
   {
      key ="345";
      value="Bob";
   }
   if (i==1)
   {
      key ="123";
      value="Mary";
   }
   if (i==2)
   {
      kcy-"999";
      value="Sue";
   }
   if (!tree.containsKey(key))
   {
      System.out.println("Adding node - key: " + key + " value: "
        + value);
      tree.put(key, value);
      }
   else
   {
      System.out.println("Generated duplicate key: " + key);
   }
}
System.out.println("\nIn order traversal of tree:");
displayInOrder(tree);
System.out.println("\nSize of tree before removing nodes: "
      + tree.size());
System.out.println("\nRetrieving a value from the tree:");
value = (String)tree.get("123");
if(value != null)
{
   System.out.println("Found key: " + key + " value: " + value);
}
System.out.println("\nRemoving a node from the tree:");
```

```
        if(tree.containsKey("123"))
        {
            System.out.println("Removing key: " + key);
            tree.remove("123");
        }
        System.out.println("\nIn order traversal of tree:");
        displayInOrder(tree);
        System.out.println("\nSize of tree after removing nodes: "
                + tree.size());
    }
    private static void displayInOrder(TreeMap tree)
    {
        Set keys = tree.keySet();
        Iterator ii = keys.iterator();
        while(ii.hasNext())
        {
            String key = (String)ii.next();
            String value = (String)tree.get(key);
            System.out.println("key: " + key + "\tvalue: " + value);
        }
    }
}
```

Quiz

1. What is a tree?

2. What is the relationship between parent node and child nodes?

3. What are a key and a value?

4. What is a root node?

5. What is the purpose of a left child node and a right child node?

6. What is a leaf node?

7. What is the depth of a tree?

8. What is the size of a tree?

9. How do you calculate the size of a tree?

10. Can a tree have a duplicate key?

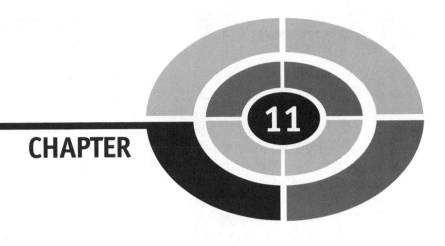

CHAPTER 11

What Is a Hashtable?

Hashtable is one of those programming terms whose definition is illusive. *Hash* means "mishmash," and a table is the organization of data into columns and rows, but a table containing mishmash data seems useless to an application. Not necessarily! Programmers use a hashtable to store and retrieve large amounts of information efficiently. You'll learn how this is done and how to use hashtables in your application in this chapter.

A Hashtable

Object-oriented applications that mimic real life must store and retrieve large amounts of information. Previously in this book, you learned that information is associated with an object and stored in an instance of a class that represents the object within the application.

Objects are stored using one of a number of data structures. The choice of data structure depends on the nature of the application. A hashtable is a common data structure to store objects that have a key/value relationship.

A hashtable is an array of pointers to data. Data takes the form of a user-defined structure that consists of up to three elements: the key, the value, and a pointer to the instance of the next structure in the hashtable. The pointer is used only if your collisions are handled in the manner described in this chapter; otherwise, it is not required.

The key uniquely identifies the value. Each user-defined structure in the hashtable must have a unique key. The value is data that is associated with the key, and it can appear more than once in the hashtable. Think of a key as a student ID and the corresponding value as a student's name. Each student is assigned a unique student ID, but two or more students can have the same name.

What makes a hashtable interesting is the way in which the program assigns a user-defined structure to an array element of the hashtable. The program hashes the key of a user-defined structure to determine which array element is assigned the user-defined structure.

A bit confused? If so, you're not alone, because this concept isn't intuitive. To clear up any confusion, look at Figure 11-1, which shows three entries in the hashtable. I simplified this illustration by using blocks to represent each instance of the user-defined structure that contains the key/value of the entry. Later in this chapter, you'll see the actual user-defined structure used for hashtable entries.

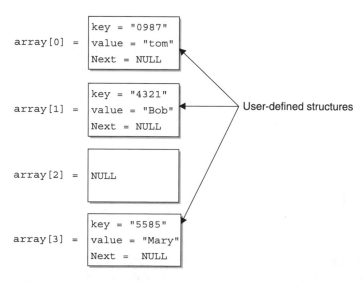

Figure 11-1 The hashtable is an array whose elements point to user-defined structures that contain data.

Figure 11-1 also shows the index that represents the hashtable. Notice that each array element points to a user-defined structure. The user-defined structure contains the actual data for the entry of the hashtable.

Each user-defined structure is assigned to a specific array element based on the user-defined structure's key. The key is translated into a number that is the array index. This number is called a *hash value* and is created by using the process called *hashing*. The hash value becomes the array index of the array element that points to the user-defined structure whose key is hashed. Each index in Figure 11-1 is the hash value of the key of the user-defined structure.

You can think of hashing as a way to come up with the index of the array element associated with an entry in the hashtable. You'll learn how to perform hashing in your application later in this chapter.

Hashing achieves an even distribution of index values, which makes finding information faster than if a string of bits is in a natural order. In a natural order, words and names follow a predictable pattern. By shuffling the bits that make up words and names, a program no longer treats those bits as a text string and instead randomizes the bits to make them more efficient to search.

Hashing is a high-speed scheme for taking a key that has natural sequence (alphabetical or numerical order) and pseudo-randomizing it. If the key is a name, certain letters appear more often than other letters, and certain sequences of characters occur more frequently than other characters. Hashing moves the bits around to produce an even distribution of hash values, which is needed to quickly search a hashtable.

The result of hashing is a number that has no real significance, but it is used as an array index to store and retrieve information that is associated with an entry that is stored in a hashtable. Indexes shown in Figure 11-1 are hash values of the corresponding key of the user-defined structure pointed to by the array element.

Problems with Hashing

Hashing is not perfect. Occasionally, a collision occurs when two different keys hash into the same hash value and are assigned to the same array element. Programmers have come up with various techniques for dealing with this conflict.

A common way to deal with a collision is to create a linked list of entries that have the same hash value. For example, say that the key of each entry hashes to the same hash value, and this results in both being assigned to the same array element of the hashtable, as shown in Figure 11-2.

Because two entries cannot be assigned the same array element, the programmer creates a linked list. The first user-defined structure is assigned to the pointer in the array element. The second isn't assigned to any array element and is instead linked to the first user-defined structure, thereby forming a linked list.

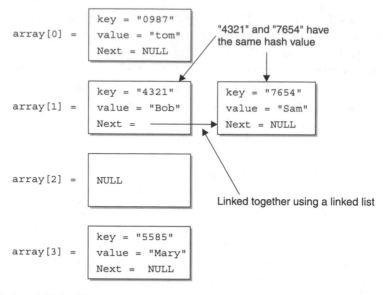

Figure 11-2 A linked list connects user-defined structures whose keys hash to the same hash value.

As you'll see later in this chapter, the program locates an entry in a hashtable by referencing the hashed value of the entry. The hash value is the index of the array element that points to the entry. You can probably see the dilemma: the index points only to the first entry, not the second.

Programmers work around this problem by having the program read the key of the first entry. If the key isn't the one the program seeks, the program looks at the next entry in the linked list. It continues down the linked list until the program finds the desired entry or reaches the end of the linked list.

Developing a Hashtable

Creating and using a hashtable in your application is a two-step process. The first step is to define a user-defined structure similar to the way you defined nodes in a tree or a linked list. The second step is to define a Hashtable class. The Hashtable class declares an instance of the user-defined structure and defines member data and member functions that are used to add, remove, and manipulate information stored in the hashtable.

The Hashtable Class

The first step to using a hashtable in your application is to define a user-defined structure and then define the `Hashtable` class, which interacts with the hashtable within the application.

Begin by defining the user-defined structure, as shown here:

```
typedef struct Metadata
{
    struct Metadata(char* key, char* value)
    {
        strcpy(this->key, key);
        strcpy(this->value, value);
        next = NULL;
    }
    char key[SIZE_KEY];
    char value[SIZE_VALUE];
    struct Metadata* next;
} METADATA;
```

I called this structure metadata because *metadata* is data that describes data, similar to a column name on a spreadsheet. You'll assign data to the structure once an instance of metadata is declared in the `Hashtable` class.

The metadata structure has three members. The first member is a char array called key that stores the key of a key/value pair. The second member is a char array called value because it stores the corresponding value of the key/value pair. The last member is a pointer to another metadata structure, which is called next. This enables the application to link together structures at a given index.

The size of both character arrays is determined by the value of the `#define` macro called `SIZE_KEY` and `SIZE_VALUE`. These are defined in the `HashTable.h` header file (see "Hashtable Using C++").

You'll notice that a constructor is defined inside the structure definition. This enables the application to pass the structure initial values for the key and value, which are then assigned the corresponding character arrays. It also initializes the pointer to the next node in the linked list. You'll see how this is used later.

Once the metadata structure is defined, you need to define the `Hashtable` class, which declares an instance of the metadata structure and defines member functions that interact with the metadata structure.

Here's the definition of the `Hashtable` class:

```
class Hashtable
{
    private:
```

```
        int tablesize;
        METADATA** table;
        int size;
        METADATA* current_entry;
        int current_index;
        long hashString(char* key);
        METADATA* find(char* key);
    public:
        Hashtable(int tablesize = DEFAULT_TABLESIZE);
        virtual ~Hashtable();
        bool put(char* key, char* value);
        bool get(char* key, char* value);
        bool contains(char* key);
        bool remove(char* key);
        void removeAll();
        int getSize();
        void initIterator();
        bool hasNext();
        void getNextKey(char* key);
};
```

The Hashtable class is organized into the private access specifier and public access specifier sections. The private access specifier section contains five data members and two member functions.

The first data member is an integer called tablesize, which is later assigned the size of the array of pointers that stores entries in the hashtable. Next is a pointer to a pointer called table, an array of metadata pointers that will store information in the hashtable. Each entry in the table is a pointer to a linked list of entries. NULL indicates there isn't an entry at this index.

The third data member of the Hashtable class is an integer called size that is later assigned the number of entries in the hashtable. The last two data members are current_entry and current_index. The current_entry data member is a pointer to the current entry in the metadata structure, and the current_index is an integer representing the current key. Both iterate entries in the hashtable.

Two functions are declared within the private access specifier of the Hashtable class: hashString() and find(). The hashString() function hashes a key in a key/value pair and returns the hash code. The returned hash code is the index where the entry resides in the hashtable, the index in the array of metadata pointers. The find() function searches a hashtable for a particular key and returns a pointer to the metadata structure that contains that key. Both functions are called by other member functions and are described in detail later in this chapter.

The public access specifier section of the `Hashtable` class contains member functions that create and interact with the hashtable. Each of these functions is discussed in forthcoming sections of this chapter.

Constructor and Destructor

The constructor of the `Hashtable` class initializes data members and creates the hashtable, as illustrated in the following code snippet. The size of the array of pointers (`tablesize`) is passed to the constructor when the application declares an instance of the `Hashtable` class. The value passed to the constructor must be an integer, which is assigned to the `tablesize` data member of the `Hashtable` class.

The constructor allocates an array of metadata pointers, which will store the data in the hashtable. This array is assigned to the `table` member of the class. Previously, you learned that the `table` data member is an array of pointers that point to metadata structures.

Once the instance of the `Hashtable` class is declared, the constructor uses a `for` loop to initialize elements of the `table` array to NULL. The `size` data member is initialized to zero, indicating there aren't any entries in the hashtable. However, you can increase the size of the hashtable by passing the `tablesize` to the constructor. In Figure 11-3, the hashtable size is five elements.

```
Hashtable(int tablesize)
{
    size = 0;
    this->tablesize = tablesize;
    table = new METADATA*[tablesize];
    for(int i=0; i<tablesize; i++)
    {
        table[i] = NULL;
    }
}
```

The destructor of the `Hashtable` class is shown in the next code snippet. It performs two actions. First, the destructor calls the `removeAll()` member function to remove all entries from the hashtable. After entries are deleted, the constructor deletes the array of pointers referenced by the table data member. It does this by using the `delete` operator.

```
~Hashtable()
{
    removeAll();
    delete[] table;
}
```

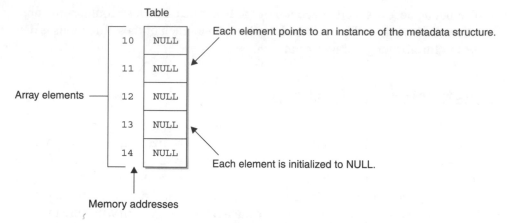

Figure 11-3   The constructor declares an array of pointers where each element of the array points to an instance of the metadata structure.

Inserting a New Entry

You insert a new entry into the hashtable by calling the put() member function, which is available directly to the application because it is declared in the public access specifier section of the Hashtable class.

The put() function is shown in the following code snippet. It requires two arguments. The first argument is a char pointer called key that contains the key of the new entry. The second argument is a char pointer called value that references the value of the new entry. The put() function returns a Boolean true if the new entry is inserted into the hashtable; otherwise, a Boolean false is returned.

As you'll recall, each key must be unique. Before the new entry is placed in the hashtable, the put() function determines if the key already exists by calling the find() member function and passing find() the key.

The keys stored in the hashtable are exactly the same as the key passed into the find() function. The hash determines which bucket it goes in, and then find() compares keys to find the desired key. You'll learn how the find() function works later in this chapter.

The find() function returns a NULL if the key isn't found; otherwise, the find() function returns a pointer to the metadata structure that contains the key. If the find() function doesn't return a NULL, the key is already in the hashtable, and the put() function returns a false.

However, if the find() function returns a NULL, a new entry is placed in the hashtable by first declaring a new instance of the metadata structure, which is then passed the key and the value of the new entry. Reference to the instance is assigned to a pointer called entry.

Next, the hashString() member function is called and passed the key of the new entry. The hashString() function hashes the key and returns a hash number that is used as the array index for the entry in the hashtable. The hash number is assigned to the integer called bucket. You'll learn how the hashString() function operates later in this chapter.

The bucket integer is then used as the array index of the table data member of the Hashtable class. As you'll remember from previous section of this chapter, the table data member is an array of metadata pointers. This means that the table[bucket] references the element of the hashtable that will be assigned the new entry.

Before the entry is assigned to this element, the current element in that bucket is assigned to the next member of the instance of the metadata called entry that is declared in the put() function. After this assignment, the new entry is assigned to the table[bucket] element of the hashtable. In effect, what this does is make the new entry the first entry in a linked list defined at this point in the array. If there was no entry at this index, the value of the index would be NULL. This would assign NULL to the next pointer of the new entry, which is okay because the new entry is the only entry in the linked list.

The put() function then increments the size data member of the Hashtable class, indicating an additional entry has been placed in the hashtable. The put() function then returns a Boolean true. Figure 11-4 illustrates the hashtable if you pass 111 as the key and Bob as the value to the put() function.

```
bool put(char* key, char* value)
{
    if(find(key) != NULL)
    {
        return false;
    }
    METADATA* entry = new METADATA(key, value);
    int bucket = hashString(key);
    entry->next = table[bucket];
    table[bucket] = entry;
    size++;
    return true;
}
```

Retrieving a Value

You can retrieve a value stored in a hashtable by calling the get() member function, which is illustrated in the next code snippet. The get() function requires two arguments. The first argument is a char pointer that references the key of the entry that you

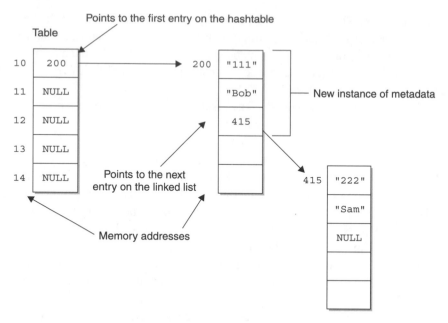

Figure 11-4 Here's what happens after the first entry is placed on the hashtable by calling the put() function.

want to retrieve. The second argument is a char pointer that references the value of the entry. The get() function copies the value of the entry from the hashtable to this char pointer if the key is found in the hashtable. If the key is found, then a Boolean true is returned by the get() function; otherwise, a Boolean false is returned.

The get() function searches the hashtable by calling the find() function and passing it the key received as the first argument to the get() function. The find() function hashes the key before searching for the key in the hashtable. The find() function then either returns a reference to the metadata structure that contains the key, or returns a NULL.

The get() function assigns the return value of the find() function to a pointer called temp, which is a pointer to a metadata structure. The get() function then determines if the temp pointer is NULL. If so, then the first array element of the value argument is assigned the NULL character (sets value to an empty string) and the get() function returns a Boolean false, indicating that this key does not exist in the hashtable.

If temp isn't NULL, it means the find() function found the key in the hashtable and it returns a reference to the metadata that contains the entry. The value of the entry is then copied to the value argument, and the get() function returns a Boolean true.

```
bool get(char* key, char* value)
{
    METADATA* temp = find(key);
    if(temp == NULL)
    {
        value[0] = '\0';
        return false;
    }
    else
    {
        strcpy(value, temp->value);
        return true;
    }
}
```

find()

You called the find() member function several times in other member functions.
Now let's take a close look at how the find() member function works. As you'll
recall, the purpose of the find() function is to search the hashtable for a key. If the
key is found, then the find() function returns a reference to the metadata structure
that contains the key and the corresponding value. If the key isn't found, then
find() returns a NULL.

The find() function requires one argument, a reference to the key. The key is
then passed to the hashString() member function, which hashes the key and returns a hash number that corresponds to the key. It does this because keys stored in
the hashtable are hash number representations of the actual key. Therefore, the key
must be converted to its corresponding hash number for the find() function to locate the entry in the array of pointers.

The hash number returned by the hashString() function is assigned to the
bucket integer, which is used as the index to identify the entry in the table array that is
the hashtable. The value of the table array element is a reference to a metadata structure, which is then assigned to the temp pointer of the metadata structure.

As long as the temp pointer isn't NULL, the find() function uses the strcmp()
function to compare the key element of the metadata structure pointed to by temp with
the key passed to the find() function. At this point, the temp variable is being used to
iterate the linked list. If there is a match, then the metadata structure pointed to by the
temp pointer is returned. If there isn't a match, then the next member of the temp
metadata structure is assigned to the temp pointer, and the find() function continues
by making another comparison.

If there isn't a match after the `find()` function has examined all the entries in the hash index, then the `find()` function returns a NULL.

```
METADATA* find(char* key)
{
    int bucket = hashString(key);
    METADATA* temp = table[bucket];
    while(temp != NULL)
    {
        if(strcmp(key, temp->key) == 0)
        {
            return temp;
        }
        temp = temp->next;
    }
    return NULL;
}
```

contains()

The purpose of the `contains()` member function is to determine if a key exists in the hashtable. As you can see by the following definition, the `contains()` function is simple to construct, but it has a critical role in working with hashtables.

As you learned previously in this chapter, each key of a hashtable must be unique. The `contains()` function enables your application to ensure that keys are unique by determining if the key already exists in the hashtable.

The `contains()` function requires one argument, which is a reference to the key that you want to know exists in the hashtable. The `contains()` function returns a Boolean `true` if the key exists or a Boolean `false` if the key isn't found.

The `contains()` function determines if the key exists by calling the `find()` function and passing it the key. In the previous section of this chapter, you learned that the `find()` function returns either a reference to the metadata that contains the key or a NULL. The `contains()` function determines which of these is returned.

If a NULL is returned by the `find()` function, then the `contains()` function returns a Boolean `false`; otherwise, if the `find()` function returns reference to the metadata that contains the key, a Boolean `true` is returned.

```
bool contains(char* key)
{
    if(find(key) == NULL)
    {
        return false;
```

```
   }
   else
   {
      return true;
   }
}
```

Remove an Entry

You'll need to call the remove() member function whenever your application needs to remove an entry from the hashtable. The remove() function, shown in the next code snippet, requires one argument, which is a reference to the key of the entry that you want to remove from the hashtable. If the key is found and the entry successfully removed, then the remove() function returns a Boolean true; otherwise, a Boolean false is returned.

The remove() function hashes the key of the entry you want to remove by calling the hashString() function and passing it a reference to the key received as the argument to the remove() function. The hashString() function returns the hash number for this key, which is then assigned to an integer called bucket.

The bucket is used as the array index of the table data member of the Hashtable class. The table[bucket] references the element of the hashtable that contains the linked list, which must be searched to find the entry. This value is assigned to a temp pointer that will be used to iterate the list.

The remove() function then determines if the entry exists by comparing the temp pointer to NULL. If it is NULL, then a Boolean false is returned to the statement that calls the remove() function. If temp isn't NULL, then at least one entry exists in the linked list, and the remove() function determines where the entry appears in the hashtable linked list.

First, the remove() function determines if the entry is the first node on the linked list by using the strcmp() function to compare the key of the entry to the key passed to the remove() function. If they match, then the strcmp() function returns a zero, and the remove() function knows that the entry is the first node on the linked list. If the entry isn't the first node, then the remove() function must iterate through the linked list to locate the entry.

If the entry is the first node, then the remove() function switches entries on the linked list. As you learned earlier in this chapter, the temp metadata contains three elements: the key, the value, and a reference to the next entry called next.

Reference to the next entry is assigned to the table[bucket] array element, which currently contains reference to the entry that is being removed from the hashtable. This makes the next entry the first entry in the linked list because the current entry is the first entry in the linked list.

After this switch is made, the `remove()` function uses the `delete` operator to deallocate the current entry, which is pointed to by the temp pointer. It is at this point the entry is removed from the hashtable. The `remove()` function then decrements the size data member to reflect the removal of the entry and returns a Boolean `true`, indicating that the entry was successfully removed.

If the entry isn't the first node on the linked list, the `remove()` function must step through the entire linked list looking for the entry. It does this by assigning reference to the next metadata structure, which is the next entry, to the `temp_next` pointer. As long as the `temp_next` pointer isn't NULL, the `remove()` function calls the `strcmp()` function to compare the key member of the `temp_next` metadata structure to the key passed as an argument to the `remove()` function.

If they match, the entries are switched using the same steps as if the entry is the first node on the linked list. If they don't match, then the next entry (metadata structure) is assigned to the `temp_next` pointer and the search continues. If the key cannot be located in the linked list after the search is exhausted, the `remove()` function returns a Boolean `false`.

```cpp
bool remove(char* key)
{
    int bucket = hashString(key);
    METADATA* temp = table[bucket];
    if(temp == NULL)
    {
        return false;
    }
    else if(strcmp(key, temp->key) == 0)
    {
        table[bucket] = temp->next;
        delete temp;
        size--;
        return true;
    }
    else
    {
        METADATA* temp_next = temp->next;
        while(temp_next != NULL)
        {
            if(strcmp(key, temp_next->key) == 0)
            {
                temp->next = temp_next->next;
                delete temp_next;
                size--;
                return true;
```

```
          }
          temp = temp->next;
          temp_next = temp_next->next;
      }
   }
   return false;
}
```

Another way to remove entries from a hashtable is to call the removeAll() function. The removeAll() function, shown in the next code snippet, deletes all entries in the hashtable. To do this, the removeAll() function uses a for loop to iterate all the entries in the hashtable. At each entry, the while loop executes to transverse the linked list to delete all entries that are linked to the hashtable entry. Once entries on the linked list are deleted, the for loop moves to the next entry in the hashtable and repeats the process until all linked entries and all entries on the hashtable are removed.

It begins by declaring a pointer called temp that points to a metadata structure. The temp pointer is then assigned the first element in the hashtable array, which is called table.

As long as the temp pointer isn't NULL, the removeAll() function assigns reference to the next metadata associated with the current entry (metadata structure) to the next pointer. The key and value of the current entry are then displayed on the screen before the delete operator is called to remove the entry pointed to by the temp pointer.

The entry pointed to by the next pointer is then assigned to the temp pointer, and the removeAll() function returns to the top of the while loop and continues by removing the next entry from the hashtable. This continues until the temp pointer is NULL, which means that the hashtable is empty. (When temp is NULL, one linked list is finished, then Java returns to the outer loop again to process the next linked list.) The removeAll() function then sets the size data member of the Hashtable class to zero, indicating there are no entries in the hashtable.

```
void removeAll()
{
   for(int i=0; i<tablesize; i++)
   {
      METADATA* temp = table[i];
      while(temp != NULL)
      {
         METADATA* next = temp->next;
         cout << "Removing node - key:" <<  temp->key <<
             "\t" << temp->value << endl;
         delete temp;
         temp = next;
```

```
      }
   }
   size = 0;
}
```

getSize()

The getSize() member function is the simplest function of the Hashtable class because it reads the size data member of the Hashtable class and returns its value to the statement that calls the getSize() function. The getSize() function definition is listed in the next code snippet.

Why should you use the getSize() function instead of giving the application access to the size data member? To protect the integrity of the data. If you gave the application direct access to the size data member, statements within the application could assign an incorrect value to size. By controlling access to size to only function members of the hashtable, you protect the integrity of the data.

```
int getSize()
{
   return size;
}
```

hashString()

The hashString() member function is another function called by other member functions of the Hashtable class whenever a function needs to convert a key to a hash number key. The hashString() function requires one argument, a char pointer to the key that is being hashed. The hash number that corresponds to the key is then returned by the hashString() function as a long.

The definition of the hashString() function is listed in the next code snippet. The hashing process begins by first determining the length of the key by calling the strlen() function. The length is assigned to an integer that we call n. You'll also declare a long called h and initialize it to zero to store intermediate values of the hash key during the hashing process.

The hashing process works at the bit level of the key and, in effect, randomizes bits that comprise the key. The hashString() function iterates through each character of the key by using the for loop. During each iteration, the bits that comprise the value of the h variable are shifted ($h << 2$), and the bits of the current character of the key are added to the shifted bits. The result is then assigned to the h variable. This process continues until the last character of the key is hashed.

The hashString() then calculates the modulus value, the final hashed value (h), and the table size (h % tablesize). The modulus value can be either a positive or negative value. However, the hashed key must be a positive value. Therefore, the hashString() function returns the absolute value of the hashed key (abs(h % tablesize)).

```
long hashString(char* key)
{
    int n = strlen(key);
    long h = 0;
    for(int i=0; i<n; i++)
    {
        h = (h << 2) + key[i];
    }
    return abs(h % tablesize);
}
```

NOTE: *The goal of hashing is to take a data set of keys and produce a nicely distributed sequence of indices. Although programmers agree that the hashtable size should be a prime number, there are various algorithms for hashing. However, all hashing algorithms have one thing in common: they use bit shifting.*

There isn't a perfect hashing function. Some hashing functions work better on a given dataset than others. Programmers typically test a wide variety of hash functions on a dataset before settling on the best one to use for a specific dataset.

initIterator()

The initIterator() member function initializes some class variables that traverse all the entries in the linked list. The initIterator() function doesn't require any arguments and doesn't return any value, as shown in the next code snippet. The initIterator() is called by the displayAll() function that is defined by the application to display the content of the hashtable. You'll learn more about the displayAll() function in the "Hashtable Using C++" section of this chapter.

When called, the initIterator() function assigns values to two data members of the Hashtable class. The current_entry data member is assigned NULL, and the current_index data member is assigned the value of the tablesize data member.

Next, a for loop finds the first entry in the hashtable. During each loop, the current element of the table array is compared to NULL. If the element is NULL, the search continues to search for the element of the table array that isn't NULL. The first element that isn't NULL is the first entry in the hashtable.

Once the first entry is found, the value of the corresponding element of the table array is assigned to the current_entry. This value is a reference to the metadata structure that contains the key and value for that entry. The index of the element is then assigned to the current_index data member. The initIterator() function then returns.

The initIterator() function is used by the displayAll() function to determine the first entry in the hashtable before the hasNext() and getNextKey() member functions are called. Both these functions directly access the current_entry and current_index data members of the Hashtable class. These functions are discussed in detail in the next section of this chapter.

```
void initIterator()
{
    current_entry = NULL;
    current_index = tablesize;
    for(int i=0; i<tablesize; i++)
    {
        if(table[i] == NULL)
        {
            continue;
        }
        else
        {
            current_entry = table[i];
            current_index = i;
            break;
        }
    }
}
```

hasNext() and getNextKey()

An application iterates the hashtable by calling the hasNext() and getNextKey() member functions. These two functions are used together with initIterator() to retrieve all the keys from a hashtable. The hasNext() function determines if there is another entry in the hashtable based on the current state of the iterator. As illustrated next, the hasNext() function doesn't require any arguments and returns a Boolean true if another entry exists or a Boolean false if the end of the hashtable is reached.

The hasNext() function makes this determination by comparing the value of the current_entry data member to NULL. If the value of the current_entry is

NULL, then the hasNext() function returns a Boolean false; otherwise, a Boolean true is returned.

```
bool hasNext()
{
    if(current_entry == NULL)
    {
        return false;
    }
    else
    {
        return true;
    }
}
```

As you'll recall from the "initIterator()" section, the current_entry and current_index are data members of the Hashtable class. The current_entry data member contains a reference to the current entry in the hashtable, and the current_index holds the index value of the table array that references the current entry.

The getNextKey() function retrieves the key of the entry pointed to by the current_entry data member. The getNextKey() function then moves to the next entry in the hashtable by first trying to go to the next element in the linked list. If the next element is NULL, it moves to the next array index and iterates the array to find the next entry.

The following code snippet is the definition of the getNextKey() function. In it, the getNextKey() function requires one argument. The argument is a char pointer to an array called key. The getNextKey() function copies the key of the current entry to this array, which is then accessed by the statement that calls the getNextKey() function.

Before the process begins, the getNextKey() function determines if the value of the current_entry is NULL. If so, a NULL character is assigned to the first element of the key array (it sets key to an empty string), and the getNextKey() returns without further processing.

If the value of the current_entry data member isn't NULL, then the key of the metadata structure that contains the current entry is copied to the key pointer by calling the strcpy() function. Once copied, the getNextKey() function sets out to locate the next entry. It does this by referencing the next member of the metadata structure that contains the current entry.

The value of the next member is compared to NULL in an if statement. If the next member isn't NULL, indicating there is another entry in the linked list at this index, the value of the next member is assigned to the current_entry data member, making the next entry the current entry of the hashtable.

However, if the value of the next member is NULL, then the `getNextKey()` function steps through each element of the `table` array to find an array element whose value isn't NULL. When it finds one, the `getNextKey()` function copies the value of the array element to the `current_entry` data member and copies the index of that array element to the `current_index` data member. The `getNextKey()` function then returns to the statement that called it.

If the remaining elements of the table array are NULL, there are no more entries in the hashtable. The `getNextKey()` function then assigns a NULL value to the `current_entry` and assigns the value of the `tablesize` data member to the `current_index` data member. These keys and values are pulled from the hashtable in no particular order; generally, hashtables do not support ordering of the data.

```
void getNextKey(char* key)
{
    if(current_entry == NULL)
    {
        key[0] = '\0';
        return;
    }
    strcpy(key, current_entry->key);
    if(current_entry->next != NULL)
    {
        current_entry = current_entry->next;
    }
    else
    {
        for(int i=current_index+1; i<tablesize; i++)
        {
            if(table[i] == NULL)
            {
                continue;
            }
            current_entry = table[i];
            current_index = i;
            return;
        }
        current_entry = NULL;
        current_index = tablesize;
    }
}
```

Hashtable Using C++

Now that you understand how the components of the Hashtable class work, it is time to assemble them into a working C++ application. I organized the application into three files: the HashtableDemo.cpp file that contains the application; the HashTable.h file that contains the definitions of the metadata structure and the Hashtable class, and the Hashtable.cpp file that contains the implementation of member functions. You'll find all three files in the code at the end of this section. In this section, we'll focus on how to use the Hashtable class in an application. You already learned how member functions and data members of the Hashtable class work.

The application begins by declaring an instance of the Hashtable class and assigning reference to it to the hashtable pointer. You then declare two char arrays using the SIZE_KEY and SIZE_VALUE macro defined to set the size of the array. These arrays store strings that contain the key and the value of data that you'll be entering into the hashtable.

Next, the strcpy() function is called to copy the key and value to the key and value arrays. Before you can insert these into the hashtable, you must first determine if the key already exists in the hashtable by calling the contains() member function of the Hashtable class. The contains() member function returns a Boolean true if the key already exists; otherwise, a Boolean false is returned. Notice the not operator (!) reverses the logic of the return value. You do this to execute statements contained within the if statement.

If the key doesn't exist in the hashtable, then the application displays a message on the screen telling that the key and value are being inserted. The actual insertion occurs by calling the put() member function of the Hashtable class. The put() function requires that the key and the value be passed as arguments.

This process is repeated in order to insert two additional key/value pairs into the hashtable. Each of these is also displayed on the screen as shown here. Figure 11-5 illustrates the hashtable.

```
Adding node - key: 389 value: Mary
Adding node - key: 415 value: Henry
Adding node - key: 999 value: Joe
```

Once all three new entries have been inserted into the hashtable, the application calls the displayAll() function. The displayAll() function is a stand-alone function and not a member of the Hashtable class. Its sole purpose is to display the content of the hashtable. The displayAll() function is defined beneath the main() function in this example.

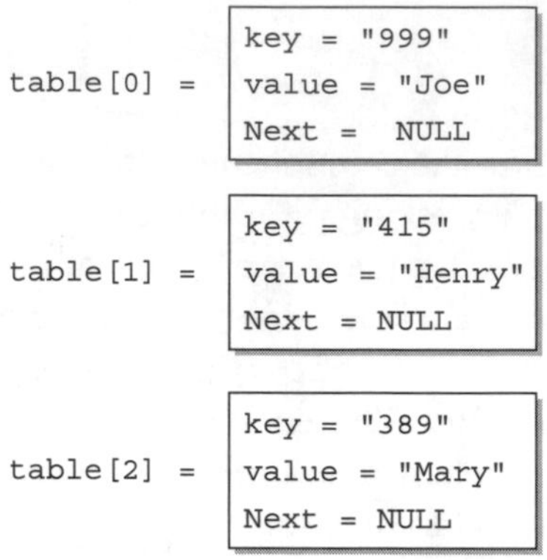

```
                        ┌─────────────────────┐
                        │ key = "999"         │
            table[0] =  │ value = "Joe"       │
                        │ Next =   NULL       │
                        └─────────────────────┘

                        ┌─────────────────────┐
                        │ key = "415"         │
            table[1] =  │ value = "Henry"     │
                        │ Next = NULL         │
                        └─────────────────────┘

                        ┌─────────────────────┐
                        │ key = "389"         │
            table[2] =  │ value = "Mary"      │
                        │ Next = NULL         │
                        └─────────────────────┘
```

Figure 11-5   The hashtable created after the put() function is called for the last time

Here's what is displayed on the screen when this function is called:

```
Current nodes in hashtable:
key: 415          value: Henry
key: 999          value: Joe
key: 389          value: Mary
```

The application then calls the remove() member function of the Hashtable class to remove the entry that has 415 as its key. Once again, the displayAll() function is called to demonstrate that the entry was actually removed from the hashtable.

```
After removing 415:

Current nodes in hashtable:
key: 999          value: Joe
key: 389          value: Mary
```

In its final step, the application destroys the hashtable by using the delete operator. The destructor is automatically called before the hashtable is destroyed. The destructor calls the removeAll() member function of the Hashtable class, which displays each entry before removing them from the hashtable. Here's what is displayed on the screen when all the entries are removed:

```
Destroying hashtable:
Removing node - key:999 Joe
Removing node - key:389 Mary
```

```
//HashtableDemo.cpp
#include <iostream.h>
```

```
#include <time.h>
#include <stdlib.h>
#include <string.h>
#include <stdio.h>
#include "Hashtable.h
void displayAll(Hashtable* hashtable);
void main()
{
   Hashtable* hashtable = new Hashtable();
   char key[SIZE_KEY];
   char value[SIZE_VALUE];
   strcpy(key, "389");
   strcpy(value, "Mary");
   if(!hashtable->contains(key))
   {
      cout << "Adding node - key: " << key << " value: "
         << value << endl;
      hashtable->put(key, value)
   }
   strcpy(key, "415");
   strcpy(value, "Henry");
   if(!hashtable->contains(key))
   {
      cout << "Adding node - key: " << key << " value: "
         << value << endl;
      hashtable->put(key, value);
   }
   strcpy(key, "999");
   strcpy(value, "Joe");
   if(!hashtable->contains(key))
   {
      cout << "Adding node - key: " << key << " value: "
        << value << endl;
      hashtable->put(key, value),
   }
   displayAll(hashtable);
   hashtable->remove("415");
   cout << "After removing 415:" << endl;
   displayAll(hashtable);
   cout << "\nDestroying hashtable:" << endl;
   delete hashtable;
}
void displayAll(Hashtable* hashtable)
{
```

```
    char key[SIZE_KEY];
    char value[SIZE_VALUE];
    cout << "\nCurrent nodes in hashtable:" << endl;
    hashtable->initIterator();
    while(hashtable->hasNext())
    {
        hashtable->getNextKey(key);
        hashtable->get(key, value);
        cout << "key: " << key << "\tvalue: " << value << endl;
    }
}


//HashTable.h
#include <string.h>
#define SIZE_KEY32
#define SIZE_VALUE256
#define DEFAULT_TABLESIZE101
typedef struct Metadata
{
    struct Metadata(char* key, char* value)
    {
        strcpy(this->key, key);
        strcpy(this->value, value);
        next = NULL;
    }
    char key[SIZE_KEY];
    char value[SIZE_VALUE];
    struct Metadata* next;
} METADATA;
class Hashtable
{
    private:
        int tablesize;
        METADATA** table;
        int size;
        long hashString(char* key);
        METADATA* find(char* key);
        METADATA* current_entry;
        int current_index;
    public:
        Hashtable(int tablesize = DEFAULT_TABLESIZE);
        virtual ~Hashtable();
        bool put(char* key, char* value);
```

```
        bool get(char* key, char* value);
        bool contains(char* key);
        bool remove(char* key);
        void removeAll();
        int getSize();
        void initIterator();
        bool hasNext();
        void getNextKey(char* key);
};

//Hashtable.cpp
#include <iostream.h>
#include <stdlib.h>
#include "HashTable.h"
Hashtable::Hashtable(int tablesize)
{
    size = 0;
    this->tablesize = tablesize;
    table = new METADATA*[tablesize];
    for(int i=0; i<tablesize; i++)
    {
        table[i] = NULL;
    }
}
Hashtable::~Hashtable()
{
    removeAll();
    delete[] table;
}
bool Hashtable::put(char* key, char* value)
{
    if(find(key) != NULL)
    {
        return false;
    }
    METADATA* entry = new METADATA(key, value);
    int bucket = hashString(key);
    entry->next = table[bucket];
    table[bucket] = entry;
    size++;
    return true;
}
bool Hashtable::get(char* key, char* value)
{
```

```cpp
    METADATA* temp = find(key);
    if(temp == NULL)
    {
        value[0] = '\0';
        return false;
    }
    else
    {
        strcpy(value, temp->value);
        return true;
    }
}
bool Hashtable::contains(char* key)
{
    if(find(key) == NULL)
    {
        return false;
    }
    else
    {
        return true;
    }
}
bool Hashtable::remove(char* key)
{
    int bucket = hashString(key);
    METADATA* temp = table[bucket];
    if(temp == NULL)
    {
        return false;
    }
    else if(strcmp(key, temp->key) == 0)
    {
        table[bucket] = temp->next;
        delete temp;
        size--;
        return true;
    }
    else
    {
        METADATA* temp_next = temp->next;
        while(temp_next != NULL)
        {
            if(strcmp(key, temp_next->key) == 0)
```

```cpp
            {
                temp->next = temp_next->next;
                delete temp_next;
                size--;
                return true;
            }
            temp = temp->next;
            temp_next = temp_next->next;
        }
    }
    return false;
}
void Hashtable::removeAll()
{
    for(int i=0; i<tablesize; i++)
    {
        METADATA* temp = table[i];
        while(temp != NULL)
        {
            METADATA* next = temp->next;
            cout << "Removing node - key:" <<  temp->key <<
                "\t" << temp->value << endl;
            delete temp;
            temp = next;
        }
    }
    size = 0;
}
int Hashtable::getSize()
{
    return size;
}
METADATA* Hashtable::find(char* key)
{
    int bucket = hashString(key);
    METADATA* temp = table[bucket];
    while(temp != NULL)
    {
        if(strcmp(key, temp->key) == 0)
        {
            return temp;
        }
        temp = temp->next;
    }
```

```
      return NULL;
   }
   long Hashtable::hashString(char* key)
   {
      int n = strlen(key);
      long h = 0;
      for(int i=0; i<n; i++)
      {
         h = (h << 2) + key[i];
      }
      return abs(h % tablesize);
   }
   void Hashtable::initIterator()
   {
      current_entry = NULL;
      current_index = tablesize;
      for(int i=0; i<tablesize; i++)
      {
         if(table[i] == NULL)
         {
            continue;
         }
         else
         {
            current_entry = table[i];
            current_index = i;
            break;
         }
      }
   }
   bool Hashtable::hasNext()
   {
      if(current_entry == NULL)
      {
         return false;
      }
      else
      {
         return true;
      }
   }
   void Hashtable::getNextKey(char* key)
   {
      if(current_entry == NULL)
```

```
{
    key[0] = '\0';
    return;
}
strcpy(key, current_entry->key);
if(current_entry->next != NULL)
{
    current_entry = current_entry->next;
}
else
{
    for(int i=current_index+1; i<tablesize; i++)
    {
        if(table[i] == NULL)
        {
            continue;
        }
        current_entry = table[i];
        current_index = i;
        return;
    }
    current_entry = NULL;
    current_index = tablesize;
}
}
```

Hashtable Using Java

The Java version of the hashtable application is simpler than the C++ version because the Java version defines the Hashtable class in the Java Collection Classes that are defined in the java.util package. The java.util package contains two classes that are designed to work with hashtables: Hashtable and HashMap class. The primary difference between them is the way they work with thread access.

The Hashtable class is a synchronized class, which means instances of the Hashtable class are safe to use for multiple thread access. The HashMap class is not synchronized and therefore is safe to use only when one thread uses an object. You can think of a thread as a process that accesses an object. Multiple processes can access an instance of the Hashtable class concurrently without any errors. However, a single process can access an instance of the HashMap class.

Let's take a look a how to create a Java version of the C++ application that you saw in the previous section of this chapter. The application is shown in the code at the

end of this section. Begin by declaring an instance of the `Hashtable` collections class and assigning this instance to the reference called hashtable.

Next, declare two instances of the `String` class called key and value and assign each the first key and value that will be inserted into the hashtable. Before entering these into the hashtable, you must determine if the hashtable already contains the key. You do this by calling the `containsKey()` member method of the `Hashtable` class. This is the equivalent of the `contains()` member function in the C++ version of this application.

The application displays the key/value pair on the screen before calling the `put()` member method of the `Hashtable` class to insert the key/value pair into the hashtable. The `put()` method is the Java version of the `put()` member function that you built in the C++ application.

This process is repeated twice, resulting in three entries being placed into the hashtable. Here's what appears on the screen once all three key/values are in the hashtable:

```
Adding node - key: 389 value: Mary
Adding node - key: 415 value: Henry
Adding node - key: 999 value: Joe
```

Next, the application retrieves the entry that has 415 as its key. It does this by calling the `get()` member method of the `Hashtable` class and passing it the key. The `get()` method returns either the object containing the key/value or NULL. The return value is cast to a String object and assigned to the value's string. If the value doesn't contain NULL, the application proceeds to display the value on the screen, as shown here:

```
Retrieving a value out of the hashtable:
Found key: 999 value: Henry
```

The application then displays the size of the hashtable and all the entries contained in the hashtable. The size of the hashtable is determined by calling the `size()` member method of the `Hashtable` class. The size is displayed on the screen, as shown here:

```
Size of hashtable before removing nodes: 3
```

Entries are displayed by calling the `displayEntries()` method. The `displayEntries()` method is a stand-alone method that is defined below the `main()` method in the application.

The `displayEntries()` method works by creating a key set of keys contained in the hashtable. As you'll recall from your Java programming course, a *set* is an object that contains a set of values that can be manipulated by an iterator. An iterator is another class that has member methods to move up and down values in the set and interact with those values.

The keySet() member method of the Hashtable class creates the set that contains keys from the hashtable. Once the set is created, the displayEntries() method creates an iterator. The hasNext() and next() member methods of the iterator step through the set of keys.

First, the hasNext() method is called within the condition expression of the while loop to determine if there is a next entry in the set. The hasNext() method returns a Boolean true if there is another entry; otherwise, a Boolean false is returned.

If there is another entry, the application calls the next() method, which moves to the next entry in the set and returns the key of that entry. The key is returned as an object, so you need to convert the object to a string, which is assigned to the key string. The key is passed to the get() method of the hashtable to retrieve the value associated with the key. The get() method returns an object that must be cast to a string so it can be assigned to the value string. Both the key and value are displayed on the screen, as shown here:

```
Contents of the hashtable:
key: 415    value: Henry
key: 999    value: Joe
key: 389    value: Mary
```

Next, the application removes the entry that has 415 as its key by calling the remove() member method of the Hashtable class. After the entry is removed, the application displays the size of the hashtable and the contents of the hashtable, as shown here:

```
Removing an entry from the hashtable:

Size of hashtable after removing node: 2

Contents of the hashtable:
key: 999    value: Joe
key: 389    value: Mary
```

```
import java.lang.*;
import java.text.*;
import java.util.*;
public class HashtableExample
{
   public static void main(String[] args)
   {
      Hashtable hashtable = new Hashtable();
      String key;
      String value;
```

```
key = "389";
value = "Mary";
if (!hashtable.containsKey(key))
{
    System.out.println("Adding node - key: " + key +
        " value: " + value);
    hashtable.put(key, value);
}
key = "415";
value = "Henry";
if (!hashtable.containsKey(key))
{
    System.out.println("Adding node - key: " + key +
        " value: " + value);
    hashtable.put(key, value);
}
key = "999";
value = "Joe";
if (!hashtable.containsKey(key))
{
    System.out.println("Adding node - key: " + key +
        " value: " + value);
    hashtable.put(key, value);
}
System.out.println("\nRetrieving a value out of the
        hashtable:");
value = (String)hashtable.get("415");
if(value != null)
{
    System.out.println("Found key: " + key + " value:
        " + value);
}
System.out.println("\nSize of hashtable before
        removing nodes: " + hashtable.size());
System.out.println("\nContents of the hashtable:");
displayEntries(hashtable);
System.out.println("\nRemoving an entry from the
        hashtable:");
hashtable.remove("415");
System.out.println("\nSize of hashtable after
        removing node: " + hashtable.size());
System.out.println("\nContents of the hashtable:");
displayEntries(hashtable);
}
```

```
private static void displayEntries(Hashtable hashtable)
{
   Set keys = hashtable.keySet();
   Iterator ii = keys.iterator();
   while(ii.hasNext())
   {
      String key = (String)ii.next();
      String value = (String)hashtable.get(key);
      System.out.println("key: " + key + "\tvalue: "
         + value);
   }
}
}
```

Quiz

1. What is hashing?

2. Why is it necessary to hash?

3. What is a hashtable?

4. What is the result of hashing?

5. How is a key hashed?

6. Can a key entered by an application be directly compared to a key in a hashtable?

7. What programming technique is used for hashing in all hashing functions?

8. Why are data members of the Hashtable class stored in the private access specifier?

9. At what level is hashing performed?

10. Is there one hashing function used in all applications for hashing?

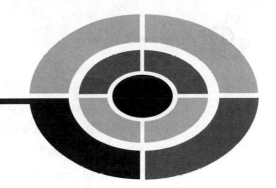

Final Exam

1. What is a numbering system?
2. What is the binary numbering system?
3. What is the purpose of an abstract data type?
4. What is a variable?
5. What is the integer abstract data type group?
6. What does the term "floating-point" mean?
7. What is a character?
8. What is the difference between single and double precision?
9. What is an instance of a structure?
10. What kind of data type is a structure?
11. How do you reference an element of an instance of a structure?
12. What are three major elements of every class definition?
13. What is the difference between a class definition and a structure definition?
14. What is the hexadecimal numbering system?
15. How do you assign an address to a pointer?
16. What value is stored in a pointer variable?

17. Why do you use pointer arithmetic?

18. What is a pointer-to-pointer variable?

19. What is an array of elements?

20. What is an index?

21. What is an array of pointers?

22. What is a multidimensional array?

23. What is the purpose of using a multidimensional array?

24. What is the relationship between a pointer and an array?

25. What is the relationship between a stack and an array?

26. What is the action called that places data on a stack?

27. What is the action called that removes data from a stack?

28. Using an array, how do you determine whether the stack is empty?

29. Using an array, how do you determine whether the stack is full?

30. What is a queue?

31. Where is data organized in a queue stored?

32. What does the term "circular queue" mean?

33. What is the modulus operator used for with respect to circular queues?

34. When would you implement a queue using a linked list instead of an array?

35. What is the action called that places data on a queue?

36. What is the action called that removes data from a queue?

37. What is a linked list?

38. What is an entry in a linked list called?

39. How are nodes linked together in a linked list?

40. What is a doubly linked list?

41. What is the purpose of a doubly linked list?

42. What is used to define a node of a linked list?

43. How do you delete an element from the middle of a linked list?

44. How do you delete a node from the front of a linked list?

45. How do you append a node onto a linked list?

46. How do you put a new node onto the front of the linked list?

47. What condition tells you the linked list is currently empty?

48. What condition tells you there's only one node on the linked list?

49. What is the size limitation on a linked list?

50. What is the destructor typically used for in a linked list?

51. What is a hashtable?

52. What is the key used for in a hashtable?

53. What is hashing?

54. What is the result of hashing?

55. What is the significance of a hash value?

56. What major problem occurs with hashing?

57. How do you overcome the major problem that occurs with hashing?

58. Ideally, how should a hash function behave with respect to the values it generates? If you feed in a list of keys, what would you expect for the output?

59. Many different hashing algorithms have been developed to provide a more even distribution of hash values. What is the essence of the hashing algorithm—in other words, what do these functions typically have in common?

60. With a hashtable, suppose your dataset gets unexpectedly large and you have an excessive number of collisions. How could you deal with this?

61. How do you insert a node into a hashtable?

62. How do you delete a node from a hashtable?

63. How do you look up a value in a hashtable?

64. How do you list out all the values in a hashtable?

65. How would you check if a hashtable is empty?

66. What is a binary tree?

67. What is the purpose of a branch node in a binary tree?

68. What is the starting node of a binary tree called?

69. What is the node in a binary tree called that spawns another node?

70. What are nodes at the end of a binary tree called?

71. If you have 1,000 nodes in a balanced binary tree, approximately how many comparisons do you need to do to find a particular node?

72. How is the maximum depth of a tree defined?

73. If a binary tree is well balanced, approximately how many nodes are in the tree given the depth of the tree?

74. What condition do you check for to see if a node in a binary tree is a leaf node?

75. How do you delete a node from a binary tree that has two child nodes?

76. How do you delete a node from the binary tree that has one child node?

77. How do you delete a leaf node from a binary tree?

78. What is the basic rule for where the nodes get placed into a binary tree?

79. How do you insert a node into a binary tree?

80. How would you check if a binary tree is empty?

81. What is a recursive function?

82. When searching for a key in a binary tree, what stops the recursive function calls?

83. What is the sequence of function calls to do an "in order" traversal of a binary tree?

84. What is a pointer?

85. What is memory allocation?

86. What does the `new` operator return?

87. Does Java use pointers?

88. How do you declare an array of pointers?

89. How do you declare an array of pointers to pointers?

90. If an `int` pointer is incremented using pointer arithmetic, how many bytes is the pointer incremented?

91. How is a binary tree's depth defined?

92. What is a balanced binary tree?

93. Must all binary trees be balanced?

94. What is the purpose of a key in a binary tree?

95. What is metadata?

96. What is the purpose of the `this` operator?

97. What does a private access specifier do?

98. If `next` and `previous` are pointers to the next and previous nodes, then what does this statement do?

    ```
    node->next->previous = NULL;
    ```

99. What is fifo?

100. What is the purpose of a public access specifier?

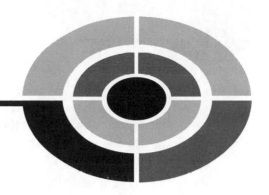

Answers to Quizzes and Final Exam

Chapter 1

1. An abstract data type is a keyword of a programming language that specifies the amount of memory needed to store data and the kind of data that will be stored in that memory location.

2. An integer: `byte`, `short`, `int`, or `long`.

3. Each memory address represents 1 byte of memory. Some abstract data types, such as an `int`, reserve 2 bytes of memory. Technically, data stored in this memory location has two memory address: one address for the first byte of memory and another address for the second byte of memory. However, the computer references only the address of the first byte of memory when accessing that memory location.

4. The `double` abstract data type is used to store real numbers that are very large or very small and require double the amount of memory that is reserved with a `float` abstract data type.

5. Precision refers the accuracy of the decimal portion of a value.

6. Memory consists of a series of switches called transistors. Each transistor stores a binary digit (bit). Transistors are logically organized into groups of 8 switches called a byte. Each byte is uniquely identified by a memory address.

7. A numbering system is a logical method used to count and perform arithmetic using digits to represent items. Each numbering system has a different number of digits. The decimal numbering systems has 10 digits, from 0 through 9. The binary numbering systems has 2 digits, 0 and 1. All numbering systems can be used to count and perform arithmetic, regardless of the number of digits contained in the numbering system.

8. The binary numbering system is used in computing because it contains 2 digits that can be stored by changing the state of a transistor. Off represents 0 and On represents 1.

9. A programmer doesn't specify the exact number of bytes to reserve in memory because the computer language determines the most efficient number of bytes to represent a data type.

10. The sign takes up 1 bit of memory that could otherwise be used to represent a value. For example, a `byte` has 8 bits, all of which can be used to store an unsigned number from 0 to 255. You can store a signed number in the range of −128 to +127.

Chapter 2

1. A user-defined data type is a group of primitive data types defined by the programmer.

2. The size of a structure is the sum of the sizes of all the primitive data types within the structure.

3. You use a structure to group together related data.

4. When you declare an instance of a structure, memory is reserved for all the primitive data types defined within the structure.

5. You access parts of a structure by referring to the name of the instance of the structure followed by the dot operator, which is then followed by a primitive data type that is defined within the structure.

6. A pointer is a variable and can be used as an element of a structure and as an attribute of a class in some programming languages such as C++, but not Java. However, the contents of a pointer is a memory address of another

location of memory, which is usually the memory address of another variable, element of a structure, or attribute of a class.

7. You use a pointer in a program in order to reduce the number of times data is copied within memory.

8. A pointer to a pointer is a variable whose value is an address of another pointer variable.

9. You use a pointer to a pointer in a program in order to arrange data without having to move data in memory.

10. The address is shown on the screen if you display the content of a pointer variable.

Chapter 3

1. The name of a variable references one memory location. The name of an array references one or multiple memory locations when used in conjunction with an index. If a programmer needs to access multiple variables, the programmer must explicitly specify variable names within the program. If a programmer needs to access multiple elements of array, the programmer can use the array name followed by an index value within a for loop.

2. An array of pointers is an array whose elements store memory addresses of variables or elements of another array.

3. You assign a memory address to an element of a pointer array by using the address operator, which is the ampersand (&), in an assignment statement such as

```
ptLetters[0] = &letters[2];
```

4. An array of pointers to pointers is an array whose elements can store a memory address. This memory address is the memory address of either a pointer variable or an element of a pointer array.

5. You assign a value to an element of an array of pointers to pointers by using the address operator, as shown here. However, the value must be a memory address of a pointer.

```
ptPtLetters[0] = & ptLetters[0];
```

6. You display the contents of the memory addresses stored in an element of a pointer array by preceding the element with an asterisk, as shown here:

```
cout << * ptLetters[0] << endl;
```

7. You would use an array of pointers to pointers to reorder large amounts of data stored in memory without having to move the data. Instead of moving the data, you reorder reference to the data's memory address.

8. An array is declared by specifying the data type, array name, and number of elements contained in the array, as shown here:

```
char letters[3];
```

9. You display the contents of the memory addresses indirectly referenced in an element of an array of pointers to pointers by preceding the array name with two asterisks, as shown here:

```
cout << * ptPtLetters[0] << endl;
```

10. Elements of an array are stored sequentially in memory.

Chapter 4

1. A stack is the way you groups things together by placing one thing on top of another and then removing them one at a time from the top of the stack.

2. The `push()` member method places a value onto the top of a stack.

3. The `pop()` member method removes the value from the top of a stack, which is then returned by the `pop()` member method to the statement that calls the `pop()` member method.

4. The `isFull()` member method determines if there is room for one more value on the stack.

5. The `isEmpty()` member method determines if a value is at the top of the stack and is called before an attempt is made to remove the value.

6. The value at the `top` attribute is an index.

7. The `top` attribute is initialized to –1 because when the attribute is incremented by the `push()` member method, the new value of the `top` attribute is zero, which is the index of the first element of the array used to create the stack.

8. The keyword `private` means that the attribute or member method is accessible only by a member method. The instance of the class cannot directly access a private member of the class.

9. The keyword `public` means that the attribute or member method is accessible to member methods and from the instance of the class.

10. A constructor is a member method of a class that is called when an instance of the class is declared. A destructor is a member method of a class that is called when the instance of the class falls out of scope.

Chapter 5

1. A queue is an organization of data where data is stored at the back of the queue and removed from the front of the queue using the first in, first out method.

2. Data stored in a queue is actually stored in an array. The queue tracks which array element is at the front of the queue and which array element is at the back of the queue.

3. The index of the front and back of the queue is calculated by modulus division. First, the value of either the front or back attribute is incremented depending on whether you are calculating the index of the front of the queue or the index of the back of the queue. The result is then divided by the size of the queue using modulus division. The remainder is the index of the array element that is either the front or the back of the queue, depending on which you are calculating.

4. The enqueue process places data at the back of the queue.

5. The dequeue process removes data from the front of the queue.

6. The isFull() member method is called within the enqueue process to determine if there is room to place another item in the queue.

7. The isEmpty() member method is called within the dequeue process to determine if there is an item in the queue to be removed.

8. Removing data from the queue does not remove data from the underlying array. The data remains in the array after the data is removed from the queue.

9. The default size of the queue prevents an error should the programmer forget to pass the size of the queue to the constructor of the Queue class.

10. The destructor in the C++ version of this program removes the underlying array from memory once the instance of the Queue class goes out of scope. Java doesn't have a destructor. Instead, Java has a garbage collector that automatically removes the underlying array from memory some time after the instance of the Queue class goes out of scope. Therefore, there is no need to explicitly remove the array from memory in the Java version of this program.

Chapter 6

1. A linked list is a data structure consisting of elements called nodes. Each node points to the next and the previous node, thereby linking nodes together to form a linked list.

2. The benefit of using a linked list is to join together large amounts of data and manipulate the data without having to rearrange data in memory.

3. A node is an element of a linked list.

4. A node has three elements. These are the current data and pointers to the previous node and the next node on the linked list.

5. A linked list can grow and shrink in size dynamically at runtime, whereas an array is set to a fixed size at compile time.

6. Yes, a node can reference more than one data element if the current data element of the node is a pointer to a group of data such as an instance of a class, a structure, or an array.

7. The add() method of the LinkedList class in Java requires that an object be passed to it rather than a primitive data type. You must use a Java wrapper class to create the object. The Java wrapper class contains a primitive data type used to store data.

8. You can insert a node in the middle of a linked list by repointing the previous and the next elements of existing nodes to the new node.

9. A doubly linked list is a linked list consisting of nodes that have both the previous and next elements. This links the node to the previous node and the next node.

10. A single linked list is a linked list consisting of nodes that have only the next element and not the previous element. This links the node to only the next node in the linked list. There is no way for the node to reference the previous node in the linked list.

Chapter 7

1. A stack-linked list is a data structure that uses a linked list to create a stack.

2. A stack-linked list accesses data last in, first out; a linked list accesses data first in, first out.

3. The benefit of using a stack-linked list is that the number of nodes on the stack can increase or decrease as needed while the program runs.

4. The front of the stack in a stack-linked list is at the back of the linked list.

5. There can be a nearly unlimited number of nodes on a stack-linked list, restricted only by the amount of available memory in the computer.

6. Yes, a node on a stack-linked list can have more than one data element, which is also true of a node on a linked list.

7. The StackLinkedList class inherits the LinkedList class because the StackLinkedList class uses attributes and member functions of the LinkedList class.

8. The constructor of the StackLinkedList class is empty because the constructor of the LinkedList class is called when an instance of the StackLinkedList class is declared. The constructor of the LinkedList class initializes the node and attributes that are later used by the StackLinkedList class.

9. The destructor of the StackLinkedList class is empty because the destructor of the LinkedList class is called prior to the destructor of the StackLinkedList class. This is because the LinkedList class is inherited by the StackLinkedList class.

10. When you push a new node onto a stack, the new node is placed at the front of the linked list.

Chapter 8

1. A queue linked list is a data structure that organizes data similar to a line in the supermarket, where the first one in line is the first one out.

2. The size of a queue linked list can change during runtime. The size of an array queue is set at compile time and cannot change at runtime.

3. A queue linked list can expand and shrink in size when an application runs, depending on the needs of the application.

4. New nodes are added to the back of the queue.

5. The node at the front of the queue is removed when the dequeue() member method is called.

6. Yes, a node on a queue linked list can have more than one data element if you redefine the node structure to accommodate additional data.

7. First in, first out is the method used to access nodes on a queue.

8. The constructor of the QueueLinkedList class is empty because initialization of data members of the LinkedList class is performed by the constructor of the LinkedList class. The constructor of the LinkedList class is called before the constructor of the QueueLinkedList class is called.

9. The QueueLinkedList class inherits the LinkedList class because the LinkedList class contains data members and function members that are necessary to manage the linked list that is used for the queue.

10. When `dequeue()` is called, the value of the data member of the node at the front of the queue is returned to the statement that called the `dequeue()` member function. The front node is then deleted from memory and the next node on the queue is designated the front of the queue.

Chapter 9

1. A linked list index is an integer that represents the position of a node in a linked list.

2. The value of the first index is zero.

3. The `removeNode()` requires a reference to the node that is to be removed, while the `deleteNode()` function requires the value of the data element of the node that is being removed.

4. The return value of the `findNode()` function is the index position of the node.

5. The `insertNodeAt()` function specifies the index of where to insert the new node into the linked list. The `appendNode()` function appends the new node to the list without requiring the programmer to specify where to place the new node in the linked list.

6. Functions that use an index value always determine if the index passed to them is valid before using the index value. If an invalid index is received, the function terminates without further processing.

7. Yes, a linked list can store data other than integers. Integers were used in this chapter as an example, but you can modify the data type of the data in the definition of the node to change the kind of data stored in the linked list.

8. You use the `getSize()` function instead of having the application access the size of the linked list directly to protect the data from inadvertently being changed by the application. If the application needs to change the data, then the appropriate function is called and the function changes the data.

9. Yes, the `insertNodeAt()` function can place a node at the front or back of a linked list if you pass the appropriate index to this function.

10. You enhance the functionality of the `LinkedList` class to more easily manipulate a linked list.

Chapter 10

1. A tree is a data structure where data is stored in nodes. Nodes are arranged in branches where each node can expand into 0, 1, or 2 other nodes.

2. A parent node is a node that branches into one or two other nodes, which are called child nodes.

3. A key is a component of a node that identifies the node. An application searches keys to locate a desired node. A value is also a component of a node that is used to store data.

4. A root node is another term for a parent node.

5. The left child node has a key that is less than the key of its parent node. The right child node has a key that is greater than the key of its parent node.

6. A leaf node is the last node on a branch and does not have any child nodes.

7. The depth of a tree is the number of levels of a tree.

8. The size of a tree is the number of nodes on the tree.

9. You calculate the size of a tree by using the following formula:

$$size \approx 2^{depth}$$

If the depth is 5 levels, then the size is 32, as shown here:

$$32 \approx 2^5$$

10. No, a tree cannot have a duplicate key.

Chapter 11

1. Hashing is the technique of scrambling bits of a key into a hash number.

2. Hashing assures that the format of keys is uniform and unique.

3. A hashtable is a table in which each entry consists of a hashed key and a value; the hashed key retrieves entries.

4. Hashing results in a hash number that has no real significance beyond it being used as the key for an entry.

5. A hash key is created by bit shifting a hashed value and then adding to the value bits of a character of the key entered by the application.

6. No. A key entered by the application must be hashed before it can be compared to a key in the hashtable.

7. Bit shifting is the common programming technique used for hashing in all hashing functions.

8. Data members of the Hashtable class are stored in the private access specifier to ensure the integrity of the data. Only member functions can assign and retrieve values of these data members.

9. Hashing occurs at the bit level.

10. There isn't one hashing function that's used in all applications for hashing. Developers test a wide variety of hashing functions before determining the best to use on a particular dataset.

Final Exam

1. A numbering system is a way to count things and perform arithmetic.

2. The binary numbering system is a number system that uses two digits to count things and perform arithmetic.

3. The purpose of an abstract data type is to specify the amount of memory needed to store data and the kind of data that will be stored in that memory location.

4. A variable is a reference to the memory location that you reserved using the declaration statement.

5. The integer abstract data type group consists of four abstract data types used to reserve memory to store whole numbers.

6. The term "floating-point" refers to the way in which decimals are referenced in memory. There are two parts of a floating-point number. The first part is the real number, which is stored as a whole number. The second part is reference to the position of the decimal point within the whole number.

7. A character is represented as an integer value that corresponds to a character set. A character set assigns an integer value to each character, punctuation, and symbol used in a language.

8. Single precision refers to the accuracy of the first 7 numbers to the right of the decimal point. Double precision refers to the accuracy of the first 15 numbers to the right of the decimal point.

9. A structure definition is like a cookie cutter in that it describes the shape of something. A cookie cutter describes the shape of a cookie. A structure definition describes the size and data type of a group of primitive data types. You use a cookie cutter to make cookies. You use a structure to declare an instance of the structure in memory.

10. A structure is a user-defined data type.

11. An element of an instance of a structure is referenced by using the dot operator, such as `myStudent.grade`.

12. Keyword class, class name, and class body.

13. A class definition defines both data and methods/functions. A structure definition defines only data.

14. The hexadecimal numbering system consists of 16 digits that are represented as 0 through 9 and A through F.

15. An address of a variable is assigned to a pointer variable by using the address operator (&).

16. A pointer variable stores the address of another memory location.

17. Pointers are used to step through memory sequentially by using pointer arithmetic and the incremental (++) or decremental (– –) operator. The incremental operator increases the value of a variable by 1 and the decremental operator decreases the value of a variable by 1.

18. A pointer to a pointer is also a variable that contains a memory address except a pointer to a pointer contains the memory address of another pointer variable.

19. An array element is similar to one variable except it is identified by the name of the array and an index value.

20. An index value is a number used to identify an array element.

21. An array of pointers is nearly identical to a pointer variable except each array element contains a memory address.

22. A multidimensional array consists of two or more arrays defined by sets of array elements. Each set of array elements is an array.

23. A multidimensional array is useful in some situations to organize subgroups of data within an array.

24. There is a close-knit relationship between a pointer and an array. The array name is like a pointer variable in that the array name by itself references the address of first element of the array.

25. A stack and an array are two different things. An array stores values in memory. A stack tracks which of the array elements is at the top of the stack.

26. Push is the action that places data on a stack.

27. Pop is the action that removes data from a stack.

28. The value of the top index is –1.

29. The value of the top index is equal to the number of elements in the array minus 1.

30. A queue is a sequential organization of data. A queue is like the checkout line at the supermarket where the first customer is at the front of the line

and the second customer is next in line, and so on, until you reach the last customer who is at the back of the line.

31. Data organized in a queue is stored in an array or a linked list.

32. A circular queue is a queue implemented using an array. When the elements at the end of the array are used up, you start over at the beginning so the queue chases itself around in a circle.

33. The modulus operator can be used to make a linear pattern into a circular pattern. When the last element is used up, the modulus operator will take you back to the first element.

34. When you don't know the number of nodes ahead of time. The linked list implementation is only limited by the amount of memory on the machine.

35. Enqueue is the action that places data on a queue.

36. Dequeue is the action called that removes data from a queue.

37. A linked list is a data structure that makes it easy to rearrange data without having to move data in memory.

38. An entry in a linked list is called a node.

39. Each member of a node points to the next node in the linked list.

40. A doubly linked list is a linked list where each member of a node points to the previous node and to the next node in the linked list.

41. A doubly linked list is used to enable a program to move up and down the linked list.

42. A structure definition is used to define a node of a linked list.

43. Declare a temporary pointer to the node being deleted. Change the next pointer in the previous node to the value of the next pointer in the node being deleted. Change the previous pointer in the next node to the value of the previous pointer in the node being deleted. Delete the node.

44. Declare a temporary pointer to the front node. Change the value of the front pointer to the next pointer in the node being deleted. Change the value of the previous pointer in the next node to NULL. Use the temporary pointer to delete the node.

45. Use the back pointer to get a reference to the last node on the linked list. Change the value of the next pointer in the back node to the address of the new node. Set the previous pointer of the new node to the current back node. Change the back pointer to the address of the new node.

46. Use the front pointer to get a reference to the first node on the linked list. Change the value of the previous pointer in the front node to the address of the new node. Set the next pointer of the new node to the current front node. Change the front pointer to the address of the new node.

47. The front and back pointers are both NULL. You only need to check one of them.

48. The front and back pointers both point to the same node.

49. The size is limited by the amount of memory on the machine.

50. The destructor typically releases all the memory that was allocated for the linked list.

51. A hashtable is a common data structure used to store objects that have a key value relationship.

52. A key is translated into a number that is used as the array index of the array element that references the value that is associated with the key.

53. Hashing is the process of translating the key into the array index of the array element that references the value that is associated with the key.

54. Hashing produces a hash value.

55. There is no real significance of a hash value other than it is a number used as an array index.

56. Hashing is not perfect. Occasionally, a collision occurs when two different keys hash into the same hash value and therefore are assigned to the same array element.

57. A common way to deal with a collision is to create a linked list of entries that have the same hash value.

58. In the most ideal case, the hash function should produce an even distribution of values for a given set of keys. The result is a minimum number of collisions.

59. Hashing typically uses bit shifting to pseudo-randomize the generated values. How could you deal with this?

60. You could make the hashtable array larger, then rehash all the keys and insert them accordingly into the new hashtable.

61. Call the hashing algorithm with the key. Go to the array and see if the value in the array index is NULL. If it is, then change this value to the address of the new node. If the array index is not NULL, then set the next pointer in the new node to the value at the array index and set the array index to the address of the new node. This makes the new node the first entry in the linked list.

62. Call the hashing algorithm with the key. Go to that index in the array. Traverse the linked list and find the value, and then delete this entry from the linked list. The entry is deleted by setting the next pointer in the previous node to the next pointer of the node being deleted.

63. Call the hashing algorithm with the key. Go to that array index and traverse the linked list until you find that key. Return the associated value.

64. Iterate the array. At each index, if it contains a value other than NULL, iterate the linked list and list out the values.

65. Iterate the hashtable array and see if all the values are NULL. If all the values are NULL, the hashtable is empty.

66. A binary tree is a tree where each stem has not more than two branches Typically the stem has two branches, but there can be situations when the stem has one branch or simply terminates resulting in no additional branches.

67. The branch node is the fork in the road that links the root node to two branches.

68. The starting node is called the root node, which is the top-level node in the tree.

69. A parent node spawns another node in a binary tree.

70. Nodes at the end of a binary tree are called leaf nodes.

71. Ten. $2^{10} \sim= 1000$.

72. The depth is the number of hops to get to the "lowest" node in the tree.

73. $2^n - 1$ where n is the depth of the tree.

74. Both the child node pointers are set to NULL.

75. Replace the node being deleted with the leftmost child of the right subtree. You could also replace it with the rightmost child of the left subtree.

76. Change the value of the pointer in the parent node to the value of the child node, and then delete the node.

77. Change the value of the pointer in the parent node to NULL, and then delete the node.

78. All the nodes to the right have a key greater than the current node and all the nodes to the left have a key less than the current node. This rule applies to each and every node of the tree.

79. Start at the root of the tree. If the key is greater than this node, move to the right. If the key is less than this node, move to the left. Continue until a NULL pointer is found, and then change the value of this pointer to the address of the new node.

80. The tree is empty if the root node of the tree is NULL.

81. A recursive function is a function that calls itself.

82. One of two conditions—either the key is found or a NULL pointer is found.

83. For each node, look to the left, process the node, and then look to the right.

84. A pointer is a variable whose value is an address of a location in memory.

85. Memory allocation is the task of reserving memory in order to store data in memory.

86. The `new` operator returns an address of memory.

87. It is a misnomer that Java doesn't use pointers. Java does use pointers, but a programmer doesn't explicitly declare pointers. You can declare an array whose data type is a Java Object—an array of pointers. The value of each array element is an Object. When you switch those values to other array elements, you are moving memory addresses and not the Object itself.

88. An array of pointers is declared by preceding the array name with an asterisk.

89. An array of pointers to pointers is declared by preceding the array name with two asterisks.

90. An `int` pointer is incremented by the number of bytes of an `int`.

91. The number of nodes on the tree defines a binary tree's depth.

92. A balanced binary tree is where each node except for a leaf node has two children nodes.

93. No.

94. The key and the search criteria are compared to each other.

95. "Metadata" is the term that refers to data that describes other data such as how an employee ID can be used to get the employee's name.

96. The `this` operator tells the compiler that you want to refer to the data element of this instance of the structure instead of the parameter that was passed in.

97. Members defined within the private access specifier area of the class definition can only be accessed by member functions of the class.

98. This statement assigns the NULL value to the next node's previous pointer.

99. First in, first out.

100. Members defined within the public access specifier area of a class definition can be accessed by member functions of the class and from outside the class.

INDEX

INTERNATIONAL CONTACT INFORMATION

AUSTRALIA
McGraw-Hill Book Company
Australia Pty. Ltd.
TEL +61-2-9900-1800
FAX +61-2-9878-8881
http://www.mcgraw-hill.com.au
books-it_sydney@mcgraw-hill.com

CANADA
McGraw-Hill Ryerson Ltd.
TEL +905-430-5000
FAX +905-430-5020
http://www.mcgraw-hill.ca

**GREECE, MIDDLE EAST, & AFRICA
(Excluding South Africa)**
McGraw-Hill Hellas
TEL +30-210-6560-990
TEL +30-210-6560-993
TEL +30-210-6560-994
FAX +30-210-6545-525

MEXICO (Also serving Latin America)
McGraw-Hill Interamericana Editores
S.A. de C.V.
TEL +525-1500-5108
FAX +525-117-1589
http://www.mcgraw-hill.com.mx
carlos_ruiz@mcgraw-hill.com

SINGAPORE (Serving Asia)
McGraw-Hill Book Company
TEL +65-6863-1580
FAX +65-6862-3354
http://www.mcgraw-hill.com.sg
mghasia@mcgraw-hill.com

SOUTH AFRICA
McGraw-Hill South Africa
TEL +27-11-622-7512
FAX +27-11-622-9045
robyn_swanepoel@mcgraw-hill.com

SPAIN
McGraw-Hill/
Interamericana de España, S.A.U.
TEL +34-91-180-3000
FAX +34-91-372-8513
http://www.mcgraw-hill.es
professional@mcgraw-hill.es

**UNITED KINGDOM, NORTHERN,
EASTERN, & CENTRAL EUROPE**
McGraw-Hill Education Europe
TEL +44-1-628-502500
FAX +44-1-628-770224
http://www.mcgraw-hill.co.uk
emea_queries@mcgraw-hill.com

ALL OTHER INQUIRIES Contact:
McGraw-Hill/Osborne
TEL +1-510-420-7700
FAX +1-510-420-7703
http://www.osborne.com
omg_international@mcgraw-hill.com

Th fast nd e sy w y to understanding computing fundamentals

- No formal training needed
- Self-paced, easy-to-follow, and user-friendly
- Amazing low price

0-07-225454-8
Available May 2004

0-07-225363-0
Available April 2004

0-07-225514-5
Available July 2004

0-07-225359-2
Available March 2004

0-07-225370-3
Available May 2004

0-07-225364-9
Available March 2004

For more information on these and other McGraw-Hill/Osborne titles, visit www.osborne.com.

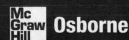

Complete Your Shelf

Expert authors, comprehensive coverage, timely topics...Complete References

C#:
The Complete Reference
Herbert Schildt
0-07-213485-2

J2EE™:
The Complete Reference
Jim Keogh
0-07-222472-X

Business Objects:
The Complete Reference
Cindi Howson
0-07-222681-1

Java™ 2:
The Complete Reference,
Fifth Edition
Herbert Schildt
0-07-222420-7

Crystal Reports® 9:
The Complete Reference
George Peck
0-07-222519-X

SQL:
The Complete Reference,
Second Edition
James Groff & Paul Weinberg
0-07-222559-4

Know How

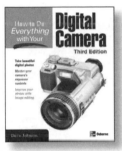

How to Do Everything with Your Digital Camera
Third Edition
ISBN: 0-07-223081-9

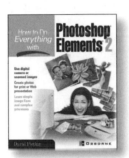

How to Do Everything with Photoshop Elements 2
ISBN: 0-07-222638-2

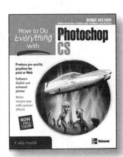

How to Do Everything with Photoshop CS
ISBN: 0-07-223143-2
4-color

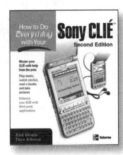

How to Do Everything with Your Sony CLIÉ
Second Edition
ISBN: 0-07-223074-6

How to Do Everything with Macromedia Contribute
0-07-222892-X

How to Do Everything with Your eBay Business
0-07-222948-9

How to Do Everything with Illustrator CS
ISBN: 0-07-223092-4
4-color

How to Do Everything with Your iPod
ISBN: 0-07-222700-1

How to Do Everything with Your iMac,
Third Edition
ISBN: 0-07-213172-1

How to Do Everything with Your iPAQ Pocket PC
Second Edition
ISBN: 0-07-222950-0

Sound Off!

Visit us at **www.osborne.com/bookregistration** and let us know what you thought of this book. While you're online you'll have the opportunity to register for newsletters and special offers from McGraw-Hill/Osborne.

We want to hear from you!

Sneak Peek

Visit us today at **www.betabooks.com** and see what's coming from McGraw-Hill/Osborne tomorrow!

Based on the successful software paradigm, Bet@Books™ allows computing professionals to view partial and sometimes complete text versions of selected titles online. Bet@Books™ viewing is free, invites comments and feedback, and allows you to "test drive" books in progress on the subjects that interest you the most.